Life
IN THE
Spirit

Life IN THE Spirit

ROBERTSON McQUILKIN
FOREWORD BY PHILLIP YANCEY

BROADMAN
&HOLMAN
PUBLISHERS

Nashville, Tennessee

0–7394–1083–0

Published by Broadman & Holman Publishers, Nashville, Tennessee
Editorial Team: Vicki Crumpton, Janis Whipple, Kim Overcash
Typesetting: TF Designs

Dewey Decimal Classification: 231
Subject Heading: HOLY SPIRIT / SPIRITUAL LIFE—CHRISTIANITY

Table of Contents

Life in the Spirit

Activity Four—Indwelling

Activity Five—Transforming

Activity Six—Filling

Activity Seven—Overcoming

Activity Eight—Gifting

Contents

Activity Nine—Sending

Activity Ten—Glorifying

Foreword

$\mathcal{D}$orothy Sayers tells of a Japanese convert struggling to grasp Christian theology. "Honorable Father, very good," he said to his missionary teacher. "Honorable son, very good. But Honorable Bird, I do not understand at all." Misunderstanding swirls around the third member of the Trinity, which is a great irony, for the Holy Spirit is the most personally intimate of the three. The Spirit lives inside us and prays on our behalf when we know not what to pray.

I readily admit to my own problems in understanding the Holy Spirit. I grew up in churches that used—and misused—the Spirit like some kind of magic genie. "The Spirit told me . . ." the pastor would say to justify some of his bizarre schemes. Members of the congregation talked about being "filled with the spirit" and living the "victorious Christian life" even as they manifested glaring faults. In a denomination down the street, other churchgoers fell down in a trance after being "slain in the Spirit." As an adolescent, I developed a hard-shell resistance to talk about the Holy Spirit.

To break through this resistance, I needed a very wise guide: one who was down-to-earth, practical, and who lived out the Spirit-filled life in a consistent, attractive way. I found such a guide in Robertson McQuilkin.

Robertson McQuilkin was reared in a home that hosted many of the leaders of the victorious Christian life movement. Growing into a mature faith, he always managed to keep his feet on the ground and his head in the clouds. He never lowered the lofty standards of the Christian life as described in the New Testament, yet neither did he deny his very real struggles with temptation and doubt. Twelve years in Japan, as a missionary in one of the cultures most resistant to Christianity, increased that sense of realism and forced a daily dependence on the Holy Spirit.

I got to know Robertson McQuilkin after he returned from Japan and became president of Columbia Bible College, where I was attending. There, I had the opportunity to observe his life at close range. As a teacher, he genuinely listened to students and their point of view. He never acted as if he were dispensing propaganda from on high; rather, he gently and persuasively presented his own beliefs and perspectives. From that example, I learned that the Holy Spirit does not coerce, but rather coaxes and prompts.

Serving as president for more than two decades, McQuilkin led the school to a new plateau. For the first time the school attained fully accredited status from regional associations. New buildings were constructed, board members squabbled, faculty members came and went. I watched McQuilkin manage each of these challenges with a rare combination of humility and strength.

More important than these accomplishments, though—and I'm sure he would agree—I also observed McQuilkin in the role of father and husband. His oldest son, Bob, was my close friend until he died tragically at the age of 36 while scuba diving. Through Bob's eyes, I saw a long-suffering father who would let his children choose their own paths while praying earnestly for their spiritual welfare. Then in 1990, at the peak of his career, Robertson McQuilkin shocked the Bible College community by announcing his resignation. His beloved wife, Muriel, had developed an advanced case of Alzheimer's disease, and he resigned in order to become a homemaker and care for her.

McQuilkin has written two articles about his experience caring for Muriel, which have been reprinted around the world. The Christian life is put to the ultimate test when a man feels called by God to leave a position of prestige and influence in order to clean, change diapers, and care for the shell of a person who has been his partner and lover for forty years. To students at Columbia Bible College, McQuilkin's decision offered a profound close-up example of sacrificial love. "Husbands, love your wives, just as Christ loved the church and gave himself up for her," Paul urges (Eph. 5:25). I know of no more poignant illustration of Christ's love for us His church. The daily ministrations of Robertson McQuilkin for a wife whose mind is nearly vacant, who is in need of his constant attention, is a picture of this love.

McQuilkin himself seems genuinely shocked that anyone would view his actions as exceptional. "I took marriage vows, didn't I," he protests. In his own mind, he is merely living out in quiet faithfulness the promises he made nearly half a century ago. In the end, it is that kind of faithfulness that defines life in the Spirit—and you will learn from a master as you read through this book of intense practicality.

—Philip Yancey

Introduction

"When you come right down to it, we're all unitarians," Bill said. Pastor of a large Presbyterian church, he'd come to talk about sanctification—what the Bible teaches on how to live the Christian life successfully. He knew I'd written a book about what the Holy Spirit does to make that possible. He continued, "We Presbyterians believe in God the Father, you Baptists believe in God the Son, and the Pentecostals believe in God the Spirit."

Maybe Bill's quip isn't far off the mark. How did we get to such a point?

The twentieth century could be called the century of the Holy Spirit. In 1901 the modern Pentecostal movement was born, and for the first time some identified speaking in tongues as the necessary evidence of being filled with the Spirit. The Pentecostal movement had phenomenal growth worldwide. Then in mid-century it broke out into mainstream denominations in what came to be called the "charismatic movement." Finally, toward the end of the century, the missionary enterprise was inundated with an emphasis on "power encounter," emphasizing the need for visible demonstrations of supernatural power to accomplish world evangelism. Many in that movement seemed to focus more on the enemy, the unholy spirits, than on the Holy Spirit. Still, "power encounter" has grown directly out of the Pentecostal and charismatic context.

In reaction to this, many Christians have rejected all demonstrations of the Spirit's activity and have been afraid to emphasize the ministry of the Spirit at all. A major research project in the mid-nineties revealed that only a third of "born-again" Americans believe in a personal Holy Spirit at all. We humans find it easier to take one side of biblical truth to one extreme or the other, neglecting the balancing truths of Scripture, rather than finding the center of

1

biblical balance. In this book we'll try to discover the core biblical teachings about the person and activity of the Holy Spirit. We'll explore the glorious truths on which we can all agree.

We want to do this because to neglect the Spirit is sad. He's the source of all spiritual blessing! The Spirit is the administrator, the executive officer, of our triune God. He's the one commissioned to take a broken piece of humanity like me and transform it into the likeness of God Himself, a fit companion for the Holy One.

Even so, many who truly believe in the third person of the Godhead tend to ignore Him. Or misunderstand Him. Discipleship leaders from around Texas had gathered for a workshop on *Life in the Spirit,* the interactive study on which this book is based. They were preparing to lead their people in experiencing the energizing power of the Spirit in daily life. After the first session, Fred called me aside to tell me a story. The night before, at his church's Wednesday Bible study, the preacher had said, "I know you don't know much about the Holy Spirit, so tonight I'm going to teach you all about it. The reason we don't know much is that the Bible doesn't say much about it. In fact, our passage for study tonight, John 14–16, tells us most of what little we know."

How did a Bible authority—a seminary graduate—come up with such an appalling misunderstanding of a key Bible teaching? And even more dreadful— why do multitudes of his colleagues in the pulpit never teach on the Spirit at all? The purpose of this book is to help correct that fatal flaw in the contemporary evangelical church. But not with just a theological exposition of the person and work of the Holy Spirit, important as that is. (It's so important, in fact, that I've sought to ground this teaching solidly on such a theological understanding.) Rather, *Life in the Spirit* has a much more practical objective— to help us experience the transforming work of the Spirit. God wants to be one with us in an intimate love relationship, and the Spirit is out to change us into the kind of people who are capable of such a friendship.

Who then would benefit by such a book? After studying about life in the Spirit with a group of pastors and lay leaders, I asked them that question—who is this study for? Here are some of the answers we came up with:

~ People who are curious about who the Spirit is, what He does, and how to relate to Him

~ People who feel frustrated in their Christian life, who think there must be something more to it than a well-worn routine

~ Those who are tired of failing to measure up to expectations or discouraged by defeat in the battle to overcome temptation

~ Those who are confused and frustrated by various teachings on the Spirit

~ People who are afraid of the Holy Spirit

Introduction

- ~ Those who have found that programs and techniques haven't filled them with excitement and purpose
- ~ Those who want to be more like Jesus, to experience a miracle quality of life that isn't merely the product of their natural qualities and hard work
- ~ People who know something is missing but are not sure what
- ~ People who want to see more evidence of power in their service to God and His church
- ~ Those who feel spiritually dry and thirsty
- ~ People who would like a road map for the Christian journey
- ~ Those who long for a closer relationship with God

In response to these longings many of us feel, we'll examine the ten major activities of the Spirit designed by God to bring us into intimate companionship with Him through changing us more and more to be like Jesus. People have told me that a particular truth in *Life in the Spirit* has revolutionized their lives, but the curious thing is this: they don't name the same activity! Each one found a different activity of the Spirit as *the* transforming truth. (My own favorite is the tenth activity, but it became that only as I prepared this study!) So I invite you to join me in experiencing life in the Spirit through participating in every one of His incredible activities.

Chapter 1

The Holy Spirit and I

*I*n all my life, I've never heard a single sermon on the Holy Spirit." Ruth wept as she told me, but they were tears of joy. She'd just been introduced to the third person of the Trinity and she exclaimed, "Why, it's just like being born again all over." It was the Spirit who had given her "new birth" in the first place, of course, but for years He was to her the Great Unknown.

It's possible to recite the Apostles' Creed every Sunday morning, "I believe in the Holy Ghost," and give no more thought to Him than to the air we breathe. Yet Scripture tells us the Spirit holds the keys to all the doors of God's vast treasures. The tragedy is that many church members don't know the Keyholder and thus are locked out of God's promised blessings. They live impoverished lives of defeat before temptation, and the only joy or peace they know can be explained by their circumstances. Their growth toward likeness to Jesus is so stunted, those around them seldom think, "Why, he reminds me of Jesus!" But God never intended life to be that way.

If we allow Him, the Holy Spirit will open doors of understanding for us to enter and discover treasures we never knew existed. And He will do even more. He will enable us to actually experience true freedom and fulfillment—in fact, to be filled to "all the fullness of God" (Eph. 3:19). He wants us to experience His presence and power every day. All day. What could be more exciting than life in the Spirit? Yet . . .

"The Holy Spirit—what's that?" I'd just been introduced to a church leader as author of *Life in the Spirit*. He wanted to drive home the point that in his

5

church God's Spirit was mostly a stranger. *Why is that?* I asked that question to a group of pastors and lay leaders. The answers popped:

~ "Ignorance," several said. "We never heard about it. It's hard to say, 'Him'."

~ "Fear," one pastor said. "There's so much wildfire around the Spirit we keep our distance—don't want to get burned." Later another said, "If we turn Him loose He might take over." Then he added, "And that's what I'm paid for!"

~ "It's just plain spooky," said another. "We call it the Holy *Ghost*."

Later I thought of a couple of other possibilities:

~ Maybe we so fill up on techniques and programs there's no space left for Him. Who needs the Spirit?

~ There may be just plain disinterest. A Gallup poll in 1996 indicated that eighty-five percent of Americans are content with their present spiritual condition.

So we lock Him away safely in our theological closets—and suffer the consequences. He's the energizer, the third person of the triune God who's the one responsible to carry out the purposes of the Godhead. When we ignore Him or neglect Him, we risk cutting ourselves off from the source of divine power and having to sputter along as best we can, relying on our own resources.

Of course, we can go to the other extreme. Some people are so intoxicated with the glorious biblical truths about the Spirit they go beyond Scripture, building doctrine on subjective impressions or neglecting the Father and the Son. We don't want to ignore the Spirit or fear Him, but neither do we want to misunderstand Him. Yet we want more than merely to understand what Scripture teaches about Him—we want to experience Him. More than that, we want to companion intimately with the Holy Spirit of God each day of our lives; we want to love Him as He loves us.

If we're serious in this quest we must make sure not to be ignorant, indifferent, or detached.

Don't Be Ignorant

We don't need to be ignorant because the Spirit of God is named almost three hundred times in Scripture, and many times, as in John 14–16 and Romans 8, His activity is described in great detail. When we study this great body of truth about the Spirit, there are certain errors we'll find corrected:

~ Don't think of the Holy Spirit as a God-force or influence, much less a term to describe how God thinks or feels—"God's spirit." He's a person.

~ Don't think of the Holy Spirit as a high angel or messenger of God. He is God.

The Holy Spirit and I

~ Don't think of the Holy Spirit as an alternate name for God. He's distinct from the Father and the Son.

The Holy Spirit Is a Person

One of the great frustrations of the electronic age is the automated telephone response. After about the third "press two" we want to scream, "Give me a *person!*" We want someone who will listen and talk. The Holy Spirit listens and talks; a force doesn't do that, only persons do.

Best of all, we like to talk and listen to someone who understands us, who feels just the way we do, who has more than a plastic smile and a courteous, fits-all-in-this-category response. The Spirit not only talks to us (Acts 13:2; 16:6–7; Rev. 2:7); He listens when we cry out. He understands us better than we understand ourselves, actually. He hurts with us, weeps with us, joins in our joys (Rom. 8:26–27). The Spirit can be hurt. He grieves when we won't listen to Him or follow His directions (Eph. 4:30; Heb. 10:29). The Holy Spirit is a person who has emotions, who communicates, not a cosmic force or a synonym for the mind of God.

The Holy Spirit Is God

His name is used interchangeably with God (Acts 5:3–4; Luke 1:35). He does things only God can do, like create (Gen. 1:2; Ps. 104:30), know everything (1 Cor. 2:10–11), be everywhere (Ps. 139:7–10). His name is linked with the Father and Son—Jesus commanded us to baptize in the "name of the Father and of the Son and of the Holy Spirit" (Matt. 28:19). The apostle Paul prayed, "The grace of the Lord Jesus Christ, and the love of God, and the communion of the Holy Spirit be with you all" (2 Cor. 13:14, NKJV). He's not a high angel, not even the highest, nor some mysterious emanation from God. The Spirit is a divine person, one member of the Godhead.

The Holy Spirit Is Distinct from the Father and Son

The Holy Spirit is not an alternate name for God. He talks to the Father (Rom. 8:26), He is sent from the Father and Son (John 14:16, 26; 16:7), He came upon the Son (Matt. 3:16), He is listed as a third member of the triune God, not an alter ego of Father or Son. He has a mind of His own (1 Cor. 12:11; Rom. 8:27; 1 Cor. 2:10–11). He is distinguished from the Father and the Son: "Jesus Christ our Lord was shown to be the Son of God when God powerfully raised him from the dead by means of the Holy Spirit" (Rom. 1:4, NLT).

Among the three persons of the Trinity, this glorious person has a distinct function. Theologians sometimes summarize it this way: "All things from God the Father, all things through God the Son, all things by God the Spirit." They speak of the Spirit as the administrator, the executive of the Trinity. He is the one charged with carrying out the will of God, as we shall see throughout this book.

Don't Be Indifferent

It's quite possible to know all the facts of Scripture about the Holy Spirit and not be excited about Him, not appreciate Him, not see the connection between His life and mine. It is sort of like a scholar's analysis of some great historic personage—accurate, complete, something to write a book about or discuss over afternoon tea. But in preparing this study I've discovered something very exciting about this grand Person. I've discovered that every major activity of the Spirit from Creation to the marriage banquet at the end of time is directly related to me. Yes, me, insignificant though I am, and late in time, 2,000 years after the Spirit revealed Himself in Scripture, in fact. But every one of those activities was designed by the Spirit to impact my life today. And in a very personal way. He didn't send His gracious gifts to me UPS, keeping His distance in outer space, nor record them in some dusty archive for me to dig out on my own. He intends personally to hand-deliver every one of those blessings. It's hard to remain indifferent to such a Person and His many gifts.

Don't Be Detached

Some people know the facts about the Spirit and are really excited about connecting with His activity, but it's sort of impersonal. That's sad. Here He is, wooing us into an intimate love relationship, and we treat Him more like a distant relative. He's our constant companion, our *inside* companion in fact, but we don't even talk with Him. Some people are startled to think of talking to the Spirit. In fact, one lady wrote an irate letter to the publisher, accusing me of heresy by even suggesting the possibility of talking to the Spirit. Since she raises an issue central to the theme of this book, let me share some of my response to her:

---

*Q*uestion: Is it biblical to pray to the Holy Spirit?

*A*nswer: It depends. What do we mean by "biblical"? If we mean, "Does the Bible command us to pray to the Spirit?" the answer is, "No, there is no such command." The question is an important first question, and for some it settles the matter. But it shouldn't. If that were the only question to ask—does the Bible directly teach it?—we would not build church buildings or have choirs, we wouldn't oppose abortion or pornography. And we wouldn't pray to Jesus, either, since we are nowhere instructed to. So the second question is, "How do we best apply Bible teaching and biblical principles to be obedient to God's will?"

The Church

If a person means then by that question, "Is prayer to the Holy Spirit compatible with Bible teaching? Does what the Bible teaches about the Spirit mean we should talk to Him?" the answer of the church through the ages has been a resounding, "Yes!" For example, in *The Baptist Hymnal* (Broadman Press, 1975), twelve full hymns are addressed to the Spirit and an additional thirteen hymns have one verse addressed to Him, such as in the well-loved hymn, "Come Thou, Almighty King," where, in verse three we pray, "Come Holy Comforter . . ." A total of twenty-five prayers to the Spirit! Why have Christians of all traditions always sung hymns to the Spirit? What is the biblical evidence?

The Bible

Let us admit, from the start, that there are no examples of prayers to the Holy Spirit. The book of Acts, reporting the activities of the apostles who had been with Jesus, gives no such example. Of course, none of the thirteen prayers recorded in Acts address the Father, either, in spite of the fact that Jesus said, "When you pray, say, 'Our Father, who art in heaven . . .'" In fact, twelve of the thirteen prayers are addressed to "the Lord," the example many of us follow ordinarily in prayer. The context of some of those shows that Jesus was the one addressed, though He is addressed by name in prayer only once. Following the apostolic example, we ordinarily address God, the triune. But notice that when we pray to the "Lord," we include the Spirit, whether consciously or not, for Paul says specifically, "the Lord is the Spirit" (2 Cor. 3:17).

To God the Father, through God the Son, by God the Holy Spirit

This seems to be a legitimate theological formulation of the official role of each member of the Trinity when it comes to prayer, but nowhere is this formula either taught or used in Scripture. To impose this as a rigid formula for prayer is certainly not biblical, for both the New Testament and our hymn books contain many prayers to Jesus, not just to the Father; and requests are made in the name of ("through") "the Father, Son, and Spirit," not just through the Son.

The Bible never uses the term Trinity, of course, nor explains the idea. But the overwhelming evidence of Scripture points to the deity and independent personhood of the Father, the Son, and the Spirit. Yet it presents to us only one God. So the church has wrestled with this evidence and has come up with the theological formulation, "the Trinity." In the same way, we try to do justice to all the activities of each member of the Trinity in line with clear biblical teaching and that's why we address the question of the appropriate ways to pray.

The Trinity

Suppose you were going on a long journey with three dear friends. Though you were constantly with all three, you spoke to only two of them, in spite of the fact that the third friend was the very one who did most of the talking to you. In fact, he came along as the one designated to be your intimate companion, your encourager. Such a one-way communication, while carrying on constant, animated conversation with the other two friends would be more than strange and rude. It would make your friend sad, grieve him. So with the Spirit who is named "comforter," "encourager," and to whose fellowship we have been committed (2 Cor. 13:14). "Communion" or "fellowship" without two-way communication?

On the other hand, the Holy Spirit never was intended to draw attention to Himself but ever to spotlight Jesus (John 15:26). Don't push that too far, however. Some have misunderstood the teaching, "he shall not speak of himself" (John 16:13, KJV) to mean he is to stay hidden. The English word "of," like the Greek original, could have one of two meanings: (1) "about" or (2) "from," that is, "on the authority of." Newer translations make clear what Jesus meant, that the Spirit would not speak independently, on His own authority alone. His words bear the authority of the triune God. Certainly he speaks *about* himself, for the Book He inspired is full of teaching about the Spirit.

My response to the person who raised the question of whether it is appropriate to speak with the Holy Spirit is a rather technical analysis of the question because it is important of itself. But it's also of critical importance to the central thesis of this book—that there is a wonderful Person who wants to be our encourager, our instructor, our companion. He wants to fellowship with us and share a love relationship. I hope the explanation is of some assistance to any who have never experienced conscious fellowship with the Spirit and who may be afraid of the idea. With all the explanations, though, a mystery remains . . .

Our youngest, Kent, puzzled over these questions when he was three years old. "Is Jesus God?" he asked.

"Yes."

"What about the Holy Spirit?"

"Yes, he's God too."

"I don't get it. There's s'posed to be one God, but you just said Jesus is God and the Holy Spirit is God too."

I don't get it, either. In fact, the mystery of our triune God goes beyond all our competence to understand, let alone explain. What kind of God would we have if we could figure Him out completely? Either He would be finite like us or we would have to be gods ourselves to understand the mystery! But even if we can't understand everything, the Bible is clear about this: the Holy Spirit is true God, partaking of all God's infinities, and He is a person distinct from the Father and Son yet one with them. The beauty of it is that you and I can know Him personally, love Him, and be loved. We can talk to Him and listen to Him, we can have His infinite life-force flow through us, even if we can't figure out how it all fits together. Something like electricity. We may not understand how the electric energy flows, but we can live our lives by its power.

And now for those ten glorious activities of the Spirit that are designed to transform my life. "The Holy Spirit and I"—that's what it's all about!

Chapter 2

Activities of the Spirit: Inward Focus

*O*f the ten activities of the Spirit we'll consider, seven are focused on changing me into something I'm not. Those activities focus inward. Then we'll turn to the three activities that focus outward—what He intends to do through me in the lives of others. First, in this chapter and the next, we'll take a brief overview before studying each activity in depth. But remember, this will not be abstract theology, merely programming our information bank, but down-to-earth and practical, considering the ten activities with which the Spirit intends to impact our lives every day.

Creating

It was the Spirit of God who hovered over the dark, empty, formless world (Gen. 1:2); and the climax of His creative work was the statement we find in Job, "The Spirit of God has made me" (Job 33:4). But He didn't make me just any way; He created me in God's own image (Gen. 1:27). And that wasn't just to test His creative powers to see what He could do. No, it was the overflow of His very character. God is love and He created humankind to share in that love relationship. But to be united in an intimate love relationship, the lovers must be compatible. So the Spirit made us God-compatible.

Remember when God was helping newly formed man find a partner compatible to him? He brought the animals, one by one, to be identified, named. "Hey, this is a big one. Let's call him 'elephant.' Too big to get under my roof, though . . . . Now here's a friendly little cuddly one. I'll call her 'kitty.' She doesn't talk much, though. I don't have a clue to what's going on in that pretty little head. Whoa, here's a likely candidate—smart, walks on two legs, sort of looks like me in a fuzzy sort of way. 'Monkey' seems like an appropriate name. But she's so deceptive and dirty—sure doesn't share my values. Better look for something better." None was compatible at the heart of it, Moses says. So God put Adam under anesthesia and did a little surgery. When he woke up, "Incredible!" Eve wasn't identical, thankfully, but fully compatible—they fit, they belonged.

So it is with God and us. Because we are made in His likeness, we can talk, we can communicate our deepest thoughts, we can create magnificent music and literature, we can probe the intricacies of the atom and of the skies and design incredible technology. But best of all, we can know God. And knowing Him, we can love Him. And loving Him truly, we can become like Him, ever more compatible. The Holy Spirit originally designed us for that high calling.

But Adam fouled the relationship. By striking out for independence from God he broke the connection and damaged the image. In fact, he disabled his God-compatibility and not only missed out on knowing God, he didn't even truly understand himself anymore. So we, his descendants, are born disoriented, confused about reality, infected by a pandemic sin virus that renders us a mere shadow of what we were designed to be. We changed, but He didn't. In his unchanging love, God reached out to repair the damage. So the next activity of the Spirit began His restoration strategy.

Revealing

Since we could no longer know God truly, nor even know ourselves accurately, the Spirit began to reveal to us who we are and who God is. "Men spoke from God as they were carried along by the Holy Spirit" (2 Pet. 1:21) so that "all Scripture," indeed, "is God-breathed" (2 Tim. 3:16) and is useful "for everything we need for life and godliness" (2 Pet. 1:3). Since the Book is from God, it's the true picture of reality, and if it's true, I'd better believe it. If it's from God, it must be of ultimate authority for how I think and how I behave. I'd better obey it.

The Holy Spirit's second great activity, then, was to inspire the authors of the Holy Book to reveal God's truth to us, without which even the most brilliant among us is condemned to wander and stumble about in the half-light of sin-distorted perceptions of reality.

However, even if we have the revelation in our hands, we can't understand it. Our receptors have been damaged. So the next great activity of the Spirit is to reprogram our dysfunctional soul-computers and reconnect us with the source of light and power.

Redeeming

Did you know that the Holy Spirit is totally involved in our redemption? Jesus provided for our redemption, to be sure, but it's the Spirit who works it out in our lives. Think about two of the redemptive activities of the Spirit, one negative, one positive.

Jesus taught that the Spirit is sent expressly to convict of sin, of righteousness, and of judgment to come (John 16:8). Very important. If the bad news of our fatal illness doesn't get through to us, we won't even be interested in the good news of a healer. James Graham was a powerful man. He'd been a boxer in the Marine Corps, and now in the years before World War II he was a powerful missionary. He was thirsty for more than he had experienced, and when he heard of revival fires blazing across the interior of China, he wanted to go and investigate. But he hesitated: the chief firebrand spreading that revival was not of his mission and, furthermore, she was a woman. Graham didn't believe in women preachers. But finally he became desperate to understand this spiritual awakening and took the long train ride into the interior. The first night he attended the service the tiny Norwegian Marie Monson was preaching on one of the Ten Commandments. The second night it was another of the commandments. When the third night brought more of the same, Dr. Graham had had it. He strode to the front and, towering over the little lady, demanded, "Why do you not leave the somber legalisms of the Old Testament to the ancient Jews to whom they were addressed and nourish us with the grace of Calvary?"

"Dr. Graham," responded Miss Monson, "until the ears of the heart are opened by the thunders of Sinai, they cannot even hear the sweet grace notes of Calvary."

So it is. First the bad news, then the good. If the bad news were all God gave me, it would serve only to crush me in despair. But the good news follows, and it's very good indeed. The Spirit not only convinces me of my helplessness and hopelessness, but when I respond in repentance and faith, He moves into my life to re-create me. That regenerative work is so total you could compare it to a birth—or a death.

As her mother enters the hospital, that tiny person in her mother's womb is the same person who a few minutes later awakens joy in the delivery room with her strong cries of protest. The same person, but what grand new potentialities! To communicate, to relate to others, to grow independently.

Or the man lying on the hospital gurney, a few moments later in the presence of Jesus—the same person. But what magnificent new dimensions of personal being, what potentialities!

The potentialities in the regenerated me are like the birth of a new me, says Jesus (John 3) or like the death of the old me, says Paul (Rom. 6). For example, the old me could do good, but it couldn't consistently choose the good. I had neither the wisdom to know the right nor the power to do it. But the new me, though it may choose to do wrong, doesn't have to. I now have the capability consistently to choose the good. But regeneration isn't all! In the Spirit's redeeming activity, He not only puts me on such a guilt trip that I turn to Him in repentance and faith and then transforms me into a wholly new kind of being; He does something even better.

Indwelling

The fourth activity of the Spirit is very personal. Not only does He re-create me, He comes to live with me! In fact, Paul says, if He doesn't live in me, I'm not one of Christ's at all (Rom. 8:9). So He doesn't remake me as a new model, wind me up, and turn me loose. It's a personal relationship He gives me. We call it "indwelling."

My sixth-grade buddy and I were having a water-gun fight during school recess. Just as I shot at him, the school bully happened to run between us and caught the stream of water on the side of his head. Twice my size, he could have twisted me into a pretzel with his bare hands, but instead he reached into his pocket and drew out a switchblade knife. Then began the Big Chase. It was chicken to go in the schoolhouse before the bell rang, so I started around the school yard with Big Jim in hot pursuit. Round and round, with all the kids, like some giant swarm of bees, following to see the slaughter. Finally, the saving bell! Into the safety of the classroom, but only for a time. Just as I suspected, when school was out, there he stood guard at the gate. I sneaked out another exit and over backyard fences the four blocks to the safety of home. Every day a different route, till finally I ran out of stratagems. A very lonely Friday afternoon found me disconsolate in a darkened hallway, contemplating my nemesis waiting patiently by the gate. I glanced out the side window, and, to my astonishment, there was a sight I'd never seen before and never since. My father was walking down the sidewalk! Down the side stairs and out to greet him with unaccustomed warmth, I put my hand in his as we marched together past the front gate. "Hi, Jim!" I said with studied nonchalance.

Victory over the sin-bullies in my life is possible not only because of the strength of the new me but also because of my inside partner. Unlike my father, He doesn't leave me: He's with me always. Like a good friend, He lifts me when I'm down, He guides me when I'm lost, He cautions me when I'm tempted, He restores me when I fall, He laughs with me when things go right, He weeps with me when things go wrong. He loves me always. But victory over the sin-bullies of my life doesn't come automatically. I've got to keep my hand in His, stay close, keep a tight connection.

So that's the way of victory—the new me with my new potentialities, plus the empowerment of my inside companion can consistently say "yes" to God and "no" to the enemy. But don't let that glorious truth lead you into unrealistic expectations. We're not perfect yet, not all we could be. That leads us to the fifth activity of the Spirit.

Transforming

When I made the big turnaround, repented and believed, He transformed me into something totally new. In fact, old things passed away and all kinds of things became new (2 Cor. 5:17). But that wasn't the end of His re-creative project, though some church testimony meetings may sound like it. It was only the beginning. You're genuinely new, but not totally new. Paul puts it this way in the verse that has become my life theme: "All of us whose hearts have been cleared of the sin-fog and who keep a steady focus on Jesus are in the process of being transformed into the original image by the Spirit of the Lord" (2 Cor. 3:18, author's paraphrase).

Notice a couple of things about that key passage on the Holy Spirit's activity in my paraphrase of 2 Corinthians 3:18. When Paul says the Spirit is transforming me, he uses the word *metamorphosis*, meaning a change in my inmost nature. It's not just behavior modification through spiritual disciplines. And it's not therapeutic adjustments to develop coping strategies. It's a radical transformation of the core me!

Does that happen automatically to everyone who's born again? Why is the church filled with people who seem to have stalled? Notice the two qualifications that make a person eligible for the Spirit's transforming work: the sin-barrier must be removed and the confident expectation must be in Jesus, not in one's own efforts or some program or technique. Another way to say it is "yield" (get rid of all the sin-smog) and "trust" (keep focused on Jesus, trusting the Holy Spirit to work the transformation He promised).

The spiral is a spiritual picture of your life. Only it's incomplete. And, of course, the way you complete it will differ from everyone else's life story. All of us begin the same—on the spiral down away from God, toward ever greater destruction. That's life without the Spirit. But life with the Spirit is another story—the story of an upward spiral toward God. That means toward ever greater likeness to Jesus and ever more intimate companionship with Him.

The glorious spiral up: the more I know Him, the more I trust Him; the more I trust Him, the more I love Him; the more I love Him, the more I obey Him; the more I obey Him, the more I become like Him; the more I become like Him, the greater capacity I have to love Him; the more I love Him . . . That's no halfway Christianity—it's full throttle! And that leads to the sixth activity of the Spirit.

Filling

The New Testament often uses picture language to describe the relation the Spirit desires to have with us. The picture word he uses is "full." We are to be constantly filled with the Spirit, Paul teaches (Eph. 5:18). But what does "full" mean literally? There are three ways the word is used in Scripture to describe what happens between you and the Spirit. So if you asked me, "Are you Spirit-filled?" my answer would depend on which idea you have in mind. Depending on your meaning, I might say, "Yes" or "Sometimes" or "You tell me!"

Occasionally in the New Testament "full" describes a relationship between two people, and you're full of the Spirit when He's in full control. So if you mean who's in charge in your life, I'd have to say, "God is, so far as I know my own heart."

But sometimes the Bible seems to refer to a subjective feeling—a person *feels* full, just as he does when he finishes Thanksgiving dinner. "Filled with joy in the Holy Spirit," Scripture says. For many people that's what they have in mind when they say they're filled with the Spirit—they have that ecstatic inner sense of God's presence. If you have that meaning in mind when you ask whether I'm Spirit-filled, to be honest I'd have to answer, "Sometimes."

By far the most common Bible use of the phrase *"filled with the Spirit,"* however, is something else entirely. It's the *result* of the relationship, the visible evidence of God being in charge. If a person is truly Spirit-filled, there'll be lots of evidence in a supernatural quality of life: attitudes and actions that defy human analysis, and abilities to make an eternal impact through ministry to others. If that's what you have in mind when you ask if I'm Spirit-filled, I'd have to respond, "You tell me." For in Scripture you never find a person claiming to be Spirit-filled. It's always used to describe others: "They, filled with Spirit . . ." For example, the evidence might have been a supernatural response to adversity—courage or joy or peace when you would have expected fear or discouragement. Or the evidence might be in powerful ministry. Others saw that and identified the source as full-blown Holy Spirit activity.

Overcoming

But suppose my talk and walk don't give much evidence of being filled with the Spirit? Suppose I go down before the same miserable temptations to lose my temper, to say unkind words, to lust for things or sex, to take credit that belongs to God, to worry instead of trust? What happened to the seventh activity of the Spirit, the overcoming activity? He promises to empower me to overcome (Rom. 8:37), but maybe it's not happening. What's wrong?

Usually it's because I'm not filled with the Spirit in the only sense I can control: am I unconditionally yielded? If not, the fog drifts back in. Maybe I get too busy about other things to invest the time I need to stay close to Him, or maybe there's been some little compromise and rationalization to justify doing what I want to do. A "no" will do it in an instant.

Perhaps there's no barrier between us that I know of, however, but I've not been proactive, I've not been acting with Him, using the weapons He provides—prayer, Scripture, the church, suffering. Perhaps I need a battle strategy. We'll develop such a strategy in chapters 30–33, but for now, remember that the Holy Spirit is the Overcomer, not I. Yet I must proactively participate with Him in using the weapons He provides—constantly, seriously, intentionally, vigorously.

What a wonder the Spirit is! He created us God-compatible for loving oneness with Him, but when Adam broke the relationship and thus broke himself, the Spirit shined into our darkness the bright light of truth. My sin-damaged receptors couldn't make sense of that revelation, though; so the Spirit pursued me till He put me on a guilt trip, convinced me of my own hopeless condition. When I responded in faith, He transformed me into an altogether new person, putting me on the spiral up toward a restored image. He moved in with me as my inside partner, filled me up with Himself and started transforming me in my inmost being. He didn't do it all by Himself, though—He provided weapons for me to participate with Him in fighting the spiritual battles, empowering me to overcome. What a wonder He is!

All the activities of the Spirit we've introduced so far have focused on personal holiness, spiraling up toward ever greater likeness to Jesus. The Spirit was given, however, not merely to make us godly in our thinking and behavior. He was given also to produce God-sized impact on others. We turn now to the activity of the Spirit through us in the lives of others.

Chapter 3

Activities of the Spirit: Focus Outward

In studying the activities of the Spirit, we could become very introspective, even self-oriented. We live in an age of radical individualism, and some people might see "spiraling up" as a very exclusive relationship between God and them. But the Holy Spirit won't let that happen! We were born in community and we were designed to live in community. Furthermore, the more like God we become, the more we'll be oriented outward, preoccupied with others, not with self. And the startling thing is this: an infinite, all-powerful God has chosen to do His work in the world through us lowly mortals! So a major activity of the Holy Spirit is to get God's purposes on planet Earth accomplished through His people reaching out.

Gifting

Churches tend to make a grave error in one of two opposite directions. Either they ignore the gifting activity of the Spirit and have to muddle along on their own very limited resources, or they become preoccupied with it, defining gifts in ways the Bible never does or seeking them in ways God never intended. After periods in my life swinging to each of those extremes, I've settled on what I hope is a more biblical balance. Seeing in Scripture what God intends His church to be and do, I trust the Spirit of God to provide the abilities necessary to do it. He gives at least one ability to every believer (1 Cor. 12:4, 7, 11); so if some member is not functioning, the "body"—as Paul calls the church—is crippled by that

19

much. In some churches fifteen percent of the members try to function for the whole body. No wonder such churches are weak and powerless!

God uses our natural abilities, our experience, and our training, but those resources alone won't accomplish spiritual impact. So the Holy Spirit gives abilities to do what we can't do on our own. The mark of the Spirit's empowerment is spiritual impact. Do lives change when the Bible is taught, songs are sung, money is managed? That's the Spirit at work! If all the impact could be explained in terms of a person's natural ability—no supernatural transformation takes place—the Holy Spirit must have been left out.

The Holy Spirit distributes gifts as He sees fit, to be sure, but don't just wait for the Spirit to move in. He says we're to be proactive about it: "Earnestly desire the higher gifts" (1 Cor. 12:31, RSV). Go after it, as the term implies, persistently asking God and simultaneously working at it—individually and as a church. Does something important need doing? Does some ministry hobble that God intends to soar on the wings of the Spirit? Then go for it! Paul's command to "desire" is very strong; that's why in the King James Version it's translated "covet." Later I'll tell you how I coveted the gift of evangelism and how God answered. But it wasn't so I could feel fulfilled or become famous. I felt the impelling of the Spirit into pioneer missionary work, but I didn't feel gifted for it—I wasn't successful in evangelism, not consistently. So for the glory of God and the extension of His kingdom I kept on asking for the Spirit-given ability to do what needed to be done. That personal experience leads to the next activity of the Spirit.

Sending

The ninth activity of the Spirit is sending: "You'll receive power when the Holy Spirit comes on you" (Acts 1:8, author's paraphrase)—power to do what? To live godly? To experience warm fellowship and great feelings? *Power to be Christ's witnesses* is what He said. If I belong to Jesus, I'm commissioned as a witness—that's part of the deal! But even better, I'm *empowered* to witness, to show and tell. To show by my life an authentic reflection of Jesus and to talk about Him, telling what I have personally experienced. It's the Spirit who lives and speaks through me.

Some are gifted to go beyond witnessing. They have the ability consistently to win people to faith. We call it the gift of evangelism. Every church should have a few of those. If most members of a church show and tell—faithfully witness by lives that draw people and talk that alerts people to the possibilities—and if that church has a few people who are good at closing, that church will grow.

The Spirit was given not merely to send His people to those near at hand, however; He commissioned the church to send some of those gifted in evangelism to reach the rest of the world. God is an all-the-world loving God. We tend to love our own. But if we're truly Spirit-filled, His heart will be ours and we'll become all-the-world loving people. If we're anywhere near godly—like God, that is—we'll love the whole world and devote ourselves, as He did, to saving it. Especially the dark half of the world: one out of two people on planet earth live out of reach of present gospel witness.

If a church had God's heart, how many of its own sons and daughters would it send? God sent 100 percent—His only Son. I was invited to speak about missions in a church in Virginia that was only fifteen years old but bursting at the seams. They had only three hundred members, but, with crowds of seekers and newborns, there were six hundred in attendance! I asked how many missionaries they supported with prayer and finances and was told "seventy-five."

"How many of those are from your church?" I asked.

"Oh," they said in mild surprise at the question, "seventy-five."

Twenty percent of the membership serving at the frontiers, in obedience to Jesus' last command, helping complete His great commission. Twenty percent! They had caught the Spirit. Or, I should say, He had caught them! How about my church? Twenty percent is a little much, you say. Well, how about one percent? The largest denominational mission board in America sends one twentieth of one percent of the church's membership. And we say we love the world? Are we listening to the voice of the Spirit? He is ever the sending God.

Glorifying

The final activity we shall study is, naturally, the marriage supper of the Lamb at which the Spirit presents the Bride to the Bridegroom. There is coming a day when the Spirit will complete His task of remaking us into the very likeness of Jesus, uniting us to Him in total oneness of heart. I call it His glorifying activity—the glorifying of us when the Holy Spirit gives real, total life to our bodies (Rom. 8:11); but more importantly, the glorifying of Jesus by the gift of a Bride, without spot or blemish (Rev. 19:6–9; 22:17).

That's why I include this in the "focus outward" group of the Spirit's activities. Not what He does for me, but what I do toward Him. Glorifying God, however, as I join on that grand day the thunder of a billion voices in loud praises to God, doesn't begin then. That final activity of the Spirit actually begins now, not then, and it points to the goal of all the Spirit's activity. The ultimate goal is not power-packed ministry, exciting as that is. Nor is the goal merely to make us godly in character. No, the holy life is a means toward the ultimate goal, for only as we are like him, God-compatible, can we respond in the kind of loving intimacy He designed us for. Oneness with God—that's His ultimate purpose. Listen to these incredible words of Jesus' prayer: "I am praying not only for these disciples but also for all who will ever believe in me because of their testimony. My prayer for all of them is that they will be one, just as you and I are one, Father—that just as you are in me and I am in you, so they will be in us, and the world will believe you sent me. . . . I have given them the glory you gave me, so that they may be one, as we are—I in them and you in me, all being perfected into one" (John 17:20–23a, NLT).

In the twentieth century, the legitimate application of this passage to the unity of the church has virtually eclipsed its more basic and utterly stunning meaning: our union with God the Father, Son, and Spirit. That's why it's so sad that many of His people treat the Spirit as a friendly stranger or lock Him out altogether. Sad, not merely because it shuts them off from becoming all they were designed to be, but sad because we were created and saved to be God's constant, loving companions. That's what He's after! And without that we may not be alive enough to be lonely, but He's lonely. And that's sad.

I've entered the golden years, which by interpretation means grandfather-hood! Grandchildren are the most wonderful invention! When I held the first one—little Eric, in my arms—how adorable. And how I loved him! He was clearly created in my image, but he couldn't understand me or talk with me. Happily, he grew. When he broke into teen age, he came for a visit and I asked for his major prayer request. Studies? Sports? Something he wants? His major prayer request was for the unsaved in his youth group. We were on the same wavelength.

When I told Tosha, in Japan, a gift was in the mail, she exclaimed excitedly, "Oh, I'll *love* it!"

I said, "How do you know? You haven't even seen it."

"Why, Pawpaw," she responded, "it's from *you*. Anything from you I'll love." She was only six, but she missed me, loved to be with me, exulted in every letter and gift. Pawpaw-compatible, you might say. I loved those children—all eight of them—when they were infants, but I also loved to see them grow. And the more they grow, the more their potential for loving intimacy. That's the way it is with God. He loves us when we're newborn, but He wants us to grow in knowing Him, loving Him, exulting in His companionship, delighting in every gift and letter. What if it didn't happen? It doesn't always, you know.

I remember when Muriel was fifty. Beautiful—she looked thirty-five—viva-cious, talented, God-lover. A daily, intimate companion of twenty-five years. As the song says, she was "the wind beneath my wings." Then she began to grow backwards. I remember the pain when she passed briefly through what seemed a confused, volatile teen reincarnation. But before I could adapt, she quickly reached the likeness of a five-year-old, then three, then one. And today? An infant in my arms. I feed her and specialize in diapers, talk to one who doesn't hear and can't respond. How my heart leaps when occasionally our eyes connect and she smiles so gently, just like the old days. Oh, I love her dearly—maybe more than ever before. But I ache because she can't love me back.

So it is with God. Which direction are you growing? Are you more like a rebel teen or wailing infant than an intimate companion, maturing in beauty and strength? How sad it makes the Spirit. That's not what you were designed for. That isn't what His ten activities aim at. That's not what glorifies God, brings Him joy. Oh, you still bear the imprint of His likeness, may even have been re-created in a sense. He loves you still. But the Spirit yearns for so much more. The goal of all that transforming grace is to be His intimate companion. Today and every tomorrow.

That's a brief overview of what the Spirit is up to, but to help us fully participate in all He intends to do in us, we'll now examine each of the Spirit's activities in greater detail. I sense a reawakening in God's church, here and there, a fresh breeze of the Spirit. I've seen it in pastors and lay leaders weeping, crying out for the Spirit's forgiveness for neglecting Him so, asking Him for revival quickening. The Spirit is moving. Hoist your sails and catch the Wind!

Activity One
Creating

Chapter 4

Designer Model

$\mathcal{S}$he was beautiful, intelligent, and articulate—not exactly your average American, at least by outward appearances. But the off-duty flight attendant sitting by me on the plane may have been a very typical American in her unseen, spiritual dimension. She was active in her church and she had heard Billy Graham on TV occasionally. Yes, she believed what Billy taught, though she herself was of "another faith." What about her husband? "Well, he doesn't have any use for church." She paused briefly, and then added, "But he's very spiritual." Spiritual? What did she mean?

She meant what most Americans mean by "spiritual." She meant he believed in an unseen world and was interested in it, just like her. And this represents a mega-shift in Western thinking. With the dawn of the "scientific" era, people in general came to view the unseen world as non-existent or at least irrelevant. But no more. Newspapers, magazines, talk shows are full of angels, magic, reincarnation, prayer, horoscopes, God, the occult, "born-again" experiences. Maybe it came from the "spiritual" East with New Age thinking, maybe it came from Christian novels about demons. Some say it came from widespread disillusionment with a sterile, rational approach to life—the "scientific" outlook, if you please—because science, it turned out, wasn't solving our basic human problems. Wherever it came from, here it is—in force. And what do we make of it? Do we cling to the old "scientific" view and live as if the realm of the spirit did not exist, or do we go with the flow of fascination with the unseen?

Perhaps we do neither. Surely we reject the old "scientific" or naturalistic view of things and take Scripture seriously, recognizing that the visible world is not all there is to life, not even the most important part. "For we fix our attention, not on things that are seen, but on things that are unseen. What can be seen lasts only for a time, but what cannot be seen lasts forever" (2 Cor. 4:18, TEV).

To treat what we can see, hear, touch or taste as if the world we see were everything—or even the most important thing—will lead to disaster sooner or later, and the modern has begun to suspect that. On the other hand, though we are grateful that people are beginning to recognize an unseen, "spiritual" realm, we think it very important to know just what really is out there, what part of that unseen world is good and what is not. If we want to understand spiritual reality and to link up only with the good part, we need to get better acquainted with the source of all spiritual good, the Holy Spirit of God. When we do, we'll discover that He created us spiritual—that is, we're not just complex material organisms. We have an unseen dimension.

The first great activity of the Holy Spirit recorded in Scripture was creation (Gen. 1:1–2; Job 33:4; Ps. 104:30). But that was long ago—what does that have to do with my life today? Everything, actually, because the way God made us determines our potential. Potential, for example, to communicate with God, to think and behave the way Jesus did. If we weren't "in His image" we couldn't do that. So the original design is very important. "Then God said, 'And now we will make human beings; they will be like us and resemble us . . .' So God created human beings, making them to be like himself. He created them male and female" (Gen. 1:26–27, TEV).

We see that family resemblance mirrored in our human families. "Just look at that boy! Why, he's the spittin' image of ol' Joe!" I'm not sure how the "spittin'" got in there, but we get the picture: the boy is a replica of his father—looks like him, walks like him, talks like him. So with us. In some mysterious way we are on the model of God Himself. In a strategic planning session deep in eternity, the Father, Son, and Holy Spirit agreed, "Let us make man in our image." To be like God at least means we're spiritual, not just material, because "God is spirit" (John 4:24). But what does that spiritual dimension look like?

Alexander the Great, Caesar, King Nebuchadnezzar, even Herod had something in common. Two things, actually: they claimed to be god and they hated cats. They grasped for supreme authority and the cats were the only ones who wouldn't obey! Supreme authority, power. That would be in God's image, wouldn't it? Or wisdom. Did you ever wonder why certain university professors or even some preachers are insufferably arrogant about what they know? It would almost seem they aspire to be like God in His infinite knowledge and wisdom, standing in self-confident judgment over all. In the twentieth century we are rapidly achieving corporately what some of the ancients futilely tried to achieve as individuals. With our computers we seem to have accumulated close to infinite knowledge capabilities, and with our jets and telecommunications we approach a degree of omnipresence. But these were not the aspects of God He intended us to share. Not omnipotence. Not omniscience. Not omnipresence.

Of course, we do have high potential for knowing and doing, created as we are on His model. That's why so much human achievement in the arts and sciences is truly magnificent. But God's infinities are forever beyond us. There is one aspect of God, however, in which He designed us to be just like Him.

Think about it. Porpoises communicate with signals, they tell us; but no dictionaries yet. Pandas make tools—they break off a stick to dig out the food they want; but no automobiles yet. Ants build incredibly complex cities and even keep aphid-cows to milk; but no churches or temples have ever been found in those cities. Monkeys misbehave; but none has been known to blush. When God created a special being in His own likeness, He designed one unlike the animals he had already created—one with an immortal spirit who could communicate, create, know right from wrong, and, above all, love and be loved by God Himself. That's His "image," the stamp of the Designer.

Theologians debate the meaning of "image." Since the Bible doesn't give a concise definition, we have to draw from the rest of Scripture to find the meaning. Here are some of the conclusions various theologians have reached about what it means to be in God's likeness:

- we are essentially spiritual beings
- we have the ability to communicate
- we have the ability to think rationally
- we have a moral sense, ability to distinguish right from wrong
- we were designed to have attitudes and moral behavior like God
- we have emotions, the ability to love and be loved, to feel joy and sorrow
- we have the ability to choose

We are indeed a "designer model"—modeled after the Designer Himself. And that was the work of the Holy Spirit in His first activity, creating us in God's image. As the old English has it, we are an "exceeding magnifical creation"! But why did God design such a being?

Muriel was pretty, vivacious, talented, fun, a great lover of God—and lover of me! Finally she agreed to be mine, and everything in life was aimed toward the wedding day, August 24. I was so intoxicated with love for Muriel I constantly did irrational things. Like subsisting on one meal a day so I could save for the Great Day. Like reading her love letters the minute they arrived, no matter that they consistently preempted my history class. Writing, calling, sending gifts. Shortly before The Day, I gathered some of my family in South Carolina, borrowed my father's car, and headed for Nebraska. In a long, sweeping curve through the wheat fields of Kansas we were slowed by a tractor which had backed up traffic for what seemed miles. Finally my chance came. I could see around the curve, ahead of dozens of creeping cars, and no one was coming toward us. I whipped out into the left lane of that two-lane highway and put it to the floor. Not very smart. But I was crazy in love. I had one objective: to get to my beloved.

Half-way through that curve, a speeding car appeared from nowhere, aimed right at us. I headed for the shoulder. "Oh, no! Why did they put that telephone pole there?" The thought barely had time to flash through my mind as I closed my eyes and aimed at the narrow gap between the approaching car and the pole. We left one of my father's fenders on that pole and limped on to Beaver City. And there it was that Muriel and I began a lifetime odyssey of exquisite delight.

And now? Now Muriel lies in bed, unable to stand or walk or feed herself and knowing nothing, really, a victim of Alzheimer's Disease. But her contented smile sometimes breaks through the dimness and brightens my day. People speak of my care of her as if it were something heroic. Far from it. I love her more now than ever I did on that mad dash to Nebraska. When I'm away on a speaking engagement, I miss her more, I long to be with her, to feel the squeeze of her hand. But there's a big difference. The love flows mostly one way. There's no connecting point now. We used to share our dreams, our work, our play, our children, our laughter, our tears. And we drew ever closer to one another. Became more and more like one another, actually. But we're not much alike now. The mutuality is almost gone.

Perhaps that's the way it is with God and you. He created you to be like Him so you could share His life and love. A mutually satisfying love affair is what He had in mind. It started out so gloriously, didn't it? You wanted to be with Him always, found Him your highest joy. But for many Christians, something has happened. Oh, God still loves them and lavishes love-gifts on them daily. But how do they respond? Communication is sporadic; love has lost its passion. Perhaps they can't even identify with Him because they are so unlike Him, now. Like Muriel, they can't stand alone, don't walk with Him, can't understand His words, can't even feed themselves, and someone has to clean up after them. Sad, isn't it? But that was never the Designer's plan, a plan modeled after the very nature of our triune God.

From all eternity God the Father, God the Son, and God the Holy Spirit were bound together in bonds of living love, for God by nature is love (1 John 4:7, 16). And from the overflow of His loving nature He wanted a being who would love Him back. For communication and love to flow freely, such a being would have to be like Him, would have to be the same kind of person. So the plan was to create us God-compatible. If that compatibility weren't there, in-depth communication would not be possible, intimate companionship would be missing. To make possible that companionship with God is the reason the Holy Spirit created humankind on God's own pattern. As a result, Adam and Eve walked with God in the garden of Paradise, sharing His life. They were created to love God and be loved of Him, and they were created in His likeness so that could be.

If that is God's purpose, what is mine? If you're a serious Christian, perhaps your supreme purpose in life is . . .

~ To serve in the church faithfully
~ To become like Christ in character
~ To win souls
~ To be successful in your life's calling
~ To love God
~ To raise children who are successful

All those purposes are worthy, but the ultimate goal of our lives is not to be like Christ in character, let alone to work hard for Him. The goal of life is loving oneness with God. "Experiencing God," you might call it. "'You shall love the LORD your God with all your heart, with all your soul, and with all your mind.' This is the first and great commandment" (Matt. 22:37–38, NKJV).

Oneness with God in eternal bonds of love—that was the purpose of creation and redemption. And since the only way to reach that goal is to become like Him, becoming like Christ is of utmost importance. So important, in fact, that how we become like Him is the major emphasis of this book.

But thinking about the character of God could lead to discouragement because we fall so far short; so next we'll consider what potential there is for actually becoming like Him. And that is the great desire of the true lover of God—to be like Him so that we can experience His purpose in making and redeeming us, an ever-deepening love relationship. That will bring Him joy—and bring us joy too!

Chapter 5

Capacity of Your Designer Model

*W*e were sightseeing in a giant computer mall. I discovered magical things like a program on which you could design your yard, "plant" shrubs and flowers, and then produce a picture of what it would look like six months later, a year later, five years later. My son, an executive with Xerox software, was trying to explain things to me in simple terms I could understand. Finally David gave up and said, "Your computer just doesn't have the capacity for that program, Dad."

Sort of like some people who, browsing through the Bible, see God's program for a growing, mature Christian. It's marvelous, but does my model have the capacity to run that program? Remember, you were designed on the model of God's own spiritual nature. Plenty of capacity! You ought to be able to reproduce any program God gives for thinking like Him or behaving like His Son, Jesus. But somehow, when you try to run the program and press the "enter" key in your mind, the response is always "not reading drive A" or some other negative response, indicating failure to bring to your life what is in the program "menu," the Bible. What's gone wrong? Why can't I get the results God promises?

Adam and Eve could do it. They knew the right and always did it. They also had the capacity to choose wrong and in the end they did that too. They disabled their "computer" so it could no longer run God's program successfully. Is there any way to fix it, to get that original capability back? If they did, what would they look like?

God's program for the Christian looks something like this: Loving responses toward the ungrateful, even the hostile; joy in the midst of unhappy

31

circumstances; peace and hope when everything goes wrong. The Christian was designed to overcome in the battle with temptation, consistently obey the laws of God, and grow in self-control, contentment, humility, and courage. Thought processes were to be so under the control of the Holy Spirit and instructed by Scripture that the normal Christian would authentically reflect the attitudes and behavior of Jesus Christ. God has first place in life, and the welfare of others takes precedence over personal desires. The Spirit planned for the Christian to have power, not only for godly living but also for effective service in the church. Above all, he or she would have the joy of constant companionship with the Lord.

The problem is the program doesn't seem to run on most Christian "computers." They lack the capacity, or if they have it, somehow the circuits are crossed up so the program doesn't run. Church members typically think and behave very much like morally upright non-Christians. They are decent enough, but there is nothing supernatural about them. Their behavior is quite explainable in terms of heredity, early environment, and present circumstances. They yield to temptation more often than not, lusting when their body craves it, coveting what they do not have, and taking credit for their accomplishments. The touchstone for their choices is self-interest, and though they have a love for God and others, it doesn't control their life; strained or broken relationships with others prove that. There is little change for the better; in fact, most do not expect much improvement and are little concerned by that prospect. Scripture is not exciting, prayer is perfunctory, and service in the church demonstrates little touch of the supernatural. Above all, their life seems to have an empty core, for it doesn't center around a constant, personal companionship with the Lord.

Perhaps you find more of yourself in the typical disabled version described in the last paragraph than in the Great Designer's model suggested in the earlier paragraph. The exciting news is that we can move from dysfunctional to functional models of our Creator God. Of course, every one of us, no matter how far the restoration process has advanced, has areas of strength and weakness—some we're aware of, some perhaps not. But God knows, and when we acknowledge our need to Him, He will move in and begin restoring our broken-down models to function as God designed them (1 John 1:5–2:2).

But "how, *how,* HOW, *HOW* can I ever live that kind of life?" The question was scribbled on a scrap of paper and passed on to me, a cry for help from a troubled graduate student who had heard me talk about a Spirit-empowered life. She was too timid to join the crowd of talkers gathered around the professor after class, but she desperately wanted an answer. This entire book is devoted to answering that question. I hope you'll discover that the model you were built on, God's own pattern, when restored by the master Repairman, can indeed run the program designed for it. You can experience daily a beautiful life of spiritual success. You can begin to resemble God, more and more, and companion with Him ever more intimately.

That will be our study, but let me summarize the answer briefly, in the words of Scripture: "For those God foreknew he also predestined to be conformed to the likeness of his Son" (Rom. 8:29). "And we, who with unveiled faces all reflect [contemplate] the Lord's glory, are being transformed into his likeness with ever-increasing glory, which comes from the Lord, who is the Spirit" (2 Cor. 3:18). "The new man . . . is renewed in knowledge according to the image of Him who created him" (Col. 3:10, NKJV). Notice that in the context of all these passages the restoration to our original design is not in a study lesson, not in a formula, but in a Person. It is the transforming presence and power of God the Holy Spirit that will enable us to be all we were designed to be.

But "how, how, HOW" do we connect to let His power flow? We connect with Him through faith. "The righteous will live by faith" was the only message of an Old Testament prophet repeated, not once, but three times in the New Testament (Hab. 2:4; Rom. 1:17; Gal. 3:11; Heb. 10:38). Indeed, faith is the up-link with divine power, whether for salvation or for being renovated into the original design. Our focus, therefore, will be on two things: God's provision for successful Christian living and our response to let that provision flow. God's provision is the activity of the Holy Spirit, and our response, releasing the flow of power, is faith.

And what is faith for a twenty-first-century, show-me kind of person? We will examine this from many angles, but for now, faith means believing what God has said. It also means trusting God, putting your life in His hands and leaving it there even when it looks like everything is going wrong. And it means having confidence in His love and knowledge of you and His ability to order your life for your greatest blessing. And what if you don't feel any of that today? What if you just can't believe it with your whole heart? Well, that's okay—faith covers that, too. Faith is active when you tell yourself you're going to go ahead anyway and live your life as if all of that was true. Faith chooses to go for it even when you don't feel good about it. And through that choice to obey, faith will grow. You'll see how as our study unfolds.

God and faith, then, are the two key words of this book. God is the standard for my life—His character is what I was meant to be. God is also the Restorer, the Enabler of my life; the Holy Spirit alone can make it happen. I connect with Him through faith. This study is designed to examine and help you experience those truths in all their exciting dimensions.

We have discovered that to be "spiritual" is much more than merely giving attention to the invisible world. God Himself is spirit in nature and He created us on the same model—we are spirit beings—so we could join His circle of love. We broke that love bond and, in doing so, broke ourselves. But God pursued us with passionate love, intent on repairing us, remodeling us into His moral likeness so we would again be God-compatible. Only thus could we rejoin the circle of love, one with the Father, the Son, and the Holy Spirit. Before we go further into this incredible love story, however, we pause in our next four chapters to check out a road map of the grand journey He has designed for us. That will let us see where we're going and how all the parts fit together.

Activity Two

Revealing

Chapter 6

The Great Unveiling

*S*omeone is pursuing a friendship with you, let's say, but you aren't so sure. How do you make sure? At least two things are needed:

~ You have to know a person
~ You have to like what you know

Of course there are other things needed to develop a friendship, like spending time together and doing things that please the other person. But first you must know a person and like what you know or you won't even want time together nor have much of an inclination to please. So how is your friendship with God? He is pursuing you; He wants your friendship. But are you pursuing Him? Are the two starter ingredients there? Do you know Him? Do you like what you know?

In pursuit of your friendship, God has reached out in many ways. For example, through what He has made God reminds us daily that He exists, a God of might and infinite wisdom: "For since the creation of the world God's invisible qualities—his eternal power and divine nature—have been clearly seen, being understood from what has been made, so that men are without excuse" (Rom. 1:20). And through our built-in moral consciousness we sense that God is righteous: "Indeed, when Gentiles, who do not have the law, do by nature things required by the law, they are a law for themselves, even though they do not have the law, since they show that the requirements of the law are written on their hearts, their consciences also bearing witness, and their thoughts now accusing, now even defending them" (Rom. 2:14–15).

The Great Unveiling

So everyone can know some things about God: that He is, that He is powerful, that He is holy. But that knowledge might drive us from God, not draw us into seeking His friendship. We might be intimidated by so awesome a God or simply feel that one so powerful is out of reach. Even if I admire a person, I may not want him as a friend. On the other hand, because of a bad conscience I might feel guilty or resent God's holiness. That's why most people ignore God or even hate and oppose Him. What we learn from creation or our moral consciousness is simply not enough to get us on a path toward friendship with God. No, if we are ever to get together, we need to know things about God that would draw us to Him and assure us that we can indeed be friends.

But those are things we can't find out on our own. Left to our own resources, we can't know God enough to want to seek Him out as a friend. So, in His never-say-die love, God chose to overcome our handicaps and reveal Himself to us. The Holy Spirit intervened on our behalf—He gave us a written record of everything we need to know about God and about our human condition. The great unveiling, we could call it. The Bible. Now we can know God, now we can love God, now we can become His friends!

The first activity of the Holy Spirit we found in Scripture was creation; now we turn to His second great activity, revelation, God's Spirit's revealing truth to us so we need no longer stumble around in a spiritual twilight zone but may know God, and knowing Him, love Him. True life in the Spirit begins with understanding the Bible and applying it to our daily lives. God is talking. How carefully am I listening? He is courting my friendship; am I pursuing His?

Here's a little of what the Bible says of itself:

~ "The holy Scriptures . . . are able to make you wise for salvation." (2 Tim. 3:15)

~ "Faith comes by hearing . . . the word of God." (Rom. 10:17, NKJV)

~ "Your word is a lamp to my feet and a light for my path . . . the joy of my heart . . . more precious . . . than . . . gold." (Ps. 119:105, 111, 72)

~ "If . . . my words dwell in you, ask what you will, and you shall have it . . . If you heed my commands, you will dwell in my love." (John 15:7, 10, NEB)

~ "All Scripture is inspired by God and is useful for teaching the truth, rebuking error, correcting faults, and giving instruction for right living, so that the person who serves God may be fully qualified and equipped to do every kind of good work." (2 Tim. 3.16–17, TEV)

Several technical terms describe the revealing activity of the Spirit: revelation, authority, inspiration, interpretation, application, and illumination. The Spirit discloses truth about the universe, about humanity, and about God—truth we would otherwise not know. We call this self-disclosure *revelation*. Because the Bible is from God, it's our *authority*, the only completely dependable means through which God has fully revealed Himself. The Holy Spirit gave that authoritative revelation through a process we call *inspiration*. Now we have the privilege and the responsibility to determine what each passage meant through *interpretation* and what it means for me today through *application*. And for the task of understanding and applying the Bible we have the Holy Spirit to guide us through his work of *illumination*. Let's consider each of those important concepts in order.

Revelation

I was an agnostic. Though raised in a Christian home and educated in a Christian college, I began to doubt the basic truths of the Christian faith. Determined to be truly scientific, I decided never to believe anything without proof, and since I couldn't prove God scientifically, He was the next casualty. It's always that way—first you doubt the Bible, then God.

I was smart enough not to be an atheist and affirm there is no God. After all, I hadn't even been to the other side of the moon, and as a true "scientist" I couldn't deny something that was beyond my experience. But I didn't know, I didn't believe. I was agnostic.

My world gradually darkened as I discovered that it was not just the Bible I doubted. I began to feel that nothing was for sure because I could never get all the evidence on anything. As a result, I could believe less and less about more and more. I tried to be brave, but it was a lonely business, this trusting no one or nothing. Finally, the obvious broke through: if you are so "scientific," McQuilkin, why have you ruled out in advance any investigation of the possibility of God? So, for the first time in a long while, I prayed. My prayer was simple, if a little arrogant, since I asked Him to meet me on my terms: "God, if you exist, will you give me some objective evidence?"

I was surprised to find the evidence right in my hand. That ancient book, which I felt was riddled with errors, had something in it that was definitely beyond natural possibility. Even accepting, as I did, the criticism of those scholars who tried to make of the Bible a thoroughly human, error-filled book, there was still something left they couldn't explain. The Old Testament predicted many details about a coming Messiah—when He was to be born, where He was to be born, what He would do, how He would die, that He would live forever. These predictions were made hundreds of years before Christ's birth. In other words, I discovered revelation. Supernatural revelation—the Bible, a miracle right in my hand. I began, ever so tentatively, to embrace God with my mind. It was a great unveiling.

If God had not taken the initiative in revealing things we can't discover through scientific investigation, how little we would have known about Him, about our lost condition, about His will for us! Without His gracious revelation, how could we have experienced salvation or the abundant life God promises?

Authority

The Bible speaks of these things, but why should we believe and obey it? Where does it get its authority? Any word gets its authority from the one who spoke it. If I say, "There will be a major earthquake in California tomorrow," you have every right to ask, "And who are you?" Once you find out, you probably won't catch the first plane out of the state. But if I turned out to be a leading seismologist who had never failed to make an accurate prediction, you probably would take immediate action. Why? The trustworthiness of a word depends on who said it. The trustworthiness of the Bible depends on who said it. If God said it, you'd better believe it. More than that, you'd better move out and do what it says! We call this book—and only this book—the Word of God. That's why it has supreme authority for our lives. We believe it; we obey it.

I said I came back from agnosticism to faith and embraced God with my mind. But the truth is I still had problems with some parts of the Bible. Like waves of fog, the doubts would blow through my mind from time to time. After about a decade of this I said to myself, "McQuilkin, you've got to get this settled. In or out." So I went to a lonely beach and camped out for three days. There I read the gospels again. And again. Something swept over me—a sense of awe in the presence of the historic person, Jesus Christ. Even if I were to accept all the explanations of the critics and do away with much of what the record says Jesus did and said, still there remains a figure who towers in lonely grandeur among men, an unprecedented revelation of God. On the third day as I stood, gazing out over the vast Pacific, I had a sense that another person was with me, as if He put a hand on my shoulder and said, "Little brother, are you smarter than I?"

"Oh, no!" I cried out, "of course I'm not smarter than you. Nor are all these highly educated critics." In that moment, all the lights turned on. And they have never gone out. I'm not smarter than Jesus! It boils down to this: Who is my authority? Jesus Christ or some scholarly critic or, worse yet, my own limited, sin-damaged intellect? From that moment, I have accepted Christ's view of the Father, of heaven and hell, of salvation, of right and wrong. And of the Bible. If Jesus repeatedly said, "Thus says the Scripture," as the basis for His authority; if He says, "not the smallest letter, not the least stroke of a pen, will by any means disappear from the Law" (Matt. 5:18); then that is my view of Scripture. There are still passages I don't understand or even that I wish weren't there, but my view from that day has been to accept the authority of the Word of God because of who said it, the living Word of God, Jesus Christ. He's smarter than I!

The power of the human intellect is awesome. It ought to be—it's designed on God's model. But it has been so disabled by sin, unaided, people can't understand the Bible—it doesn't even make good sense to them (1 Cor. 2:14; 2 Cor. 3:14–15). Even if there were no crazy mirrors of sin to distort reality, our capacities are limited. We were never designed in likeness to God's infinite capacities. We are finite. So we grope after meaning, the meaning of our own lives if not the grander meaning of the universe. We probe with our ten-watt brains, short-circuited by sin even before the search begins. On this pitiful scene breaks a great light, a mega-burst of eternal truth, truth about God and truth about His plan for our salvation, truth about the meaning of our lives. In the Bible, the Holy Spirit has turned up the lights and revealed God and His will for us. That's why we call the Bible "revelation." God said it, so we believe it. God said it, so we must obey it.

But questions may linger. A natural question would be, How did God say it? We turn now to probe that question, what theologians call "inspiration." Not inspiration as we mean when we say Shakespeare was an inspired writer, but—well, what do we mean by the inspiring activity of the Spirit?

Inspiration

The Bible claims to be inspired by God, and that makes me curious. Exactly what did the Holy Spirit do to the Bible authors? How did He make sure they wrote what He wanted to say? Since He doesn't tell us, we try to figure it out. Some conclude the Spirit must have dictated the Bible to the authors like executives dictate to their secretaries. He obviously did dictate parts of the Bible, as when He gave the Ten Commandments to Moses. Not much of Scripture, however, was dictated. Some, in fact, was written from historical research, like Luke and Acts (Luke 1:1–4).

On the human side, then, the experiences and writing style of each author are evident throughout Scripture. But in some mysterious way those authors were influenced by the Holy Spirit so that what they wrote was consistently called "the Word of God." The authors were "carried along" by the Spirit (2 Pet. 1:20–21) so that "all Scripture is God-breathed" (2 Tim. 3:16). We translate Paul's term for the Spirit's activity in that passage "inspiration," meaning "breathed-in." Our focus is what He did to the authors, but Paul's emphasis was on the source—God Himself is the origin, it's God-breathed-out. Though we may not know how the Spirit carried out this activity, we know from Scripture itself that He so guided the writing process that the human authors wrote what the divine Author wanted communicated. This cannot be said of any other book, no matter how helpful it is. Other books may be called "inspired" in the sense that they inspire the reader, but none can be said to be God-breathed as is Scripture. The Bible alone carries that guarantee.

The Great Unveiling

My son Kent, well versed in the creation story of Genesis, first encountered an alternative view of human origins in the third grade. His righteous indignation ran so hot that he conducted his own inquisition at the lunch hour. Going down the line of little people waiting to be fed, he asked each one, "Do you believe the monkey business?" When he reached his best friend, Dalwin, his friend replied, "Of course I do." ("Dalwin," I later learned, is spelled D-a-r-w-i-n. He seemed to live up to the name his parents gave him!) Kent then leveled his accusation: "Then you don't believe the Bible." Dalwin replied, "Oh yes I do, I just don't believe the part about creation." With the wisdom of his advanced years, untutored by any elder, Kent responded, "Well, how do you choose which part to believe?"

Eight-year old Kent identified the key issue. If I do what Jesus Christ never did, that is, affirm error in Scripture, then I have put myself over Scripture. By deciding what to accept and what not to accept as trustworthy, I must sit in judgment on the Book; my authority becomes superior to its authority. In that way I would reduce the authority of Scripture to the size of my intellect, and that's not a very impressive "revelation"! Paul assures us, "*all* scripture is inspired" (emphasis mine). On the beach that day, I took the step of faith and embraced Jesus' view of the Bible. I'm not smarter than He!

What a magnificent gift the Holy Spirit has given us! In the Bible, He has unveiled the hidden God. We can know God! And knowing Him we will surely love Him. It would really be a mismatched friendship, though, if we did not become increasingly like Him. So, to make that possible, the Holy Spirit gave us a fully reliable revelation of God's will for us. Next we'll look more closely at Scripture as God's revealed will for what we think and how we behave. He could have left us to stumble around in the twilight until night closed in, but He broke through with a brilliant light, liberating us with His own truth. That's what truth does—it sets free (John 8:32). What love! Hallelujah!

Chapter 7

When We Open the Book

*A*s we have seen, *revelation* means that God has spoken, telling things about Himself and us that otherwise would have remained hidden, and *inspiration* means that the Holy Spirit so worked with the authors of Scripture that they wrote what He wanted written. We have a Book we can rely on. But so what? What is it good for?

Paul answers that question in his second letter to Timothy: the Bible is useful to show lost people the way to salvation (2 Tim. 3:14–15), and it was designed to reveal what we will be like when we are spiritually mature (vv. 16–17). Here's how Paul puts it: Scripture is useful to show us what to believe: "teaching the truth and rebuking error." And it is useful for showing us how to behave, "correcting faults, and giving instruction for right living." In fact, to summarize, Scripture was given to make us "fully qualified and equipped to do every kind of good work."

Muriel always wanted to visit London. An artist, my wife never tired of visiting art museums, and London was, in certain respects, the art capital of the world. When Britannia ruled the waves, Britannia collected the art treasures of the world! But with six children at home, we only travelled where necessity demanded. There was a window of opportunity as I had a speaking engagement in England and we began to plan.

We knew well enough the glorious destination we had in mind, just like our destiny in life: we want to be like Jesus so we can be his intimate companion. And just as there are wonderful travel books to tell us about London, so God has provided a wonderful travel Book to guide us to our destination. That's why we are so eager to study His Book. In a similar way, Muriel and I studied about London. We talked with people who had been there, and we accumulated videos, travel books, maps.

We liked the videos best. In the same way, most of us like the Bible "videos," the stories of Bible characters who illustrate where we want to go—or what we want to avoid! God told a wealthy rancher to leave his home and family and go somewhere. He didn't even tell him where! Remember, Abraham had no Bible, no map. But he obeyed and left for somewhere. We see the "video" 4,000 years later and say, "What faith! I wish I could trust God that way." We watch Joseph resist his temptress; we see David fall to his temptress. Do we follow the teen-aged slave or the aging king? We watch the Bible "videos" and say, "God give me strength to be a Joseph." Towering above all illustrations of God's will for us, of course, is Jesus Christ. In fact, it is He who came to show us in detail what God is like (John 14:7–11; Heb. 1:1–3). We see Him hanging in agony of body and spirit, shamed and helpless, and we say "Oh, what love! What courage! How I long to be that kind of person."

But the Bible gives more than examples to follow. If that were all we had, we could easily draw mistaken conclusions. But like a travel book, the Bible also gives descriptions of what our destination will be like. Muriel and I read many descriptions of what London was like. We learned, for example, that the Tate Museum contained the largest collection of paintings by our favorite artist, Turner. And there are many descriptions of the Christian life in Scripture, such as what the activity of the Holy Spirit produces: "The fruit of the Spirit is love, joy, peace, longsuffering, kindness, goodness, faithfulness, gentleness, self-control" (Gal. 5:22–23, NKJV).

The Bible describes the opposite as well—what we will look like if we become more like the devil: "The works of the flesh are evident, which are: adultery, fornication, uncleanness, licentiousness, idolatry, sorcery, hatred, con-tentions, jealousies, outbursts of wrath, selfish ambitions, dissensions, heresies, envy, murders, drunkenness, revelries, and the like; of which I tell you before-hand, just as I also told you in time past, that those who practice such things will not inherit the kingdom of God" (Gal. 5:19–21, NKJV).

Our travel Book describes where to go and where not to go in life, but it also gives many principles on how to get to our destination. "Love fulfills the law" is a principle of life. The Bible does describe in detail how love will behave, but by stating the broad principle, it covers all potential attitudes and actions. That way, we can't escape by saying the Bible doesn't give any rules about racism, for example. The principle of love covers all relationships. How long would the Bible be if it gave specific examples or precise commands covering every possible attitude and activity for all people of all time? We would need a Library-of-Congress-sized collection with maximum computer capacity just to

43

record them all! Forget about finding what you need at the moment of temptation! So God gives us principles that cover all possible attitudes and actions.

But examples, descriptions, and principles would never have gotten Muriel and me to the Tate Museum. We needed specifics, a map. If we didn't find Millbank at Atterby Street, we would never get there. So God's travel guide has lots of road maps—specific commandments which we must follow or we'll never reach our destination. In fact, there are more than six hundred commands in the Old Testament and—surprise!—more than six hundred in the New Testament. For example, "Thou shalt not steal" (Exod. 20:15, KJV), or, "Do not get drunk on wine, . . . Instead, be filled with the Spirit" (Eph. 5:18). Do you want to be like Jesus? Then you must be filled with the Spirit. A command.

Think about the relationship between principles and laws. The principles and commands of Scripture are never in conflict. You can't justify violating a direct command by appealing to some broader principle. For example, "In this case it's okay to lie to fulfill the principle of love." No, the specific commands are God's official application of some principle and must be obeyed. My application of the principle doesn't have God's authority, so I must not set my interpretation in opposition to a clear directive from God. On the other hand, the fact that no command covers a specific situation doesn't set us free to do as we please. We are still bound by the principles of Scripture. Thus we need both the principles and the commands to know God's will.

The Spirit, then, in giving us a revelation of God's will for our thinking and behavior, uses examples to follow or avoid, descriptions of good or bad behavior, general life principles, and direct commands. For example,

- ⁓ A command: Thou shalt not covet.
- ⁓ An example to follow: Stephen asked forgiveness for those who were stoning him.
- ⁓ A description: Happy are those who hunger and thirst after righteousness.
- ⁓ A principle: Be holy as I am holy.
- ⁓ An example not to follow: Jonah refused to witness in Nineveh to an alien people.
- ⁓ A description: Love suffers long and is kind.

Did you notice that all of these either express a principle or could be converted into a principle? That's why we can say, "The Bible is more a book of principles than a list of rules." "Be holy as I am holy," is a command, but it is not a specific command. That is, it doesn't define "holy"—it's a general term that covers all righteous thought and action. In that sense, in the list above, the "be holy" command is the one most clearly a general principle, but all the other examples, descriptions, and commands can be converted into principles as well.

In this way, we can call the Bible God's guidebook; it clearly reveals God's standard for how He expects us to think and behave. But the Spirit didn't make up rules just to test us, let alone to plague us. His "rules" are simply a description of what He is like, and His will is that we be restored to that likeness. That's the way—the only way—we'll be truly fulfilled. More than that, that's the way *He* will be fulfilled. The more the original design is restored, the more we can become one with Him, companion with Him, be best friends. That's the exciting destiny of life: to be like Jesus so we can be one with Him. Thus His will for us is no sterile code of ethics; it is very personal. God Himself is our standard for life. What an incredible travel plan!

Revelation, then, is not merely fun truth about the unseen world to satisfy our curiosity. It is given to show us what God wants us to be and to do. It's God's standard for the Christian life. Our study of life in the Spirit will not center on God's standard, but rather on God's provision for successful living, how the Holy Spirit enables me to become like Jesus and how I link up with that power. But first we need to know the goal, what we will be like if we are like Christ. Notice that His standard isn't optional; it's the law. That's where the comparison with a London guide book breaks down. That we can take or leave; it's just good advice. Not the Bible. Since the Holy Spirit is the origin of Bible truth, the standards we discover there are for obeying.

It could be discouraging to find out how far short I fall from reaching God's standard, but there is no other place to begin. That's where the Bible itself begins because if we don't first see our need, we'll never look very hard to find out how to meet it!

Like our maps and guidebooks of London, the Bible is a road map to tell us about our destination, what we will be like when we get there, and what the signs of progress are along the "highway of holiness." "There will be a highway there, called 'the road of holiness.' No sinner will ever travel that road; no fools will mislead those who follow it . . . Those whom the LORD has rescued will travel home by that road . . . They will be happy forever, forever free from sorrow and grief" (Isa. 35:8–10, TEV).

Of course, you may choose not to follow the map. But don't be surprised if you end up at a different destination! God doesn't force us to follow His way, but any who do will be eternally grateful, Isaiah says. Should we not celebrate God's wonderful plan that we be like Him and rejoice that He has shown us exactly what that would be like in His wonderful Book? As the psalmist exults, "Oh, how I love your Law! It is my meditation all the day" (Ps. 119:97, NKJV). But why should "law," which to most people is an unwelcome intruder, be the object of such passionate affection? For two reasons.

In the first place, we want to know what will bring our Lover joy, we want to please Him by doing what He wants. Jesus said, "You are my friends if you do whatever I command you" (John 15:14, NKJV). Love makes obedience to God's rules a joy; and the rules, in turn, make love specific—they describe how love will feel and behave. We love God's standard of life because we love Jesus.

But there is another reason to love the Bible. Obedience brings *me* joy. Only on the tracks laid out by divine wisdom will I find the fulfillment of life's purpose. The headstrong little engine who thinks the tracks too narrow and confining, who opts for the freedom of the corn field, will never reach her destination! To disobey is to destroy ourselves little by little. But to run on the tracks the Spirit so carefully laid out, on the other hand, is the road—the only road—to intimate friendship with Him. Indeed, "Oh, how I love your law!"

Today, let us determine to study the Guidebook carefully and get on with the journey toward likeness to Christ.[1] But there's a problem. With any guidebook, if I don't correctly understand what the author intended to communicate, I'll never reach my destination. We have in our hands the ultimate "guidebook," an authoritative revelation of what God intends us to be and do, but not everyone is agreed on what the guidebook means. So it's our task to sort out what each biblical author intended to communicate. We call that activity "interpretation." Let's think about that for a few minutes.

---

1. These introductory comments on God's standard for our attitudes and behavior could well be frustrating for the reader who wants further light on some current or ancient issue. They might find help in a widely used textbook I've prepared, *An Introduction to Biblical Ethics* (Tyndale House Publishers, 1989, rev. 1995).

Chapter 8

Understanding the Book

*D*enise told me that Charlene was getting divorced. I innocently asked, "Does she have biblical grounds for divorce?"

"What do you mean?" Denise had an edge on her voice.

"Well," I responded, "the Bible gives a couple of legitimate reasons for divorce and I just wondered . . ."

"Oh," Denise interrupted, "that's *your* interpretation."

Interpretation? That must be the most abused word in all "Bible talk." Everyone's "interpretation" is valid, no matter how outrageously out of sync with what the Bible plainly teaches. Curiously, that view of "interpretation" is only used about religion. Can you imagine two engineers debating what 2 x 2 equals? "I say it equals four."

"Oh, that's just your interpretation."

No, by "interpretation" we mean determining what the author of a passage intended to communicate, not how my view of something can be justified by molding the passage into some other shape. When we assume the Bible is sober communication of specific meanings, some people, especially journalists, call our approach, "literalistic." When I see that word in print I want to ask, "Literalistic? Like literalistic news, history, law?" They ought to give the Bible at least the respect they give any other piece of literature. Approaching any written communication but the Bible, they assume the author intended to say something, whether literal or figurative, and their job is to understand that meaning, not impose their own. The Bible is not a batch of Silly Putty that can be shaped any way anyone wishes.

47

But even for Christians who take the Bible seriously, it may not be in control of their thinking. Elizabeth is Queen of England, but Parliament makes the rules; Elizabeth is queen, but the prime minister is chief executive. What sort of monarch is she? A "constitutional monarch," they call her. She has the title, enjoys special privileges and the affection of the people, but she has no authority. She's just a nostalgic symbol of past glory. That's what the Bible is for many Christians—it reigns supreme in theory, revered as a symbol of authority, but not exercising any controlling function in actual practice. An impotent, constitutional monarch. But if the Bible has the authority of God Almighty, it should actually function as the control mechanism of our minds. How it can do that is of critical importance to living out life in the Spirit.

The first step in understanding the Bible (interpretation) is to settle on our basic approach. There are three approaches to interpreting Scripture; two will lead you astray, but the third will help you understand what the author is getting at.

Those three approaches come from the nature of the Bible. It is both human and divine—"men spoke," to be sure, but they were "carried along by the Holy Spirit" (2 Pet. 1:21). As is so often the case, we humans tend to go to one extreme or the other, and so some church people understand Scripture strictly as a man-produced document, while others treat it as exclusively supernatural, almost magical. We will surely miss what God wants us to understand by using either one of those approaches. And that is a tragedy, since we cannot experience life in the Spirit without knowing the mind of the Spirit. We can never become truly spiritual people, grow up to maturity, become more and more like Jesus, without understanding what that life is like and how to experience it. So we must be careful how we understand and apply the Bible.

Treating the Bible as Purely Human

Some scholars set aside any miraculous event recorded in Scripture as impossible. The "feeding of the five thousand" was actually a story of sharing. A selfish crowd, who had been hoarding their lunches, responded to the generosity of a boy who was willing to share and brought out their own picnic baskets. For people using this "naturalistic" approach, a miracle kind of life—living life in the power of the Holy Spirit—is just like the stories of feeding the five thousand, of Adam and Eve created in the image of God, or of the reluctant missionary Jonah and his savior, the whale. To such "interpreters" those stories are all no more than mythological accounts given to teach spiritual lessons.

With this approach, the Bible has many errors, not only in historical accounts but in its teaching. For example, do we go to Scripture to find out what Paul meant about homosexual conduct (Rom. 1:26–27) or husbands as head of the home (Eph. 5:21–6:4) or do we go with a contemporary secular viewpoint and "interpret" Paul's clear intent away, as many religious bodies increasingly do? Much of "interpretation" is manipulation and the Word of God is not treated as a word from God. The interpreter is in charge of the meaning, not the original author. The interpreter's own natural reason sits in judgment on the Scripture, screening out the true from the false, the authoritative from the dispensable.

But it's not just the scholars. Many Christians, while saluting the "monarch," perhaps even talking about "inerrancy," nevertheless refuse to obey certain parts of Scripture because it doesn't fit what they want to do or have come to believe from other sources. They, too, are naturalistic in their approach to the Bible, since their natural reason is their basis of belief, not what the Bible says. For example, to treat the Holy Spirit as if He did not exist because it doesn't fit my earth-bound frame of reference is a "naturalistic" approach.

Treating the Bible as Exclusively Supernatural

Some interpreters throughout the ages have treated the Scripture as if it were almost exclusively supernatural, with hidden meanings to be discovered by the reader. It's a mysterious, almost magical book. There are scholars who seem to use this approach even in the twentieth century, but the more popular "supernaturalistic" approach is to use the Bible as a place of gaining insights, feeling impulses, or getting directions which may be wholly unrelated to what the Bible author intended to communicate.

Small group Bible studies sometimes do this. Members share what "hit" them as they were reading the Bible and none of the "hits" need agree with one another or with the meaning of the text. All are valid, just so long as the impression received is honestly acknowledged. Some Christians seek guidance for life in this way, treating the Bible as a magical divining rod to identify God's will supernaturally. An impression received while reading Scripture lends God's own authority to the guidance whether or not the text requires that course of action. This approach, though common, is sort of magical—we look for hidden or personalized meanings because the Bible is a supernatural book.

The Bible does view itself as supernatural, of course—God the Spirit is the Author behind the authors. But it also treats itself as truly human. The authors meant to communicate a specific meaning as the revealed truth of God. It is just like reading the newspaper. Political cartoons and comics may have a double meaning, a hidden agenda, but the bulk of the newspaper is language intended to communicate a single meaning. So the Bible has some "picture language" in which the meaning is not obvious, but the Bible is intended to convey meaning, not hide it, and the vast majority of it is plain to understand. It is *revelation*. So our objective should be to understand the meaning the author himself intended to communicate.

Treating the Bible as Divine/Human

We need to view Scripture as more than a human book from which we pick and choose, or a magical book that grants our wishes. We need a balanced view that involves looking to Scripture as a divine revelation of things we could not otherwise know; but, as with any human communication, we must search out the meaning intended by the authors.

For example, the most difficult decision we ever made was to leave Japan. We loved the land and the people and intended to "bury our bones" there, as the oriental would put it. But here was an invitation to return to our alma mater, Columbia Bible College (now Columbia International University), to lead that ministry known for training missionary leadership. What was God's will in the decision—stay or go?

Immediately, instinctively, we began to make lists of pros and cons, to consult a few wise and trusted friends. But if we stopped there how would we differ from the worldling who has no Bible at all? Just use your common sense in the decisions of life! But we knew the Bible was more than a human book, it was our guidebook; so we turned to it for direction. What did we look for? Some experience of a Bible character, some teaching of Scripture that suddenly, startlingly spoke to our immediate situation? Perhaps we discover in the Bible that God said to Abraham, "Get out of this place, leave." God has spoken to us through Scripture! Pack your bags and get moving! Or perhaps we discover a passage that says, "Do not go down to Egypt," and conclude that God is telling us to stay in Japan. That kind of "guidance" is not what Scripture was meant for. The Spirit speaks through the authors of Scripture a meaning that we must understand if the Bible is to be our guide. It's a supernatural revelation to be sure, but it's human communication that was meant to be understood. So how did the Bible help in our decision?

As was my custom when faced with a major decision, we scheduled time alone with the Lord to seek His will for our lives. In those days of fasting and prayer, what did I look for in Scripture? I wasn't looking for some personalized special hidden meaning. But God did guide us clearly through the principles of Scripture. For example, I was impressed again that in the book of Acts, God guided His servants on most occasions through His church. I resisted going to those to whom I was responsible because I knew my mission council would never agree to my leaving, nor would the leaders of the Japanese churches. And the little church I was in the process of starting—why, they wouldn't even know what I was talking about. But finally I gave in and agreed to follow the pattern I found in Scripture. To my amazement, the "church"—missionary leaders, Japanese church leaders and, yes, our little fellowship of new believers—was virtually unanimous in urging me to accept the call to Columbia as God's call.

Understanding the Book

Part of their reasoning was another principle of guidance I too had rediscovered on my retreat. The purpose of my life was not to reach my community for Christ, not even to reach Japan for Christ. My purpose was God's—to reach the world for Christ—the guiding principle of all who would follow Jesus. The only legitimate question was how I could best advance His cause of world evangelism. Would my life count more for His cause starting churches in Japan or leading that school in America?

So in my time alone with God I was using Scripture the way God intended: what does it teach me concerning His way of doing things, His purposes? What are the principles of life I should be putting into practice at this point? Perhaps He intended to use me in a larger way to reach His goal, painful as the decision was. And that is exactly what happened. Of course, there were other elements in that guidance, some supernatural to my thinking. For example, God graciously gave me a direct impulse from the Spirit in my spirit, "This is the way, walk in it." But it was my guidebook that set the course so that we never looked back to question our decision, wondering if the subjective impulses had truly been from God.

I was lured by the vision of a school that already had a worldwide reputation as a premier place for missionary preparation. But that was in the college program. The graduate school/seminary had a small enrollment and had been graduating only five or six each year. Twenty-two years later, the year I resigned to care for my wife, 175 graduated from the seminary alone, seventy percent headed for missionary service! During those twenty-two years, Columbia International University sent hundreds of missionaries around the world, many to places of strategic leadership in the mission enterprise of the church. I could not foresee all that years before when I wrestled with God in a hotel room in Tokyo. Of course, it was a whole team of people more gifted than I who made it happen, but God apparently wanted me to lead that team and He got me there, reluctant though I was, through the Word. I had learned to use Scripture for what it was intended, treating it as a divine book, with God's own authority, but treating it also as a human book in human language that can be understood. In that way the Spirit shone a great light on the Father's purposes for the world. And for me.

If our goal is to find out exactly what the Holy Spirit wants to say to us, we must treat the Book as both human and divine, not going to one extreme or the other. "Do your best to present yourself to God as one approved, a workman who has no need to be ashamed, rightly handling the word of truth" (2 Tim. 2:15, RSV).

It's a shameful thing to mishandle the Bible and it takes hard work to handle it right. But to use Scripture correctly will win God's approval, Paul assures us. If we work hard at searching out the meaning intended by the author, we will not find the Bible a complicated puzzle, much less Silly Putty to be shaped any way we please. The Spirit of God wants us to understand the meaning He intended. And by His grace we can do it![1]

But as we study, we may become confused or discouraged, so I have good news. We have more than a book; we have a Guide! The Holy Spirit comes alongside to guide us in understanding the Book. We turn now to that enlightening work of the Spirit.

---

1. We have only been able to introduce the subject of interpreting Scripture. To pursue the principles and practice further, a number of good textbooks are available, often containing the term "hermeneutics" in the title. I've written one that has enjoyed wide acceptance, possibly because it is both thorough and user-friendly, *Understanding and Applying the Bible* (Moody Press, 1983, rev. 1992).

Chapter 9

Turn Up the Lights

Everyone said I should get on the information super-highway so I could send and receive electronic mail. "Why," they said, "You can send letters to Zimbabwe free of charge! Instantly!" But I was intimidated. I'd used a computer since the mid-eighties; in fact, I lived through my fingers. But I never read one of the twelve—count 'em—thick manuals on my shelf. They might as well have been written in Chinese. If I hit a snag, I'd never read a manual; I'd call Peter, my computer expert.

Sort of like a lot of people and their life manual. The Bible sits on the shelf, so intimidating. How could I ever understand it? I'll just give the expert a call, I'll just wait to hear what the preacher says. But we surely will go astray if we don't use the Manual, get acquainted with it, figure it out, apply it to life. Yet that thick Manual can be intimidating! How can I understand it? Isn't it great that we can have our own personal guide? The Holy Spirit will guide us into all the truth we need (John 14:26). "We know these things because God has revealed them to us by his Spirit, and his Spirit searches out everything and shows us even God's deep secrets . . . And God has actually given us his Spirit . . . so we can know the wonderful things God has freely given us . . . But people who aren't Christians can't understand these truths from God's Spirit. It all sounds foolish to them because only those who have the Spirit can understand what the Spirit means" (1 Cor. 2:10–15, NLT). Without the Spirit we are sure to go astray, misread the Manual, punch the wrong keys, mess up. No wonder He's called the Comforter!

Peter, a computer whiz, was my guide. Problem is, I can see Peter, but I can't see the Spirit. How does a spirit-being "illuminate" my mind, throw light on the pages of Scripture? I don't know. It's as mysterious as His activity in inspiring the Bible writers. How He does it, we may not know, that He does it we can experience daily. I've had that experience.

I once heard a Chinese evangelist say, "No Bible, no breakfast." I thought it made sense, so I started reading my Bible every day. But it was like eating sawdust. So I let it slip—the Bible, not breakfast. Sometimes I'd have my "morning devotions," often I wouldn't. This went on for years and I was increasingly spiritually malnourished until I became desperate. Finally I made a vow to the Lord that no matter what happened I would start the day with His "bread" and "milk" and "meat," as the Bible calls itself. I thought He'd be pleased with that and work a miracle—the Bible would taste better than breakfast! But it didn't happen. It was still like eating sawdust. Still, I kept my vow, doggedly reading that Book before the day got under way. Several months later I noticed a radical change had come over me, stealthily, all unannounced. I had a ravenous appetite, I loved my time in the Book. If life pressures meant I had to miss the Bible or my breakfast, it would be no contest. I was thoroughly hooked.

Before the day begins—while I'm still in bed, in fact—I tell God good morning, thank Him that He is with me and then ask the Spirit of Christ to guide me in my study of the Manual He inspired in the first place. I have become so confident He will keep His promise, I anticipate with excitement what the Spirit will do with my mind and heart. Then as I open the Guidebook I often have an "ah-ha" experience. "Why didn't I think of that before?" or "Oops, look how this lifelong attitude needs to change!" or "Oh, now I see how to do it," or "What a wonderful God you are!" The light comes on, lifting my spirit, raising my sights, empowering my will, pointing out the right path. The Guide, the expert on my "computer," is doing His work. What exhilaration! No wonder I keep at it, even when I get bogged down in Leviticus! Just like I keep at breakfast even when it's Shredded Wheat. I need it, whether it tastes good or not.

The illuminating activity of the Spirit is available to every believer every time they open the Book. But there is a special illuminating for some. The Bible speaks of a Spirit gift of knowledge and wisdom. It wouldn't hurt to ask for the gift! In the meantime, however, it's good practice in humility to recognize that gift in others who may already have it and to use their insights. Perhaps your Sunday school teacher has such a gift. Your pastor is supposed to have it. And the Bible scholars through the ages have enriched us with books full of wisdom about the meaning of Scripture. But whatever the gifted among us may experience, the mind of every believer is enlightened by the Holy Spirit—on that you can count.

That doesn't mean everything in the Bible will be instantly clear, of course. There will remain difficult and disputed passages for the greatest of scholars; but they are few, and none impacts any important thing God wants us to know or do. If it were essential, He would have made it plain! So count on the Spirit to guide you into all the truth you need.

But there's a problem. Many Christians who have a life of intimate conversation with God begin to think that what they understand about the Bible is infallible, that it is as certain as the Bible itself. Often the "professionals"—the preachers and theologians—fall to that temptation. We must never confuse the activity of the Spirit in inspiring Bible writers and His other activity in illuminating our minds today. Both are part of His "revelation" activity. The Spirit gave us an objective record of some of God's truth and He also helps us, subjectively, to understand it. But there's a major difference. He may have inspired the Bible authors to write without error, but He does not so illuminate me. My interpretation, my understanding of the Bible's meaning, might be wrong. And the most godly and brilliant of Bible scholars can get it wrong too.

If He enlightened us infallibly, there would be no differences among Christians! There would not be charismatics and non-charismatics, Calvinists and Arminians, Baptists and Presbyterians. But don't panic. That's part of our human condition. It's not remarkable that He who didn't choose to rid our hearts of all sin in this life, should not choose to rid our minds of all error. All of us come to Scripture with colored lenses—colored by our traditions, by our cultures, by our preferences. But even if I'm on guard against such unconscious distortions, I may err. Of course, if I knew where I was in error I would change. But until the dawning of eternal day I should recognize my limitations and not claim infallibility. Even though some may act as if what they say is God's own revealed truth unmixed with error because "God told me," we need to be a bit more modest. We must recognize that though Scripture is fully trustworthy we may err in our understanding of it.

Having given that caution, however, we must return to the glory. His revelation in Scripture is so clear that Bible-believing Christians—reconditioned "computers" with God's program online—throughout church history have agreed on ninety-five percent of the Manual's teachings. And today we exult in the comforting assurance that the Holy Spirit comes alongside to help us understand it. Each time you open this special Book, ask the author to do His work and help you understand it.

Several chapters ago I asked a question: "How's your friendship with God?" He went to a lot of trouble to reveal Himself to you because He wants to be best friends. Best friends have to know one another and like what they know. They take every chance to get together and they work hard at doing what the other one likes. Do you know Him? How hard have you been working to understand His self-revelation? Do you make the time necessary to get better acquainted? Are you committed to do only what would bring Him joy? That's what the revealing activity of the Spirit is all about.

The Bible is a love letter showing us the face of our Beloved and pointing out what we'll be like when we reach our destiny of becoming just like Him and being united to Him in bonds of living love. When I reached this point in our study, I found my heart was singing. Here's what I noted in my daily journal entry for that day:

> Hallelujah! Hallelujah! Spirit of the Living God, thank you, thank you, that in ancient times You unveiled God's own life through the prophets and apostles, and that today You lift the veil of my heart to understand the Book. I want to walk with You all the days of my life, listen carefully to Your whispers, follow the light You shine on my way, and bring You some small joy. Amen.

Our entire study of life in the Spirit will be built, not on theories drawn from personal experience, but on the foundation of what the Bible says about the work of the Holy Spirit. In other words, at every step of our study, we'll apply the principles of the "revealing" activity of the Spirit we've just considered. Bible scholars call this study of Scripture, "hermeneutics," or the science of determining the meaning of a text and applying it authentically to life. In summary, because it is God who revealed truth we wouldn't otherwise know (revelation), the Bible is fully trustworthy and demands our obedience (authority). God gave this revelation by doing a special work by His Spirit in those chosen to author Scripture (inspiration) and it is our privilege and responsibility to determine what each passage means (interpretation). Then we can discover how God wants us to respond to the teaching of a passage (application). For interpretation and application we have the assistance of the Holy Spirit, guiding us into all the truth we need (illumination).

Now we turn to the "redeeming" activity of the Spirit and, just as in the revealing activity, there are several parts to His redeeming activity. For example, in redeeming, delivering us from the consequences of sin, the Spirit enabled Jesus to provide that redemption by some remarkable activity in the Savior, a study that may have some surprises. And in applying that redemption to us He does two distinct things, one negative, one positive. Again, there may be some surprises! We turn now to the glorious redeeming activities of the Holy Spirit.

Activity Three

Redeeming

Chapter 10

Outrageous Love

$\mathcal{D}$ad, I have terrible news. Bob has been badly hurt in a diving accident. Please pray." Susan's voice at the other end of the line was quiet, and though she was in control, terror lurked around the fringes of her words.

I sat at my desk, stunned. I cried out to God to spare my son. Bob had just made a fresh commitment of his life. I thought of the conversation only three days earlier when he told me, "Dad, it's time for me to stop circling the harbor and launch out to sea." He was reaching the summit of his career as a photojournalist, his marriage to Susan was idyllic, I had just received another of those exquisitely-crafted love letters he periodically wrote me. What a terrible time to die. "Please, God," I cried. I felt so helpless; dared I even hope?

Ten minutes later the phone rang again. "Dad, Bob's with Jesus . . ." Hot tears flowed as if to wash away the pain, and friends gathered to embrace me, but the wound was too deep to be healed. Sons are meant to bury their fathers, not fathers their sons.

In those days I began to think about a father's love. I would do anything to protect my son. If given a choice, how gladly I would have taken his place. I would never *choose* to let him go, not for anyone. Yet God did just that. He chose to give His son for me. That's how much God loved me. I was not a family member, not even a friend. An enemy. And, unlike me, God did not have two sons left. His only son. For me. Outrageous love.

I had always thought of Jesus' love as supreme. And perhaps it was. And yet . . . and yet . . . it is one thing to give up one's own life, but the life of your beloved son? I began to feel a little of the pain of the brokenhearted Father.

Outrageous Love

The Father's Cross

Father,
What was *your* Gethsemane?
And when . . .
And where . . .
Did you decide,
Against all heart and reason,
To abandon your beloved one?
And that for me—
Oh, worthless substitute!

Like the piercings of a sword
We hear the cry,
"My God, my God, why
"Hast thou forsaken me?"
"What love!" we say
And yet . . .
Was not the Savior's piteous lament
A mere echo
Of that broken-hearted cry
Reverberating down the endless
Corridors of heaven,
"My Son, my Son,
"My beloved Son,
"Why have I forsaken you?"

No greater human love,
Christ taught, than when one
Gives his life.
But Father's love explodes
Beyond the reach of
Highest, deepest, and most untamed
Flight of human thought—
God gave not life, but Son.
His only Son.

For me . . .
—Robertson McQuilkin

Parents may give a son or daughter for love of country; a firefighter may die in a rescue that fails. But for an enemy? Yet "God has shown us how much he loves us—it was while we were still sinners that Christ died for us" (Rom. 5:8, TEV).

Once the word *blood* had power to move us. That single word summoned a vivid image of sacrifice and death. It stabbed our hearts with the pain of torture and senseless death. But no more. Television and movies have so washed the screen with blood that the writers must work to invent fresh images of increasingly violent death to grab our emotions. And we, by our bouncy hymns about the blood of Jesus, have trivialized the most sacred of sacrifices. We repeat the word *blood* like a mantra, or chant it like a cheerleader's slogan. It no longer evokes strong passions within us.

The image of the cross also used to have powerful effect. Today we have difficulty understanding the image a cross had in the New Testament church. We have so glamorized the cross, who would be startled by the image? Who would think of wearing on his lapel the replica of a hangman's noose or an electric chair? People would think it weird and mutter, "Ugh." How do we regain the sense of loss, of outrage, of profound gratitude when we speak of the cross? Perhaps if we could put ourselves in His place . . .

> And they came to a place called Gethsemane; and He said to His disciples, "Sit here until I have prayed." And He took with Him Peter and James and John, and began to be very distressed and troubled. And He said to them, "My soul is deeply grieved to the point of death; remain here and keep watch." And He went a little beyond them, and fell to the ground, and began to pray that if it were possible, the hour might pass Him by. And He said, "Abba! Father! All things are possible for Thee; remove this cup from Me; yet not what I will, but what Thou wilt." And being in agony He was praying very fervently; and His sweat became like drops of blood, falling down upon the ground. And when He rose from prayer, He came to the disciples and found them sleeping from sorrow. (from the accounts of Matthew, Mark, and Luke)

Jesus' heart was not bouncing with some jingle about blood. He was not fascinated with a diamond-studded replica of a cross. No, He pled for a way out in a deep, deep agony of spirit. What caused such pain? It may have been the fear of death, especially so torturous a death, but I doubt it. History is full of heroes who faced death unafraid. And His death wasn't permanent, anyway; Jesus knew that He would rise again on the third day—hadn't He predicted it? Surely He shrank from that mysterious identity with our sin, the foul moral pollution of a whole world of sinners, in fact (2 Cor. 5:21). But perhaps there was something deeper.

Have you ever been betrayed by a friend? Even more painful—have you ever been abandoned by someone whom you thought would stand by you no matter what? But at the critical moment, they were silent. Or absent . . . Perhaps you have felt such pain, not from a mere friend, but from a parent. It seems to me the deep agony of Gethsemene was not the betrayal by Judas, painful as that must have been, nor the abandonment by Peter, deep sadness that it was. The agony of Gethsemene was the doom He faced, like some cosmic quake that rocks the universe, a break in the Trinity itself. From all eternity, the Son was the delight of the Father's heart, the crowning joy of heaven. And now, and now . . . as the Son embraced our sin, the wrath of the Father fell on Him instead of us, and that heart of God, in a moment of time, suffered an eternity of grief. "My God, my God, why have You forsaken Me?"

How do you feel about the cross, the blood? Have they lost their power? Isn't it time to pause now and pour out to God your astonishment, your love, your gratitude? And if you don't feel the passion, it's past time to ask Him to restore it or, perhaps, to engulf you with such love for the first time. Whatever your emotions—whether grief for His loss and gratitude for your gain, or passionless familiarity with the old story of our salvation—isn't it time to tell Him?

Life in the Spirit doesn't focus on the activity of the Father and Son, yet their incredible love is the fountainhead of all good, so in the story of our salvation there's no other place to begin. But the surprise may be that the Spirit also was intimately involved in that redemptive work from start to finish, as we shall see.

Chapter 11

Jesus Needed the Spirit Too

*W*e wait in the darkness with high anticipation. Mega-hero Dwight Eisenhower is to appear at the high school auditorium in our small town—the most historic moment in our collective memory. The school band, with remarkably few miscues, strikes up the familiar "Hail to the Chief." Now the curtain rises, lights flood the stage and Dwight D. Eisenhower strides to center stage. As the spotlight follows his every step, the crowd rises, turns, not toward Eisenhower, but toward the spotlight operator and begins to applaud his fine performance. Strange behavior, you say? But that tale is no more bizarre than is the church that replaces King Jesus at center stage with a primary focus on the activity of the Holy Spirit.

That's why we began our salvation story with the love of the Father and Son, not on our theme, life in the Spirit. That's as it should be. The work of the Holy Spirit is to keep the spotlight on the hero, Jesus, the eternal Son of the living God. Jesus is center stage. "The Spirit of truth . . . will guide you into all the truth; for he will not speak on his own . . . *He will glorify me*, for he will take of what is mine and declare it to you" (John 16:13–14, RSV, author's emphasis).

But the Holy Spirit is more than the "spotlight operator." He is the production manager, and the danger of most churches is not to replace Jesus with focus on the Spirit, but to leave off the credit lines altogether, to treat the Spirit of God as if He did not exist. That is a tragic, perhaps fatal, error because everything in the life of Jesus from birth to resurrection—the entire incarnation— was by the power of the Holy Spirit. He knew this and depended consciously on the Spirit for everything He did or said.

Jesus Needed the Spirit Too

His birth. Both Matthew and Luke credit the Holy Spirit with the mystery of the incarnation. In Matthew's account, Joseph is told in a dream that he should take Mary as his wife because "What is conceived in her is from the Holy Spirit" (Matt. 1:20). Luke tells us that the angel Gabriel announced to Mary that she would conceive. Mary asked a legitimate question: "How will this be since I am a virgin?" (Luke 1:34).

The angel replied, "The Holy Spirit will come upon you, and the power of the Most High will overshadow you. So the holy one to be born will be called the Son of God" (Luke 1:35). Both Matthew and Luke clearly attributed this miraculous event to the activity of the Holy Spirit.

His ministry. Before Jesus' public ministry began, He traveled south from Galilee to be baptized by John the Baptist. But that was only symbolic of a far greater baptism that was essential to His ministry. There by the Jordan River, in the presence of John and a large crowd of onlookers, "the Holy Spirit descended on him in bodily form like a dove" (Luke 3:22).

His prayer life, His overcoming temptation. "Jesus, full of the Holy Spirit, returned from the Jordan and was led by the Spirit in the desert" (Luke 4:1).

His teaching. "The Spirit of the Lord is on me, because he has anointed me to preach good news to the poor. He has sent me to proclaim freedom for the prisoners and recovery of sight for the blind, to release the oppressed, to proclaim the year of the Lord's favor" (Luke 4:18–19).

His healing. "One day as he was teaching, Pharisees and teachers of the law, who had come from every village of Galilee and from Judea and Jerusalem, were sitting there. And the power of the Lord was present for him to heal the sick" (Luke 5:17).

His death. "How much more, then, will the blood of Christ, who through the eternal Spirit offered himself unblemished to God . . ." (Heb. 9:14).

His resurrection. "God powerfully raised him from the dead by means of the Holy Spirit" (Rom. 1:4, NLT).

The Holy Spirit was at work in every event in Jesus' incarnation. When Jesus was conceived, when He healed, overcame temptation, taught, prayed, endured death by crucifixion and was raised again, everything was attributed to the Spirit's power. The Spirit's activity thus was essential to providing our salvation through empowering our Savior.

If Jesus had accomplished His Father's will by exercising His divine powers, then we could never hope to follow in His steps. Yet that is exactly what we are told to do: "Follow my example, as I follow the example of Christ," said Paul (1 Cor. 11:1). Paul then explained how: "If we live [that is, have life] by the Spirit, let us also walk by the Spirit" (Gal. 5:25, RSV, author's note). Jesus Himself said He was sending the Spirit to be "with you" and "in you" (John 14:16–17). So we have exactly the same resource Jesus had to live His life: the

Holy Spirit within. And that is so important, Jesus says it is more important than having Him physically present! Before He ascended, Jesus told His disciples it was to their advantage that He was going because only then would they receive the Holy Spirit (see John 16:7–14). How could that be? So essential is the Spirit to our redemption—from new birth to final resurrection—that those activities provide the themes of this book.

Shortly we'll turn our attention to those activities, but first, notice the striking parallels Scripture draws between the Spirit's work in Jesus and His work in us. If the powerful Son of God, Himself deity, needed the Holy Spirit's presence and power, how much more do you and I! Here are some of the parallel's between the Spirit's activity in Christ's life and ours:

~ *Miracle birth:* "I tell you the truth, no one can enter the kingdom of God unless he is born of water and the Spirit . . . the Spirit gives birth to spirit." (John 3:5–6)

~ *Spirit-empowered ministry:* "The Holy Spirit displays God's power through each of us as a means of helping the entire church." (1 Cor. 12:7, TLB)

~ *Prayer life:* "Praying always with all prayer and supplication in the Spirit." (Eph. 6:18, NKJV)

~ *Death:* In powerful picture language, Paul draws parallels between Christ's death and our own "death" to the old life. "We were therefore buried with him through baptism into death in order that, just as Christ was raised from the dead through the glory of the Father, we too may live a new life." (Rom. 6:4) Furthermore, Paul says Christ's death paradoxically also points to how we are to continue that new life. "If by the Spirit you put to death the misdeeds of the body, you will live, because those who are led by the Spirit of God are sons of God." (Rom. 8:13–14)

~ *His resurrection:* The apostle also draws parallels between Christ's resurrection and our own, spiritually in the past and physically in the future. "If we have been united with him like this in his death, we will certainly also be united with him in his resurrection . . . count yourselves dead to sin but alive to God in Christ Jesus." (Rom. 6:5, 11) He has already raised us to new life, but He will also, as He did in Christ, raise our bodies at the final resurrection. "And if the Spirit of him who raised Jesus from the dead is living in you, he who raised Christ from the dead will also give life to your mortal bodies through his Spirit, who lives in you." (Rom. 8:11)

We, like Jesus, from new birth to our own death and final resurrection are in complete dependence upon the Holy Spirit. Born again by the power of the Spirit, we gain any knowledge or wisdom we have through Him, and we're empowered to live godly lives and to minister with eternal impact only as He energizes us. Our future is ablaze with hope for what the Spirit will yet do.

These analogies will prove rich lodes of truth for us to mine throughout this study on how to live out our own lives in the Spirit. But for now, remember that if Jesus needed the Holy Spirit, how much more do we! With that exciting preview, let's return now to consider the activities of the Spirit in order, beginning with what He does to apply to us today the salvation He provided in Christ so long ago.

Chapter 12

Guilt Trip

*T*he greatest crisis in my life came at an early age. I was desperately afraid of hell. I went to my mother, naturally, where a fearful child is accustomed to go; but she sent me to my father. Upon hearing my fear, he asked me an old-fashioned question: "Have you sinned?"

Such a question for an innocent child! I nodded. Even worse, he followed up with, "And what was your sin?" That was my pain; I needed no heart-searching probe to find a possible answer.

Sobbing, I blurted out, "I lied." Finally it was out. Surely he would let me off the hook as a confessed sinner. But no.

"Any other sins?" I couldn't remember any more, so focused was I on that lie. So Daddy helped me remember some more.

Finally we were ready to pray. We knelt by his bed, the same bed on which I had been born the first time, and I gave my life to the Savior. Since I was only a child, I could not begin to appreciate all the Holy Spirit did in my life that day. I was sorry enough for my sin, but primarily I feared punishment. I had heard of hell, and I knew hell was for sinners. Jesus was for sinners, too. I ran to Him, opened my heart to Him, and felt His warm embrace. With that embrace came peace.

In the downward spiral of my life there was a big turnaround that day. Oh, I hadn't lived long enough to descend too far away from God toward destruction, but that was the direction I was headed. On that downward spiral, the longer we live, the less like God we become, the more like Satan. Some are on the fast track, hell-bent—literally—and some descend more slowly, but all are born headed in the wrong direction. There is hope, however, for always the Holy Spirit is working to bring us to our senses, to stop us in our tracks. In fact, that's why He was sent, said Jesus: "And when He has come, He will convict the world of sin, and of righteousness, and of judgment" (John 16:8, NKJV). That's the Spirit's first activity in applying Christ's finished work of redemption. Not everyone is pleased with that activity.

The emcee introducing me said, "Now, don't worry—we're not going to put you on a guilt trip." I was to speak on life in the Spirit and I thought, "Uh-oh, how can I speak on the Spirit and avoid the guilt trip? That's what He's for!" He has a hard job, actually. Like the emcee, we don't want to hear that we're headed the wrong direction, that we actually are guilty of sin. It's part of our fallen nature, our disconnectedness from God and His truth. In our pride-filled, self-assured view of ourselves we just naturally suppress that truth. "The wrath of God is being revealed from heaven against all the godlessness and wickedness of men who suppress the truth by their wickedness, since what may be known about God is plain to them, because God has made it plain to them" (Rom. 1:18–19).

Besides that natural resistence to information about our true condition, the Spirit's task of convincing us of our need is complicated by what we hear. The reason we see ourselves as sinners less often than did our forefathers is that leading social scientists, the media, counselors, and government social programs have all conspired to shift our focus from the Bible themes of sin and salvation to the new model for explaining the human predicament: hurt and therapy. Americans believe less and less in sin and guilt, more and more in a battered psyche that needs healing. We are no longer guilty sinners needing salvation; we are victims of someone else's hurtful behavior, and so we need to have a healthy self-image restored by education and by reorganizing society or, if those fail, by therapy.

Of course we *are* hurting people, some of us battered more than others. And most of us could use help toward healing, some by a skilled specialist. Perhaps you, like I, have watched with gratitude as a family member was restored through such a healer. But it will prove to be a fatal error if, to explain our human predicament, we replace a sin/salvation model with a hurt/therapy model. Yet that is what seems to be happening so that most of us tend to believe if we can liberate ourselves from all damaging circumstances and people, we will find fulfillment, we will be happy.

"The greatest roadblock to human happiness and fulfillment is a feeling of guilt," a therapist tells his counselee. To such a counselor, his task, unlike the old-time "doctors of the soul," is not to rid you of guilt, but to rid you of those guilty feelings. Yet what if your family doctor told you the greatest roadblock to healing and wholeness is pain? A leper, I'm told, doesn't feel pain. If he is not protected, he could fall into a fire and burn away a hand. It is the same with you and me, only ours is a leprosy of the soul, deadening our sensitivity to sin. The truth is, spiritual pain (guilt), like physical pain, is a wonderful gift. We've been given a sense of soul-pain, a conscience to warn when we are spiritually ill. The greatest danger is to feel no pain. So the counselor who persuades us of innocence when we are, in fact, guilty, is no true friend.

Too bad my father lived before the era of enlightenment! When I, a fearful six-year-old, came to ask how to avoid hell, he didn't realize that I was in danger of having my little ego further damaged by concern about such things. He didn't discuss my sister's oppressive behavior or my mother's regular abuse of my behind. He asked an old-fashioned question: "Have you sinned?" But it turned out to be OK—the Holy Spirit had got to me first. Notice what the Holy Spirit used to bring me low under conviction of sin. First He worked directly in my spirit, as Paul said He would: "Who show the work of the law written in their hearts, their conscience also bearing witness, and between themselves their thoughts accusing or else excusing them" (Rom. 2:15, NKJV).

In my case, however, there was a prior work. My parents had taught me from the Bible about truth-telling and lie-telling and the consequences of each, so the Spirit had access to my mind through what He had long since provided in Scripture: "I would not have known sin except through the law. For I would not have known covetousness unless the law had said, 'You shall not covet'" (Rom. 7:7, NKJV).

Notice, however, that I didn't make the big turn-around until a person, filled with the Spirit, explained these things to me and showed me the way: "Son of man, I have made you a watchman . . . therefore hear a word from My mouth, and give them warning from Me . . . if you warn the wicked, and he does not turn from his wickedness, nor from his wicked way, he shall die in his iniquity; but you have delivered your soul" (Ezek. 3:17, 19, NKJV).

Those are the ordinary ways the Spirit uses to do His convicting work: innate moral awareness, commonly called "conscience," the Bible, and a human witness. Though the Bible may not tell us all the ways the Spirit brings conviction, there is one other way He often uses: the example of those who sin and the consequences they suffer. Whether or not there are immediate natural consequences—and often there are not—the Spirit intends to use His church to make an example and demonstrate the consequences when sin is especially flagrant. He intends to do this through church discipline, a responsibility of the church rarely fulfilled in our permissive, tolerant age: "Those who sin are to be rebuked publicly, so that the others may take warning" (1 Tim. 5:20).

Though I had not descended to the place where that method of conviction was necessary, the Spirit had completed His convicting work in my spirit and halted me in my downward spiral. I fled to Him in fear for my eternal destiny and in remorse for my sin, and He embraced me, turned me around, and set me on the upward spiral. Never again did God see me as a polluted, self-dominated sinner, but clean and innocent as Jesus. Never again did I quake before Him as a wrath-filled judge. Hallelujah!

Both the Bible and history are filled with people whose lives were transformed by the power of the Holy Spirit. John Newton was a slave trader, without regard for man or God. After the Spirit convicted him of his sin and brought him to repentance and faith, Newton became a pastor and the author of one of the most beloved Christian hymns of all time:

> Amazing grace! How sweet the sound,
> That saved a wretch like me!
> I once was lost, but now am found,
> Was blind, but now I see.

Perhaps you, like Newton, are safe in Jesus and sure of it. For you, the Spirit's work of convicting the world of judgment to come is no longer your dread. But is there not the grief of what your sin did to Jesus, the dread of bringing Him pain yet again? Have you ever felt deeply what your sin means to Jesus? I'm ashamed to admit it, but eighteen long years passed before I shed the first tear over my sin. I'd been asked to give a message on the death of Christ. As I prepared, for the first time in my life I felt sorrow that Jesus was on that cross because of my sin. Not Hitler's. Not Stalin's. Not the world's. Mine. My heart was broken by grief, not grief for what my sins might do to me, but grief for what they did to Him.

Like a deep reservoir trapped for years beneath a stony heart, the gusher burst free and I mourned the hell I caused my Beloved. That was the work of the Holy Spirit. Not everyone will have the same outward response, but the evidence of the Spirit's work is grief for the wrong I have done my Savior. Perhaps today is the day the Spirit will break open your heart and let your love burst forth in grief and gratitude.

On the other hand, you may never have heard the convicting whisper of the Spirit. Perhaps there's a dread leprosy on your soul that deadens the pain of guilt. You're convinced your only big problems are inflicted on you by others or by your circumstances, that you are, after all, reasonably innocent of significant wrong. Error, perhaps, but not sin. Or maybe even today the Spirit has penetrated the fog of self-serving explanations of why things go wrong and has convicted you of your sin in the bright light of His righteousness and the certainty of judgment to come. Flee to Him today, admit your guilt, embrace the Son, and cast yourself upon His mercy.

Wherever you are on your spiral down or up—if you have a whole lifetime of living independent of the One who owns you and loves you, or if, as a Christian, there's some sin unrepented or unconfessed—now's the time to respond to the convicting work of the Spirit and agree with God about it. Tell Him how sorry you are to have hurt Him so much, and ask Him to wash away the guilt. Get off that guilt trip by getting rid of the guilt! Throw yourself on His mercy. He'll forgive in an instant, erase the record of all your sin, and embrace you as His dearly beloved.

Chapter 13

Ultimate Change Agent

Yesterday I received a phone call from Kimie. In Japanese she blurted out, "Kesshin shimashita!"—("I decided!")—and for a moment I wondered what she had decided: where to live? what courses to take? Then my heart leaped for joy. For weeks Kimie had been visiting me, bringing with her a gift of Japanese crackers and long lists of questions about the Trinity, God's sovereignty and her choices, the deity of Christ, and the state of her father who recently died. Gradually, this young woman who had never heard of a personal God until six months ago began to understand. In fact, last week she said she believed all I told her was true and sometimes she was excited about it all. But she wasn't ready to turn her life over to this new acquaintance named Jesus, at least not unconditionally.

Oh, Kimie knew that she was a sinner—not a notorious sinner, but a self-oriented person, not deserving God's favor. She was grateful that God loved her enough to give His Son to die for her, but what would she do about it? I said, "Kimie, you can study and study, pray and pray, and attend church faithfully, but that will never make you a Christian." She was startled. She had been sure that by doing those things and trying hard to be a better person she would gradually become what she so much wanted.

"No, Kimie," I told her last week, "you can't grow into it. Sooner or later you must make a choice. You must decide."

"But what about my feelings?" she asked.

"That depends on your personality and how you have lived out your past rebellion against God. The feelings, the joy, will follow, but first comes the choice."

"Sono uchi ni" ("one of these days"), she said as she left for school in another city. That was last week. Yesterday she called to tell me, "Sensei, I did it! I decided for Jesus!" And her joy had already begun to surge.

> If anyone is in Christ, he is a new creation; old things have passed away; behold, all things have become new. (2 Cor. 5:17, NKJV)

Notice that God does several things at the critical moment in which we turn to Him in repentance and faith. For example, as Kimie experienced so gloriously, the Father forgave her, wiped the record clean. Also, because of Jesus' payment of her sin-debt, a legal transaction took place in the courts of heaven. Theologians call it *justification* because she, wholly unjust, was declared just or right as the Judge accepted that substitute payment. Justification is an objective reality, no matter how I feel about it, but another act of God takes place at the same time which is subjective. It takes place in me, not in the courts of heaven.

Re-creation

Fathers weren't allowed in delivery rooms in those days, but our doctor was young and willing to break the rules. Could I stay in the birthing room when our firstborn arrived? I was to stand just inside the door where I wouldn't be in the way. When the time came, however, I could see nothing but a sheet-draped figure on a table across the room! Then it happened. The doctor rose from behind the sheet canopy, holding aloft a tiny creature by her heels. "Is she supposed to be blue?" I wondered. "And why is she so silent? I thought babies started off with a bawl." Nurses scurried, one to retrieve a suction syringe and—what's this?—the doctor whacked my baby across the behind! Suddenly little Mardi let out a wail, startling me with her lung power, and bringing relief to a tense delivery room.

Who was this new creature? She wasn't all that new, as any pro-lifer could tell you. She was the same little person who had been residing for a time in her mother's womb. But what new dimensions of life! She could communicate now, she breathed on her own, she could develop loving relationships, she could grow, unimpeded by the restrictions of her former life.

So it is with us, Jesus taught. We must be born again (John 3:3–8). Same person as before, but what a radical transformation! Now we can communicate with Him, we can develop a relationship of intimate companionship, we can grow up to look more and more like Him. A new creation or, as the theologians call it, regeneration. We were originally generated by God in His likeness; now we are regenerated. Born again.

Or you might liken the transformation to dying (Rom. 6:1–11). I sat on the side of my bed, head bowed, tears flowing. I was grieving the loss of my eldest son, Bob. My youngest, Kent, stood by me, trying to comfort a heartbroken father. All the what-if's paraded through my mind: What if he had caught fire for God sooner? What if I had been a better father? "Dad," said Kent, "if you ever failed Bob, I'll guarantee he has forgiven you now. And all you ever wanted him to be, he is. And more. Just like Jesus. He's free and fulfilled. Why, I'll bet he's winging it off to some distant galaxy on a photo assignment, planning exciting new adventures for you to share when you get there, like he always did here."

It was the same Bob who lay dying on a hospital gurney, but oh, what new dimensions of life, what new potentialities! So it is with us when we are born again. The same person who lived out life in a dim shadowland now has come alive in Jesus. We died, as it were, and have been resurrected to a new life. We don't know exactly how it was done or even exactly what happened, but we know there is a radical transformation into a whole new dimension of being. "The old is gone, the new has come." Sort of like a death. Or a birth. That's the work of the Spirit.

Salvation

Salvation is a glorious word that encompasses all God ever did for us and all He ever will do. Regeneration is one part of the Spirit's saving work, but *regeneration* and many other words describing bits and pieces of God's work in us are not always understood in biblical ways. Part of the reason for misunderstanding is that the Bible often uses picture language like "birth" or "death." Another part of the problem is that theologians use complicated terms to describe a truth like "regeneration" and "justification." So for some people the words are unfamiliar and threatening; for others they are blurred by a lifetime of repetition. Theological cliches, you might call them. There are many of these terms used to describe what happens around the time of our initial salvation. Let me summarize:

The Spirit first *convinces* us that we are sinners in need of a savior. His work may take a long period of time, depending on the resistance He meets. Finally, He breaks through our denial, and we recognize our need of a Savior. We believe certain basic facts about Jesus and about our own condition. We feel sorrow for our sin. We turn from our sin in repentance and trust our lives to the Savior. That is a description of complete or biblical faith. As you see, biblical faith means much more than simply believing. When we respond to God in faith, He *forgives* our sins; He blots out the record of our sin and declares us righteous. This we call *justification*, or being justified, "just-as-if-I'd" never sinned. At the same time, in some mysterious way we may never fully understand, God transforms us at the core of our nature into something wondrously new and different. We call this change *regeneration*.

Not all would agree with the order of the salvation process as I outlined it. Some would put regeneration at an earlier stage, but all would agree that the activity of the Spirit in remaking us is a glorious essential in our salvation.

The Results of Regeneration

In regeneration "everything" becomes new, that is, the Spirit changed something about every part of you—the way you think, how you feel, and what you choose. Here's a brief checklist of things that change so you can evaluate what the impact of the Spirit has been in your own life:

~ Your mind, how you think. What viewpoints changed—about what is right and wrong, important or unimportant, about who you are, who God is, what you can become?

~ Your heart, how you feel about things. What attitudes changed—what you liked and disliked, who you liked to be around, who your heroes were? Feelings about yourself and God?

~ Your will, your ability to make choices for God and against sin. The new you is empowered to do what the old you couldn't do—consistently say "yes" to God, "no" to temptation. Did any bad habits stop, good habits start? Any changes in lifestyle, activities?

You have just described a "magifical" new creation, as the old English would put it. You! The new you. How exciting! It could be likened to a fuzzy, little worm, earthbound and slow, transformed into a free, gorgeous creature of the skies. The transformation from caterpillar to butterfly is so radical we call it a *metamorphosis*. Maybe that's a good synonym for "regeneration"!

But regeneration is not the end, though some testimony meetings and church prayer meetings may sound like it. It's just the beginning of a great restoration project, which the rest of our study will pursue. There is an instantaneous transformation that takes place when we first put our trust in Christ, and this starts a transformation process that lasts a lifetime. But today we exult in the radical re-creation that has already taken place.

Before we begin that magnificent upward spiral, let's review the activities of the Spirit we have considered thus far:

Activity One: Creating

~ The Spirit created us in God's spiritual likeness. Our first parents defaced that likeness and I added my own damage.

Activity Two: Revealing

~ Then the Spirit revealed the way back to God by giving us the Bible and illuminating our minds to understand it.

Activity Three: Redeeming

~ Next He fully provided for our restoration by superintending God's master plan of sending the Son for our salvation.

~ Salvation provided, the Spirit brings home to me in convicting power my need of a savior, and when I respond in repentance and faith . . .

~ The Spirit transforms me into a new person with wholly new dimensions of personal being, new desires, new awareness and understandings, new powers.

But the Spirit doesn't just stay at a distance and send His blessings on some cosmic delivery truck, nor does He come to us and do things to us like a heavenly repairman. His relationship to us is very personal, and to that incredible truth we now turn.

Activity Four

Indwelling

Chapter 14

Inside Companion

*R*emember Jim, the school bully? Day after day he stalked me, day after day I strategized on how to elude him; but when I ran out of my own resources, the answer came unexpectedly down the street—my father! Hand-in-hand we strolled past the bully, unintimidated. What strength! What joy! There was a problem, however. Daddy was not likely to come that way ever again. What would I do tomorrow? The dread settled in again on my ten-year-old spirit. Oh, that Daddy could be with me always . . .

So it is with us. We, too, were haunted by the evil presence of some bully set on destroying us. Trapped into a lifestyle of worry—worry about a job we have or don't have, worry about the children, worry about old age, health. Ambushed by a sexy woman or a picture of one; booby-trapped by an explosive tongue when family members don't do it my way. The Bible and church are supposed to help, but they seem deadly dull. The Enemy stalking us, stalking us.

To cope with the enemy, we tried first one strategy and then another. New Year's resolutions. Popular seminar. Best-selling book. Therapy. More coffee. Pills. But nothing seemed to work. Not very long, at least. And then, one glorious day, down the street—so unexpectedly—came help. The Comforter has come! "The one called alongside" is what that name means literally. And He doesn't just shepherd us through the crisis of the moment. Unlike my father after school that day, the Holy Spirit is with us forever. Better than that, the strong Comforter no longer is merely walking beside us—He is inside us! It's an inside job. He not only gave me incredible new potentialities by re-creating me, He comes in person to accompany me each step of my journey home, as my inside companion. And "greater is he that is in you, than he that is in the world" (1 John 4:4, KJV). What release! What strength! What joy!

> I will pray the Father, and He will give you another Helper, that He may abide with you forever; the Spirit of truth, whom the world cannot receive, because it neither sees Him nor knows Him; but you know Him, for He dwells with you and will be in you. (John 14:16–17, NKJV)

The secret to living the Christian life successfully is God's Spirit within. It's not just the Holy Spirit, of course—the Father and Son are inside, too (John 14:10, 17, 23; Eph. 2:18; Eph. 3:14–19). What a mystery! He whom the heaven of heavens cannot contain, the infinite One, everywhere present, in some mysterious way lives inside me. Not exclusively, of course, but in a special sense which cannot be said of the non-believer. I don't know that I'll ever understand the physical aspect of this relationship (God's presence somewhere inside my body), but perhaps a key to unlock the mystery is the way the Bible uses the word *in*. Surprisingly the focus is not on the physical.

An Intimate Relationship

For example, Jesus speaks of being in us and our being in Him almost interchangeably (John 14:20; 15:4–5). They seem to mean the same thing, at least to point in the direction of a single reality. And what is that reality? In the marvelous passage about the vine and the branches (John 15:1–17) the little word *in* is used constantly. Most of those "in's" speak of our being in Christ and Christ's being in us, but there are a few more. When in verses seven, nine, ten, eleven, Jesus speaks of His words and His joy being in us and our being in His love, He seems to be talking of a relationship more than of a physical location. In bypassing the physical aspect, a mystery we may never fully solve, Jesus moves on to something far more important: a relationship. The *Theological Dictionary of the New Testament* calls this the "in" of fellowship.[1] We might call it "intimacy." That's it! A relationship with another Person so close that the only way to describe it is to speak of His being in me and I in Him. An identity of life, an inter-penetration so intimate you could call it being "in love" (v. 9).

Have you ever been crazy in love? Well, that's a mere shadow of what this in-love-ness was meant to be—why, the only way to describe it is to say it's the way the Father and the Son relate (vv. 9–10). That's beyond my capacity to understand. True, God is always there for me and He is constantly with me, but Jesus reaches higher and deeper—He is *in* me and I am *in* Him, in some way just like the Father and the Son love one another!

Incredible as it may seem, God has planned my life around Himself, uninterrupted companionship with the greatest Lover who ever lived! No getting an appointment a month in advance. No taking a number and waiting my turn. He doesn't just tolerate me. Outrageous mystery—God actually desires my company! In fact, He wants to be best friends. That's what it means to be "in Christ" and for Christ to be "in me"—a new relationship that defies analysis or description. While we wonder about the mysterious physical aspect of my body as a residence for God, and while we exult in that mystery, let's be sure to focus our attention on the relationship between the two of us.

What the Spirit Does Inside

As in all of God's other activities, this "inside job" is assigned to the Holy Spirit as the primary mover. The Holy Spirit not only created us in God's likeness, He not only re-created us as altogether new people; He takes up residence inside us. But what does He actually do in there?

- First of all, He gives me assurance that I belong to God; He whispers to my spirit, *Remember, the heavenly Father's your daddy* (English for "abba") *and we—the Father, Son, and I—will be here forever, no matter what bully is stalking you* (Rom. 8:15–16; 1 John 4:13).

- The Holy Spirit is the master teacher, enlightening our minds to understand all the truth we need to know about God and His will for us (John 14:26; 16:13; 1 Cor. 2:10–14; 1 John 2:20).

- He not only helps us understand Scripture; He guides us in the personal decisions of life, sometimes impressing us with the way to go, sometimes blocking the way we thought to go (Acts 13:2; 16:6–7; Rom. 8:14).

- His name is "Comforter" because that is what He does. When we are in trouble, He gives a peace and joy and hope that can't be explained by the smartest psychologist in terms of our early environment or present circumstances (John 14:16; Rom. 14:17; 15:13).

- And when we stumble, even falling, like David, into gross sin, the powerful Spirit of God lifts us up to stand and move forward with strength (Ps. 37:24). He never abandons us (Ps. 51:11, 12). In fact, He strengthens us powerfully so we need not fail, the power so great it is the same as that He used when He created the worlds and loosed Jesus from the grip of death (Eph. 3:16, 20; 1:19–20; Rom. 8:11).

- The Spirit energizes us to live godly lives (Ezek. 36:27; Gal. 5:22–23), to minister powerfully (Zech. 4:6; 1 Cor. 12:7, 11), and to witness boldly with wisdom (Matt. 10:20; Acts 1:8).

- As if all that were not enough, God's Spirit even assists us in our prayer (Eph. 6:18; Jude 20). Often we don't even know how to pray, what to pray (Rom. 8:26). But He knows, and He inspires our prayers. Even inspired prayers may fall short, however, and that's when the Spirit, who knows the mind of the Father, goes straight to the throne and tells the Father exactly what we needed to pray.

Hallelujah! With such an inside partner, nothing can stop you! A successful life in the Spirit is no fantasy land, our salvation is no "pie in the sky by and by." Here. Now. God the Spirit lives in you in such a tight relationship that everything He promises is within your reach. Hallelujah!

Our Inside Companion in person is all the resource we need to live out the Christian life successfully, to spiral upward toward ever greater likeness to Jesus and intimate companionship with our Lord. But what if it isn't happening? What if the power doesn't flow, the transformation is so slow it's imperceptible to those around me, the relationship with the Spirit distant? There's supposed to be a tight connection, but somehow there's been a disconnect. That's what we want to consider next.

But first, isn't it time to tell the Comforter how much you appreciate Him? If you've never talked directly to the Holy Spirit, why not now? Tell Him all the things about Him you especially like, how much you love Him, how grateful you are for what He has done and is doing and will yet do. After the thanksgiving, reflect for a few minutes on what you wish He would do to make you different, to improve your relationship with Him, and then ask the Spirit to do what you sense needs doing.

---

1. *Theological Dictionary of the New Testament*, vol. 2 (Grand Rapids, Mich.: Wm. B. Eerdmans Publishing Co., 1964), p. 543.

Chapter 15

Close Connection

*T*he Spirit of God lives inside and has all the resources of heaven to empower me, as we've seen. But what if I don't seem to experience a supernatural quality of life? Everything I say or do, even most of my attitudes and thoughts, could be explained by a good psychologist in terms of what I inherited and what my circumstances have been. What's wrong? I may not have a close connection with the Spirit. The divine current doesn't flow automatically—I have to throw the switch, and the "switch" is faith.

"The righteous will live by faith" (Hab. 2:4) must be an important truth: it's the only Old Testament statement quoted three times in the New Testament (Rom. 1:17; Gal. 3:11; Heb. 10:38). Not only are we justified by faith, but we live out the Christian life by that same faith. "As you . . . received Christ Jesus the Lord [by faith] so walk in Him [by faith]" (Col. 2:6, NKJV, author's paraphrase). The Holy Spirit within does His work when we throw the switch of faith. But is He really able to give me the victory over my besetting sin? Someone else, maybe, but *me*?

What Doubt Says About God

One day, when I was stumbling down a dark alley of doubt, three Bible stories startled me with what I was actually saying about God.

~ The father was distraught. Jesus' disciples had failed to live up to the advertisements. They couldn't heal the father's son of his terrifying condition. Then Jesus came on the scene and the father said, "If you can, heal my son" (Mark 9:22–23, author's paraphrase). "If you can!" What kind of lead-in is that!

~ The hired mourners had lots of experience with dead people. They knew dead when they saw it. So they slapped one another on the back and scoffed as they pointed at the itinerant preacher, "Some healer he is! He doesn't even know the kid's dead. We know better" (Luke 8:53, author's paraphrase). You know better? What kind of talk is that!

~ The wind howled and the waves lashed the little boat mercilessly, terrifying those seasoned fishermen. But there was a passenger on board who had no better sense than to lean back against a pillow in the stern and go to sleep. "Enough of this!" The fishermen shook their leader awake. "What's wrong with you? Don't you care that we're dead men?" (Mark 4:38, author's paraphrase). "Don't you care?" What kind of question is that!

I'll tell you what kind of questions they were: questions of unbelief. The father wondered if Jesus could handle his tough situation, the professional mourners were more confident in their own judgment than His, and the disciples accused Him of being uncaring. When those three Bible stories woke me to what I was actually saying about God, I saw my "innocent" flirtations with unbelief as actually calling into question the very character of God. What an insult!

When we fail to trust God, we are actually questioning His power (as the father did) or His wisdom (as the mourners did) or His love (as the disciples did). We're saying, in effect, "You're not strong enough to handle my rotten boss, to make me victorious with my impatience, to meet my needs while I'm unemployed." Or we're saying, "I'm not sure you're smart enough to figure out how to get me out of this jam, to guide me in the best way. I think I know a better way than yours." Or we're saying, "You're powerful enough, all right, and you're smart enough. You just don't care that much about me." We call into question the character of God.

What Doubt Does to God

That's the first problem with unbelief. God is displeased when we don't trust Him; He has been insulted and by a family member at that. "Without faith it is impossible to please God" (Heb. 11:6). When we don't trust Him, it makes God sad, just as it makes us sad when someone we love doesn't trust us.

What Doubt Does to Me

But there's more to the tragedy. Not only is God hurt; so are we. Unbelief short-circuits the flow of divine energy—the Holy Spirit won't act freely in the life of one who doesn't trust Him. For salvation, for growth, for success in the Christian life, for power in ministry, faith is the connector to God-power.

The Way Back to Faith

Recently, in a file of old letters, I discovered a cry for help from a young woman. It is such a poignant statement of the embattled state of so many Christians, I thought it might be of help to others. I was away from home on ministry of some kind and Muriel wrote me of her deepest concerns. I don't think she would mind if I shared it with you.

> Mrs. Hudson Taylor died at age 33, but Hudson Taylor had learned how to trust in the Lord in a way that kept him even then. He wrote his children he used to try to remember Jesus all the time and try to keep his heart from sin. Now he trusted Jesus and He reminded him and called his heart to abide. He learned about trust, and Daddy (she referred to my father) did . . . and you did . . . and so many have. Why can't something happen to me so I'll change and not return to my sinful self? I feel everything in my heart so violently and I'm so tired of living with Elaine (her middle name which she hated) and I can't be rid of me to dwell with Christ in the heavenlies. Why can't this mysterious something happen to me? Rosalind Goforth got suddenly changed and stayed changed.

> You said it's surrender and trust. According to Hudson Taylor if you really learn *how* to trust this way you needn't, as I do, *try* to keep your mind on Him. He who loves you draws your mind to His. If it's just trusting as for Salvation I wonder how I could be saved because something just eludes my grasp. I either don't understand or there's Something I need to do. I want victory. I am positive I have never had it or understood it. I think the Lord is helping me little and little to grow in grace but there is something missing. As long as I can remember I have carefully listened to Daddy tell about victory, always telling myself maybe *this* time I'll understand it. But nothing has ever happened.

> Please pray the Lord will let me see it or do something. Please don't just give me up as a bad job or hopeless case or just imagining things. Several times I've come to you and you don't seem to tell me . . . I wish you'd really preach at me and tell me off or something—sometimes when we're not too sleepy to be able to talk. I should think I'd be more help to you if I was delivered from myself once and for all. Oh wretched man that I am who shall deliver me from this dead body!

> I am not unhappy this time. And the Lord is more and more a very present help in trouble. But I'm almost thirty and have had the best Bible training and lived in the best Christian family to be found anywhere. And my heart is unreasonably tempestuous most of the time. Really you can't imagine how *fearfully* upset I get suddenly and over nothing—and all the time.

> What you need is encouragement and here is only one more problem. Poor Dear. Do come home and straighten me out once and for all and just think how good it will be to have a calm, happy, satisfied, spiritual wife to help bear your burdens! This is what I desire to be. There is no supernatural fruit bearing.

How many times in those days did I tell her it's not "something"—it's a Person and all you need is to trust Him? I didn't take her too seriously, I fear, for she was such a godly young woman, so winsome, and so incorrigibly happy. She did make progress, but there was one bully that always got her down. Twenty years passed . . .

Muriel called herself a chain worrier. With six children . . . well, what's a mother for? Worry those children through to good citizenship! One night she lay in bed doing her usual thing—but let's listen in as she tells her own story to a friend who—to this day—is a chain worrier.

Dear Grace,

I am not a theologue or Bible teacher or anything else that lends itself to helping you. But I am a mother and a woman, so I decided to take typewriter in hand and send some comfort if the Lord will help me do that.

A few years ago I was praying Jan would come home from Christmas work in town. "Lord," I prayed, "You know Jan dented the fender and that the tires are so slick and she is not very old. Please, Lord don't let anything happen to her in this downpour." Well, I didn't let it go at that. I wrung my hands in characteristic fashion and carried on at a great rate.

Jan got home fine and I was ashamed for getting myself so worked up. David didn't get home from his Christmas job downtown either. So I started in again. "Now Lord, you know David . . ." and on and on. I again was ashamed for the worry-filled prayers that had blotted out the faith needed to answer those very prayers. Well sir, you won't believe this. After supper Robertson and Tom got into the car so Tom could catch the bus in town. As it was still pouring rats and cats I went into the bedroom instead of doing the dishes so I could non-stop, three-dimensional, solid-state worry.

Now I am not one to say the Lord said this and that to me. It only happened this one time but you must agree I was in need of a voice from heaven instead of you-know-where-else. There was this blithering idiot lying on the bed of her total unbelief begging the Lord for help that wasn't even needed. The Lord clearly said to me, "Is this really the way you want to spend the rest of your life?" I knew who spoke this time and in horror I recoiled from this basket-case Christianity and saw myself for once as God did. My instant reaction was to shout back from the depths of my soul, "No, Lord, I can't stand one more minute of it!"

Well, the storm was over and sweet peace filled my soul. What a relief! I realized I was free. And I realized I would always be free. Not that I would never have times of testing. From then on the boys went off shooting the rapids, rapelling down cliffs, jumping out of planes and gliding spread-eagle not bothering to pull the rip cord till all was done that fun could imagine. But I was free . . .

Well, this might not be any help to you but it sure has made a different life for me after a lifetime of worry and fears. It is sort of like conversion—I go around telling everyone who will listen. I'm free!

Love and prayers, Muriel

That was no experience reserved for mystics hidden away in monasteries. Rather, it was the experience of a very busy mother of teens who'd been bullied by the sin of worry. Perhaps God will do it for anybody! When Muriel got desperate enough to cry for help, God intervened. As she turned those children over to the Lord, the burden lifted, and, she testified often in women's retreats and sometimes on her radio talk show, never again did she have one of those "hissy fits of worry," as she called them. Some years later one of those children did die in an accident. By then, her mind was beginning to fail so she couldn't fully understand all the circumstances, but she trusted; in her deep grief, she trusted still. Oh, she was tempted often enough, but she began that day to focus on the kind of God she had, on His glorious capabilities. He was a God she could trust! In the days following that original night-time encounter with the trust-worthy God, she penned this verse:

Anything, anytime, anywhere,
I leave the choice with you;
I trust your wisdom, love, and power
And all I need you'll do.

Notice the three characteristics of God she sang of—those same characteristics I had found myself doubting! Muriel had learned to trust—just simple faith—and that final bully went down in defeat.

How Much Faith Is Enough?

"All justified people live by faith" is a good paraphrase of the recurring passage from the prophet Habakkuk. That is, all of life is to be lived out connected with the power source, the Holy Spirit. But how much faith is needed to connect? Are there varying levels of faith? Jesus chided the disciples for their little faith (Matt. 8:26), commended the foreign woman for her great faith (Matt. 15:28), and of the Roman army officer he said, "not even in Israel have I found such great faith!" (Luke 7:9, NASB) Little. Great. Greatest.

Which level is necessary to connect with God? Jesus answered that question when the disciples asked for more faith (Luke 17:5–6). They had problems with an unforgiving spirit—couldn't trust God with the outcome if they did what He said and forgave the same person for the same sin over and over—so they asked for greater faith. At least they knew the root problem of spiritual defeat was unbelief! Jesus responded, "More faith? Why, if you had faith as large as a tiny seed, you could say to this mountain, 'Up! Into the Mediterranean,' and it would jump. The amount of your faith isn't the problem; the problem is you don't have any at all. And that leaves you disconnected with the flow of power. But if you have ever-so-little confidence in me, you'll be connected to all my resources."

Let's think back to those three Bible stories again. Notice that, though there was doubt, Jesus acted anyway. The father's timid faith was enough: he cried out, weeping, "I believe. Help my unbelief," and his son was set free. The professional mourners didn't believe, but Jairus, the religious leader whose daughter had died, did believe and the little girl rose to embrace her father. The disciples were in fear of their lives in the grip of the storm. Jesus rebuked them for their low-level faith (Matt. 8:26), but He stilled the roiling seas anyway.

In a sense, it isn't how much faith you have but what your faith is in. "Timid faith in thick ice and you'll make it across; robust confidence in thin ice and you're sunk," I once heard pulpiteer and best-selling author Stuart Briscoe say. God is trustworthy—He will bear up under your heaviest loads.

How Can I Tell If I Have Enough Faith?

How can I tell whether or not I have any faith at all when confidence seems to waver, for example, about this broken relationship that is tearing me apart? Easy. What choices do I make? Do I choose to yield to what I believe is God's will? That is the critical evidence of faith or lack of it. If I believe Him enough to do what He says, that will connect. Theologians differ as to whether yielding to God's will is part of faith or simply the necessary evidence of genuine faith. Either way, Scripture teaches that we can't connect with God without obedience. If I refuse to do what I know to be right, the deal's off. Intimate companionship is broken, Holy Spirit power won't flow.

Because there are two aspects of faith, yield and trust, we'll next think about faith as yielding to God's will and then we'll consider how we can grow in faith, trusting God the Holy Spirit to do His "inside work." There is nothing more important in the whole subject of life in the Spirit than the principle of faith. This is the indispensable connection that lets the life of the Spirit flow to us and through us. The secret to successful Christian living is trusting God to do what He says He will do. So how is your FQ, your faith quotient? Average? Above average? Miserably low? Now is the time to ask the Spirit of God to give you a robust faith. Perhaps you'd like to join me in the following prayer before we move ahead in probing further the meaning of biblical faith.

Spirit of the Living God, like the father with a demon-stressed son, I cry to You, "I believe. Help my unbelief." I want to be strong in faith so that Your power may flow freely and mightily to make me all You designed me to be. To prove that I do believe, here is my body and mind. Move in, take possession and do whatever needs to be done. I am Yours.

Chapter 16

Faith That Works

Cici's church is in turmoil. There's a movement afoot to dump the pastor, and people are lining up on each side, drawing the battle lines—none of it, on either side, conforming to biblical standards. Cici doesn't feel good about all the politicizing, but she thinks the truth is at stake so she plunges into the battle. She knows the gossip and rumormongering are wrong, she knows the problem isn't being handled from the right motives nor in a godly way, but she joins the fray. Why? Cici doesn't believe God has what it takes to protect His church from wrong-headed people, or she doesn't believe God is smart enough to know how to handle this situation, or she doesn't believe He cares enough about her or the others to work things out for their best interests. So she disobeys. She's disconnected.

But suppose she had chosen instead to obey God, refusing to violate biblical teaching on how to settle differences, even though not seeing a glimmer of hope, feeling utterly miserable and abandoned? She would have acted in faith. Timid, faltering faith, to be sure. But that obedience would be evidence she had enough faith to connect with the powerful Spirit of God. Of course, for the problem to be solved, others will have to learn faith and obedience too. But her response doesn't depend on the response of others, nor does Holy Spirit intervention in her own life wait on them. "Trust and obey, for there's no other way to be happy in Jesus . . ."

"Trust" and "obey" are so intertwined that James says you can't have one without the other.

88

Faith That Works

What does it profit . . . if someone says he has faith but does not have works? Can faith save him? . . . You believe that there is one God. You do well. Even the demons believe; and tremble! But do you want to know, O foolish man, that faith without works is dead? . . . For as the body without the spirit is dead, so faith without works is dead also. (James 2:14, 19–20, 26, NKJV)

A body without a spirit is truly a human body, but it is dead. James says it's the same way with our connection with God. "Faith" that doesn't embody obedience is no more than a corpse. There's a lot of confusion about the hard words *law, repent, obey, yield, confess,* and the soft words *love, trust, spiritual.* In order to understand the "spirit" of faith, obedience, let's try to work through that confusion.

Saved by Grace

We must begin with the grand affirmation of the Protestant Reformation: Salvation is by grace alone through faith alone. Paul makes this plain in documents like his letters to the churches in Rome, Ephesus, and Galatia. Are Paul and James at odds on this central issue? Notice carefully what James said in the passage quoted above. Does he teach salvation by works or, when you boil it all down, does he teach rather that "faith works"? Obeying God is the worked-out evidence that I have genuine faith. And what does Paul say? "By grace you have been saved through faith . . . a gift . . . not earned by your own effort. That salvation is accomplished by the work of the Holy Spirit who re-created you on purpose to do good" (Eph. 2:8–10, author's paraphrase). That was no afterthought, but God's original plan.

Paul exults in God's grace. And is there a more glorious word than "grace"—God's free gift of full salvation to those who have earned damnation! You can't earn a smidgin of it, he says. But notice that Paul ends up in the same place as James: faith works. In fact, Paul seems to say that the purpose of salvation is "works"—a changed life.

On the other hand, if my salvation depended on my goodness I would be forever insecure. Have I done well enough to make it? In fact, in my case, I wouldn't be uncertain at all; I'd be quite certain—of a guilty verdict! I know my performance, even for a moment, would never make me eligible for membership in the family of a holy God. So the glorious news that broke into history two millennia ago and into my life six decades ago is that "Jesus paid it all, all to Him I owe!" That's why we can be confident, which is another way to say, "to trust," or "have faith." Salvation is by grace alone through faith alone, but that isn't the end of the grace line.

Sanctified by Grace

Another way the Bible speaks of our salvation is to say we were "sanctified." The word literally means "set apart." When God saved you He set you apart from sin for Himself. Sometimes the word is translated "holy," and so we are called a holy or "set apart" people. Other times the word is translated "saint," and so all believers are called saints. That has a nice ring to it, doesn't it? "Saint Robertson!" So saint Robertson by new birth has been sanctified, that is, made holy, that is, set apart, from sin and its consequences to God and His use.

But there's another meaning of the term *sanctify*, the way it is most commonly used. I may be declared a saint officially on the merits of Christ, but am I saintly? "Saintly" means to be like Jesus. That's our goal, of course, but who can claim to have reached it? So the second use of the term *sanctification* speaks of the activity of the Holy Spirit in me from the time of my initial salvation till I reach heaven, the process of changing me from what I was by natural inclination, more and more to be like Jesus. So "sanctification" can refer to the *state* we have been given by God's act of grace and also it can refer to the *process* of growing in that new state. The saint becoming saintly! This second use of the word *sanctification* is the term that best describes this whole book.

The problem is that many people who know they have no part in saving themselves other than to believe, casting themselves on the mercy of God, act as if working out that salvation were all up to them. Paul calls this dumb: "Are you so foolish? Having made your start by the Holy Spirit are you now going to perfect yourselves in your own strength?" (Gal. 3:3, author's paraphrase). No, no! Just as salvation began by the Holy Spirit's activity in response to faith, so you will now be continuously sanctified, or transformed, by the activity of that same Holy Spirit. And that's grace!

Repentance for Salvation, Obedience for Sanctification

The transforming grace of God in our lives comes in response to the same kind of faith as did His saving grace in the first place. But just as saving faith included repentance or turning away from sin as well as believing what He promised, so sanctifying faith includes obedience as proof that we really do trust Him. Trust and obey, for there's no other way to succeed in the Christian life than to trust and obey.

Obedience to What?

Faith works. If I really have cast my lot with Him, the evidence will be that I follow Him. "If you have life by the Spirit, by the Spirit also walk" (Gal. 5:25, author's paraphrase). But how does He guide me in my walk, how does He tell me the difference between right and wrong? Now that the Spirit lives inside, does that mean that all the moral guidance I need comes through inner impressions He gives me? Maybe the written rules aren't needed any more? No, He went to a lot of trouble to have His will written out for us to see. We call it "the law."

The first purpose the Spirit had in giving the law was to condemn us and bring us to our senses. By the law we understood how sinful and hopeless we were, so that we would flee to the Rescuer (Gal. 3:24) and no longer need fear the law. "There is therefore now no condemnation to those who are in Christ Jesus" (Rom. 8:1, NKJV).

But the law still has a function in our lives. To the believer it serves as a guide, pointing out the attitudes and behavior that are pleasing to God. Nothing the Holy Spirit suggests to my spirit can be contrary to what He revealed in the Bible. His function is to light up God's intention expressed in the written law.

Thus, to the sinner, the law is like a light over the bathroom sink, showing the dirt, condemning, but to the saint that same law is like a flashlight, piercing the darkness to show us clearly the way to go. It is through the law, then, we understand sin, whether sinner or saint. And once the law identifies sin in our lives, we can choose what to do about it—either trusting Him enough to obey, or choosing instead to go our own way.

Faith That Saves, Faith That Sanctifies

When you first "trusted Jesus as your own personal Savior," did you deliberately repent (turn your back on your old, sinful ways)? In your agreement with God was it all "yes," or was there small print in the contract with a "maybe" about some things, or even an "excluded" part of your life? If there was, James says you're not saved, your "faith" wasn't the saving kind. The "body" of faith, says James, is no more than a corpse without the "spirit" of obedience that proves the faith is genuine. To change the analogy, if both poles, faith and obedience are not plugged in, you're not fully connected.

And if you did come to God with complete, saving faith, what about today? Remember, if your will is not totally turned over to Him, He doesn't do business. Holy Spirit power won't flow through a connection that's shorted out by disobedience. When I truly trust God's wisdom, power, and love, I'll do what He says!

Are there any reserved sections of your life where God doesn't reign? Some plan you won't give up, some bad habit you hang on to, someone you need to ask forgiveness of? Then now is the time to make certain that you have a close connection, that your faith is complete. If you have business to do with God, do it now!

Chapter 17

How to "Grow" Faith

*S*ometimes I have a hard time believing that God will do what He says He will do. Can He get me out of the mess I've worked myself into, putting things together so this will *really* work out for any kind of good—mine or God's? "All things work together for good?" Really now, *all*? Can God give me the victory over a weakness—I'm reluctant to call it what He probably does, "sin"—something that has plagued me for years. "Thanks be to God who always causes us to triumph in Christ?" Really now, *always*? Perhaps there's some sin-bully that has you on the run, some persistent temptation like a loose tongue or volatile temper or irresistible lust. Can God really give victory? Or perhaps you struggle with other promises like "my God will supply all your needs" or "I will be with you always" or "my peace I give to you." Maybe the promised fruit of the Spirit just doesn't ripen: Love for that particularly unlovable person in your life, or joy when things are truly miserable. You wish you could see the touch of Holy Spirit power on your witness or ministry—the way He promised. Sometimes it's hard to believe the promises.

If it's sometimes hard to believe absolute promises, what about trusting Him to do something He has not promised? Like healing my arthritis? Showing me *plainly* which option I should take in a decision I must make? Protecting my son who lives at the gates of hell, among the slum dwellers of Calcutta? Those are all unpleasant or scary parts of my life right now. Oh, He has promised to heal in answer to prayer, to guide, to protect. But heal *this* illness, *now*? Guide me infallibly in this particular choice? Protect all believers from all harm? There are no guarantees. Sometimes it's hard to trust Him with the outcome when He doesn't let us in on what He has in mind.

If it's sometimes hard to rely on God when He hasn't revealed His will, what if He has revealed His will and you trust Him *not* to do it? Now that would be some kind of faith! And that's exactly the kind of faith Moses had. Not just on one heroic occasion, either; it seemed to be part of Moses' friendship relation with God.

Incredible Faith

God was furious. "Out of my way, Moses," He said, "I'm going to wipe out the Israelites and start over with your descendants." In a few short weeks they had forgotten God's mighty deliverance from Egypt and gone to worshiping a gold-plated bull. What did Moses say? What would you say? Moses begged God to change His mind! He prayed against the clearly stated purpose of God (Exod. 32:11–14). What faith! How I would love to have that kind of faith! How did Moses get it? Was he born with it? Did it result from his early environment? Hardly. His early environment was in a foster home, the palace of a pagan Pharaoh! And his first attempt to serve God and His people was disastrous. In fact, he failed so badly he apparently developed a stutter and he certainly went on the lam for forty years. That was how much courage and faith he had. Sounds like I feel sometimes. How then did Moses develop such mighty faith, such a tight relationship with God? If we found out, it might give us a clue on how we can grow in faith. The story is found in Exodus, chapters 32 and 33.

Faith-Builder: Prayer

First of all, Moses spent time with God. To trust a person, we have to know him and to know him, we need to spend time with him. It's risky to trust a stranger too much. Moses spent time with God—a lot of time. So much time in fact that when he left one particular encounter with God, people could see God's own glory lingering about him (34:28ff). Notice several things about Moses' prayer life.

His times alone with God were part of his daily life. He set up a special place to meet with God, called the "tent of meeting" (33:7). There God talked with him "face to face." That's the kind of close friendship Moses had with God. Intimate. God knew him by name, not account number. God accepted him, favored him, and companioned with him.

A survey in the 1980s showed that American evangelicals, on average, spend four minutes a day in prayer. Is this enough time with God to get to be friends, to grow in faith? If you want your faith to grow like Moses' did, are you prepared to spend regular, daily, extended time alone with God?

Moses also had special times of extended fasting and prayer (32:1; 34:2). I was principal of a Christian school, the first ministry for which I was responsible. It was an impossible situation or the board would never, in desperation, have called on an inexperienced twenty-five-year-old to take over. I soon discovered it was indeed impossible. Nothing worked; I became more and more desperate. Finally I reflected on what people in Scripture did and it scared me. They prayed long enough to miss meals. For days on end. I'd never missed a meal in my life! What would I talk to God about for three days? In desperation I took a Bible, a hymnal, a jug of water and headed off into the mountains. To my surprise God met me there. It was like a second honeymoon with Him. Every one of the problems with which I had wrestled was solved through the wisdom the Spirit gave on the side of that lonely mountain lake. However, at the time I really didn't care. So glorious was the time alone with God, I got "hooked." It became a pattern of life, so I can't "survive" spiritually without that extended time alone with the Lord at least once a year.

But forty days? And remember, Moses' fasting was not the variety so popular today: "subsisting" on ample supplies of vegetable and fruit puree. It frightens me even to think about forty days, just like those three-day retreats frightened me at first. But Moses had those special times more than once.

Have you ever spent enough time with the Lord to miss a meal? Would you like to? Muriel used to say, "Honey, what do you do? I don't think I could hold out without eating. And what would I talk about to the Lord for three days? I need to stay with the children . . ." Finally, one year she said, hesitantly (Muriel rarely did things hesitantly!), "Could I go along this time and see how you do it?" She was surprised by joy, a spirit set free, a surge of faith.

Moses' prayer focused on God, worshiping Him, praising Him. He constantly reminded God of His mighty acts and magnificent promises (see Exod. 32:11–13). Praise, fixing our attention on God, is a powerful builder of confidence in Him.

It was a dry time in my pilgrimage. My life had gone stale and times of prayer had become a dull routine, so I went away on one of those retreats. "What's wrong?" I pled with God to renew me, to revive my spirit, to restore a robust faith. After several hours, I wore out on that approach and, a little listlessly, turned to praise. Once again I relearned the lesson: a heavy spirit lifts on the wings of praise. Here's what I wrote in my journal, the prayer that set my spirit free, renewed intimacy in the relationship with my Lover, induced a surge of faith:

Father, thank You for Your marvelous gifts: salvation and hope, the Savior's loving presence within and about, the blessed Spirit who transforms and empowers, Your friendship, incredible as that is. Thank You, thank You, for the wonderful Book. And thank You for the gift of such a magnificent world: the flowers, the grass and trees, the lovely birds and wondrous beasts, mountains and seas, streams and mighty rivers, rocks and sands and all things beautiful. What a glorious idea marriage was! And family. Friends so loyal and loving. And humankind, displaying Your image-imprint, creating magnificent art and literature and music. I love fine architecture and astounding technologies. You've given me work to do that counts for eternity. The gifts of health and abilities and, especially, Muriel. Thank You for Your gifts.

And thank You, Father, for what You have done, Your mighty acts. You saved me and save me and will save me, and a world of men and women besides. Creation that seems almost as infinite as You! The invincible Church, made of impossible building material. Your incredibly complex and wondrously beautiful planning and Your meticulous execution of every intricate part; Your sustaining power for all the worlds and for each sparrow. What a wonder You are!

But best of all, Father, I'm forever grateful for who You are. Every characteristic speaks Your majestic Godhood. But from among them all, in splendid array, I focus often on Your wisdom, power, and love. Wisdom to know all things, power to do all You will, and love to count me in. What more could I ask? I could ask for holiness, for what kind of god would we have if he could figure everything out, accomplish anything and felt affectionately toward us, but were crooked, no model of right and dispenser of justice? And what if You were unpredictable and given to change? How insecure we would be! And what if you had a beginning or—worse—an end? That would be the ultimate insecurity. But no, You are all there is of perfection, beyond all imagination. And today I bow in humble gratitude.

Not immortal literature, you say? But when those words burst from deep within me at three in the morning in a borrowed mountain hideaway, my hobbled, heavy spirit took flight. I was free again! Praise will do that. Moses, on a grander level, experienced a surge of incredible faith as he rehearsed to God all His excellencies.

There are other ways Moses shows the way to build trust and we'll look at them next. But first, to trust Him we must companion with Him. And in companioning with Him, thanksgiving, praise, adoration—worship, to sum it up—builds the trust bonds best of all.

Faith-Builder: the Bible

The second resource for building up our faith is the Bible, but Moses didn't have that resource! He wrote the first five books of the Bible himself; he could hardly have learned to know God through a written revelation. But he did have the stories of God's interventions in the lives of His people and he knew God's covenant promises well. In fact, he referred to those promises in all his dealings with God (e.g., Exod. 32:13). To remind God of what He Himself has said gives power to prayer, reinforces confidence. The Bible is a faith-builder. In fact, "Faith comes from . . . the word of God" (Rom. 10:17).

Haven't you found that true? Remember my return to faith from agnosticism? It was the Old Testament prophecies that brought me back to faith and the gospel account of Jesus, the great God-revealer, that delivered me finally from doubt. There are times when doubts nibble at the fringes of my consciousness even now, and my faith falters before some immovable mountain of difficulty, but it is the Word of God that restores. It even delivered Ted.

"I hate God," Ted said through clenched teeth. He'd come to my office to find help on how to love his newborn son. The love just wasn't there. Not much for his wife either. So I asked him about God. His response led to the next question: "How do you and your dad get along?" Teeth clenched again. "I hate that man." He was worried about the horizontal relationships, particularly with his son whom he had expected to bring joy into his life, but we soon discovered there was a vertical problem. He didn't trust God. Trusting God really seemed out of reach. In all probability you have never had such an experience, but if Ted found a secret to building faith, maybe it would help each of us build our confidence in God from wherever we are now.

"What can I do?" Ted pleaded in desperation.

"I'm not sure. But why not try this. Start reading the Psalms and jot down every characteristic of God you find there. If you get better acquainted, you might not hate Him so."

A slow miracle began. Weeks later Ted came again to see me to report that he was beginning to have feelings of affection for his little boy and the intensity of his hatred for God was beginning to melt, just a little. The Bible was doing its thing: building faith. It took years, not months, but how well I remember the day Ted wrote to tell me he was reconciled to his father.

An intimate companionship with God means a daily encounter with Him in His Word. How else can we get to know God? Knowing Him is the only way to strengthen those trust bonds. That's why the Holy Spirit gave us the Book.

Faith-Builder: the Church

Prayer and Bible meditation can be private, but there is one faith-builder that is very public: the church. Moses, mighty in faith, seemed capable of operating successfully on his own—a team with God and Moses should be unbeatable. But he didn't try to solo. When God suggested destroying the rebellious people and starting over with Moses' descendants, Moses pleaded with God to change His mind. Later, when Moses tried to do his work singlehandedly, his father-in-law, Jethro, told him he needed to delegate his authority to others, and Moses, called by God the meekest man on earth, agreed. In the grandest solidarity of all, Moses did an incredible thing. The people stood under judgment for their vile sins, and Moses pleaded again for their forgiveness. Then, sensing that a holy God might not be able to forgive, he offered himself as a sacrifice in their behalf (Exod. 32:30–32).

We don't think of Israel as a church, though Stephen called it that (Acts 7:38). But the solidarity of God's people was central in Moses' thinking and behavior. So it will be with us if we are to advance in faith. I'm sure there are those heroic figures throughout church history who have stayed true to God while utterly alone, as, for example, when imprisoned for their faith. But I have never personally known a professed believer who has made it without the church. I've known many who tried, and I've watched, grieving, as they drifted further and further from a living relationship with Jesus. He gave a promise, "I will build my church and the very Pentagon of hell will not overcome it or even be able to hold out against it" (Matt. 16:18, author's paraphrase). The book of Acts follows and shows what the Holy Spirit actually built: a string of local congregations across the Roman world. He did not say, "I will save Robertson McQuilkin and he will prevail." He said, "I will build my own invincible church."

So it was that the Holy Spirit came on the First Church of Jerusalem when they were gathered for prayer. The Holy Spirit visited them again a few weeks later when they were in desperate need of courage to hold on. It was in a prayer meeting at the church in Antioch that the Holy Spirit guided them to launch the missionary enterprise. It was in consultation and prayer in Jerusalem that explosive issues were settled by the Holy Spirit. Guidance, encouragement, power for service—it was through the church that the Holy Spirit worked.

For building up our faith, nothing can substitute for church. When I sing with God's people, my faith surges, and the sermon almost always reinforces my faith. I watch a lonely widow, dying of cancer, as she faithfully worships and serves others in the church, and my faith is challenged deeply. I make myself accountable to others and they encourage me, hold me to my commitments. I falter in confusion about what I should do and in prayer with God's people my faith is strengthened to take that leap into the unknown. Church builds faith.

Prayer. The Bible. Church. These are called by theologians "means of grace," for it is through them that the Holy Spirit empowers us. And one of the first things He uses them to do in us is to build our faith. And faith, as we have seen, is the indispensable connection with Holy Spirit power. What wonderful gifts God has given to build us strong in faith! And when we trust Him, what are the results we can expect? To that we now turn.

Activity Five

Transforming

Chapter 18

The Spiral

Matsuyama slumped cross-legged on the wooden floor of his third-floor apartment. Apartment? It was one room for a family of four on the second floor of a former army barracks. The ramshackle old building was now serving out its last days as housing for dozens of poor families.

"What's wrong, Matsuyama San?"

"I'm not a Christian any longer."

"What happened?"

"Oh, I got drunk, some guy bad-mouthed me, and I chased him with a baseball bat. What's worse, when I got home and told my wife, she handed me the butcher knife. She said, 'the Bible says if your right hand does wrong, cut it off.' I'm no Christian."

It was out of drunkenness that Matsuyama had been saved. An excellent electrician, he descended down the river of alcohol to poverty, taking his wife and three children with him. "Did you ever get drunk and fight before you became a Christian?" I asked.

"All the time."

"Did you feel bad about it?"

"Only if I got beat."

"Don't you see, Matsuyama San? Since the Holy Spirit lives in you, when you fail you're miserable. Your misery is proof you really *are* a Christian!"

Six months passed. Matsuyama's business had been reestablished. One Sunday morning he arrived at church with shoulders slumped, dejected. "What's wrong?" I asked. "Chase someone with a baseball bat?"

The Spiral

He smiled wanly. "No, but I really chewed out one of the young fellows who works for me. A Christian doesn't blow his top like that."

A year passed and it was the greatest celebration of them all: New Year's Day. But Matsuyama wasn't celebrating. I found him in his little office, slumped over his desk. He'd built the leading electrical contracting firm in the city by now, but he wasn't a happy man.

"What's wrong?" I asked.

"The check bounced," he said. In Japan people sometimes commit suicide when they can't pay their bills by December 31. He owed many people and was counting on getting payment from the general contractor for his work on a high-rise under construction. Finally he'd been paid by check on the thirty-first, and he rushed to the bank before closing time. But the check was worthless.

"What did you tell the contractor?" I asked.

"Nothing. But my stomach is standing up" (that is, "I'm very angry"). From drunken brawls to verbal abuse to rage held inside, Matsuyama was spiraling upward toward greater and greater likeness to Jesus. And the beautiful thing is, he didn't even see it!

But he did sense the Spirit at work. One Sunday a year later Matsuyama bounced in with that crooked, boyish grin I'd come to love. "What happened?" I asked. Then he told a story hard to believe. He discovered two of his employees had been ripping him off for months and everyone in the company knew it but no one told him. One or the other would call in sick, then take a company truck and go to a distant village to moonlight, drawing sick pay for the time off. Finally he got suspicious and phoned the home of the next employee who called in sick. The child who answered the phone said, "Oh, Daddy's gone to Hojo town."

Matsuyama rode his motorcycle to the fork in the road his "sick" employee must pass on the way home, hid his bike in the bushes and waited. As he sat there, contemplating the mayhem about to happen, he began to think about Jesus and about how God had forgiven him for a lifetime of evil and about how much loss Jesus had suffered to provide that forgiveness. "As I sat there, thinking about Jesus," Matsuyama said, "I choked up. Then I pulled out my bike and went home."

There'd be plenty of time later to tell Matsuyama biblical ways to hold people accountable, but that Sunday morning we celebrated the incredible victory of the Holy Spirit in the life of a wretched sinner saved out of Buddhist idolatry, from hopelessness to hope, from failure to success, from bondage to an explosive temper to freedom and power. Matsuyama was spiraling up.

The Bible verse that best describes "spiraling" became my life verse when I first began to spiral up. I have chosen other "life verses"—a theme verse for each season of life—but this was my first and it has molded my life ever since. It's our theme verse for *Life in the Spirit:* "And we all, with unveiled face, beholding the glory of the Lord, are being changed into his likeness from one degree of glory to another; for this comes from the Lord who is the Spirit" (2 Cor. 3:18, RSV).

That describes Matsuyama's life. He made the big turnaround when he met Jesus, and though he stumbled sometimes and groped his way, he never stopped spiraling up. Of course, he was spiraling before he met Jesus. Only then the spiral was downward, away from God and His ways. So the "spiral" is a picture of everyone's life, including yours and mine. We're either growing up more and more into Jesus' likeness or we're spiraling down toward greater likeness to the devil. Of course, not all are spiraling at the same rate—some are on the fast track and others on the slow, either direction. Matsuyama was on the fast track, first down and then up. I was on the slow track with the same temper problem—that's a story I'll tell you later.

What Does the Spiral Up Look Like?

I think it's easier to spot someone on the downward spiral. When you see a drunk, gossip, glutton, short-fused person, cheater, braggart, promise-breaker, porn addict, or wife-beater, you know which direction he's headed. On the other hand, what if you see a baptized church-goer, faithful witness, Sunday school teacher, student of the Bible who prays daily—are you certain she's spiraling up? Perhaps. Perhaps not.

But if you see a person loving unlovable people, being joyful and at peace when everything goes wrong, enduring tragedy with strength and grace, being gentle with those who are hurting and humble about personal accomplishments, and if you watch her reject sinful impulses more and more successfully, you're sure you've seen someone who's spiraling up. You know that because what I've just described is the fruit of the Spirit (Gal. 5:22–23). That's how to tell whether you're on the upward spiral. Do you feel, act, and react more and more like Jesus?

Can a Person Get Stuck in the Middle?

When I'm not in a fast descent, but not really moving upward to any visible degree either, I'd like to think I'm on a plateau spiritually. But that's not possible. We're always on the move, either up or down. The car that's in neutral on a steep grade isn't parked—it's rolling backward downhill. If your sails are not raised to the wind of the Spirit, you're not dead in the water; the tide is pushing you toward Enemy territory. "He who is not with Me is against Me," said Jesus (Matt. 12:30, NKJV).

The Spiral

Analyzing the Problem

So what's the basic problem in the life of believers who aren't "being transformed from one degree of Christ's glorious likeness to another?" One of three problems:

~ They're ignorant of which direction they're headed or of the provision the Holy Spirit would make available to spiral up.

~ They're not yielded fully to God's will, either because of gradual drift away from a tight relationship with God or through active rebellion, saying "no" to God about something.

~ They're not trusting God to keep His promise to give them the victory, haven't grown in faith to the place of expecting and receiving the power-flow of the Spirit.

You could summarize those diagnostic indicators as ignorance, unyieldedness, and unbelief. One of those deficiencies, or a combination of them, is always the root problem for the Christian who isn't spiraling up.

Those aren't academic analyses of Bible truth, however. If we don't get personal about it, the doctrine becomes death-dealing instead of life-giving. Are you confident that you're spiraling up to ever greater likeness to Christ? Can your family and fellow workers see it? If you have some uncertainty or at least you're not satisfied with your present rate of progress, reflect for a moment on which of the three problems contributes most to the slow growth: ignorance, unyieldedness, unbelief. Then take action. What action?

Turning Point: A Crisis in Life

My father was a successful young businessman and active church leader, especially with youth. But something was missing. He felt defeated by sins of the spirit, his work for God was powerless, he was agitated within. Though no one in his family or church would have guessed it, he was fighting a losing battle in his attempts to spiral up. Then came the turning point. Challenged by the "big turnaround" in the life of a friend, he went to his room and methodically yielded to God each part of his life: first the sins he was aware of, then the disputed things that some said were wrong, others said were OK; after that, he turned over to God his past, both failures and successes, his future, and finally his fiancée. Everything. In an instant his life was transformed. He said there was no special emotion, no vision, but from that time on, for the first time in his life, nothing else mattered but the will of his Lord. And for four decades the world watched in wonder as he spiraled up.

God's plan is for the newborn Christian to keep growing without interruption, like Matsuyama. But most of us, like my father, because of ignorance, drift, rebellion, or inadequate trust, slip into a downward spiral, getting out of touch with the Spirit. We need another encounter with God, we need to make a U-turn. Theologians call this a "crisis" experience, but that term can be misleading. For many, the anticipated experience must be an emotional upheaval or some miracle sign from heaven. And a person's "crisis experience" may indeed be a cataclysmic event. But it need not be that way. As with my father, it can be a rational transaction with God. The intensity of the turning experience may depend on one's personality, expectations, or on how long and how deliberately one has resisted the will of God—in other words, how difficult the turning is. But the basic meaning of the term "crisis," both in the dictionary and in biblical teaching, is simply "a turning point." And without that, no one will ever spiral upward.

Maintaining an Upward Spiral: the Process

Once the turning is complete, the Holy Spirit is free to begin the process of transforming us into ever greater likeness to Jesus. My Christian life, like this book, has focused more on the "process" than on the "crisis," possibly because my turning point was early in life. At age twelve I turned my life over unconditionally to Jesus Christ. The process that followed hasn't been steady, but I never went back on that contract I signed with God. I've stumbled, even wandered occasionally, as in my season of agnostic doubt, sometimes grew more rapidly than at other times, and often failed through ignorance. But I can't ever remember shutting God out, deliberately saying "no" and sticking with it. So the process began.

Where are you in life's spiral? More importantly, in which direction are you headed? If you aren't sure or you are quite sure you aren't spiraling up, at least so anyone would notice it, isn't it time to make a turnaround, or to make sure you have fully turned around? To "turn around" is to make an unconditional commitment to the will of God, no fine print or reserve clause in the contract. And to check out whether or not that's our heart's true condition, we don't merely consult our feelings. The Spirit gave us a Book full of specifics to use as a standard to evaluate our attitudes and behavior. So if you're ready to check out your own relationship to God, here are a few areas Scripture says must be yielded to Him:

- Your reputation (Phil. 2:3–11; Luke 14:11)
- Your future (Matt. 6:33–34)
- Your family, friends (Matt. 10:37)
- Your possessions (Luke 12:33–34)
- Your talents, abilities (1 Cor. 4:7)
- Your entire self (Rom. 12:1–2)
- Everything (Luke 14:33)

The Spiral

There may be other areas not listed here, of course, things you've been keeping under your own control—some world-like pattern of thinking, some relationship, some activity, talk, or habit. Are you ready for the big turnaround? If you are, now is the time to name each area the Spirit has convicted you about and turn it over to God. Unconditionally. Next time we'll look closer at how the Holy Spirit moves us up the spiral, but first, be sure to settle the direction you're headed. Do it now!

Chapter 19

Keeping Step with the Spirit

"Since we live by the Spirit, let us keep in step with the Spirit" (Gal. 5:25). This verse could be paraphrased, "If you came to life by the power of the Holy Spirit, by that same power spiral up!" That's an exciting prospect, but what does it mean in actual practice?

First of all, remember that the Holy Spirit is a person who invites us to companion with Him all day every day, walking with Him through life. But that fellowship is not just a mystical, internal experience. In the process of transforming us, moving us up the spiral, the Spirit puts certain tools in our hands, things we can see, touch, experience. Theologians call them the "means of grace" and point to gifts the Spirit has given, like the Bible and church, and things He energizes and transforms, like prayer and suffering.

Consider how, by faithfully using these "tools," we can participate with the Spirit in His work of remodeling our lives which sin has so defaced.

The Devotional Life: Companioning with God

One important kit of tools might be called the devotional life. That's another way of describing our companionship with God. Here are a few characteristics of a healthy devotional life:

~ A regular time to read and meditate on a passage of Scripture
~ A time for worshiping God and giving Him thanks for His many blessings

~ Prayer (intercession) not only for oneself and one's family, but also for friends, the church, the cause of Christ in world missions, the lost, the government

~ A set time daily, a "date" with God, for devotional activities like these

~ Confession of sins the moment there is failure

As you check off those activities we associate with a "devotional life," you may have experienced what I have. It can become a dry routine, a duty-driven habit instead of the vibrant personal companionship the Spirit has in mind. Of course it's better to do right, even for inadequate motives and with poor results, than to fail to do right. But why settle for that? The goal is quality time alone with the Lord so that you leave that special encounter with the exhilarating sense that once again you've connected.

One Man's Experience

Since many seem to find help in seeing how others experience God, I'll share some of my approach to the devotional life; but please remember that my way isn't the only way. In fact, it's not even the best way, but it's one way a fellow pilgrim has pursued companionship with God.

I kept a "personal quiet time" following that surrender at age twelve, but reading the Bible was more like eating sawdust; and praying—well, was God listening at all? I tried to keep that morning appointment with Him, but more often than not I skipped it in favor of more sleep or breakfast. Finally, at age twenty-one, as I mentioned earlier, I told the Lord I would read the Word daily whether it had meaning for me or not, just as an act of obedience. Things didn't change, but I kept that promise faithfully, week after weary week, eating sawdust. Then one morning I realized I *had* changed. I couldn't get along without that time with God. In fact, the Bible had come alive to me. And it's been that way ever since.

I said "morning." And that's my appointment: every morning at six o'clock. Why morning? David said God would hear his voice every morning (Ps. 5:3). Rhett, a friend of mine, said he couldn't see tuning your violin after the concert was over! I don't insist on morning since some say they aren't morning people, but it is important to have a set time or other things will crowd out your time with God altogether. The Enemy will see to that! By the way, there aren't many interruptions, I find, at 6:00 A.M.

How much time should I set aside for my "date" with God? The editor of *Christianity Today* wrote in a personal column that he cannot get along without spending fifteen minutes a day alone with God. Many Korean pastors say the same thing—only for them it's four hours that is indispensable! For myself, I can hardly unwind and settle my restless mind in fifteen minutes. I set aside an hour and it's always too short! One thing is for sure, a hasty salute toward heaven won't do. God deserves better than that. And so do you, for the goal is companionship, not dutiful routine.

Praise

First I sing a couple of hymns. That "tunes my heart to sing God's praise." He doesn't care about my lack of solo quality! A friend of mine who lives in crowded conditions had to stop singing aloud but switched to a Walkman with earphones. I can hardly wait to meet Charles Wesley and Isaac Watts in heaven; Handel and Bach, too, not to mention David. How the gifted bards from all the ages have lifted my soul to heaven! No wonder there are so many commands in the Bible to sing. By the way, I like Steve Green and Scott Wesley Brown too.

The Bible

After tuning my soul with song, I turn to the Bible. I use a different translation each time I read through the Bible to keep it fresh and gain new insights. I read consecutively through any Bible book I've chosen—the way the author intended it to be read. That way the Spirit can communicate what He intended in each of His personal "love letters" to me. That's why I often pause before reading and ask the Spirit to speak to me through His Word.

As I read I underline passages that speak to me—a new insight into God's ways, comfort for my present heartache, conviction of sin I had become numb to, a principle of life I didn't understand, or one I understood but neglected. Then I go back through and think about (meditate on) the parts I underlined, often praying these back to the Lord in His own words or asking Him to work them out in my life. If the underlined portion is something I want to remember, I type it on an index card and rotate those on my "refrigerator collection." That way I can memorize them without really working at it! That's my approach to devotional Bible reading. What's yours?

Prayer

Thanking God for His blessings, exulting in His beauty, and worshiping Him with adoring praise often come naturally through the songs or passage of Scripture. If not, I spend some time in worship, not asking for anything but just focusing on God. Have you ever tried to spend a few minutes, say five or ten, without asking God for anything? Just praise Him and thank Him. He enjoys that, just as you do when people express appreciation for you.

Then I turn to "intercessory" prayer. I commit each plan for the day to the Lord, asking Him to use me to the maximum for His purposes in each encounter and each activity, planned or unplanned. It's good to talk to God about everything in your life—He invites us to. But most Christians are egocentric in their prayers. It won't do to stop with intercession for my own needs and those of my family.

One way I pray for others is to have a current "hit list"—people who are a special concern, divided by categories: unsaved, Christians in spiritual trouble, people with health needs or bereavement, those making hard decisions, those having special ministry opportunities, etc. After praying for them, I turn to my prayer photo album. The first pages are pictures of those I pray for daily: family, close friends, and others for whom I have assumed a prayer responsibility. Then follow many pages of those I pray for less frequently. Finally, I pray for the nations and for missionaries seeking to reach them. I want to be a world Christian on my knees! God loved the world; I want to also.

Did you notice the kind of prayer I left out? During my morning time with the Lord I rarely confess my sins and failures. I don't do it then because I've formed the habit of confessing my sins to Him immediately, as soon as I'm aware of them. He forgives on the merits of Christ and buries them. So there's no need for me to exhume them the next morning! I do confess my sins each night. First I briefly review the day to see if I can recall any sin not confessed. Or I may revisit an earlier confession if the offence was particularly grievous. Then I ask the Lord to forgive all the sins I didn't even recognize, cleanse me, and counteract any bad outcomes in the lives of others that might result from my failure. I do confess sin, keeping short accounts with God, but not much in my morning time with Him. I haven't had time yet to sin that much!

Of course, our companionship with God, walking with the Spirit, is not confined to the daily devotional time. The mystics speak of "constant, conscious communion with Christ." I've not attained that, especially the "conscious" part, though I would like to. But each of us can be aware of His abiding presence and turn to Him spontaneously throughout the day, telling Him "thanks" when things go well, calling on Him to help when they don't, and just sharing our hearts with our best friend, the only friend who is always there. I'll never get over the wonder that the Infinite One actually desires my companionship!

Prayer and the Word—two wonderful gifts the Spirit gives for us to participate personally with Him in the transforming of us from who we are to who we were designed to be. But He's provided more than that: He's provided other people to join in the spiral. We turn next to those exciting truths, but first, if my experience has alerted you to something you'd like to change in your own devotional life, don't feel you need to radically change everything instantly. That may be discouraging. Just take a step at a time—that's what spiraling up is all about. But be sure to tell the Lord what you intend to do.

Chapter 20

Partnering: How Church Fits the Spiral

$\mathcal{A}$ vibrant devotional life is essential to spiraling up, but it mustn't be a solo performance. The Spirit not only partners with us in utilizing His gifts of the Bible and prayer; he uses other people too. But not just random "other people." He established the church, an organized body of believers, to provide help in the spiral up. As twentieth-century Americans we may be tempted to go it alone. We tend to live by the creed of rugged individualism, do-it-yourself independence. We're also committed to privacy. It's hard for us to believe, down deep, that we really do need one another, that God's plan is for life in community, that inter-dependence is a better way. But it is. Christ promised not to build invincible Christians but an invincible church (Matt. 16:18). Paul constantly reminds us that a major purpose of the church is the "building up" of believers, or spiritual growth. That's what we've called "spiraling up."

Actually, any activity done by a group of God's people aimed at honoring God can be used to strengthen each member of the family, but Scripture seems to emphasize six major purposes of the church. I've put them in diagram form, indicating three inward-pointing and three outward-pointing purposes. To fulfill the inward-pointing purposes—for the benefit of its own members—the church *teaches* the Bible, provides *fellowship* as a family, and holds its members *accountable*. The first outward-pointing purpose is Godward: *worship*. Then there are two purposes toward the world outside the church: *evangelism* and *service*.

110

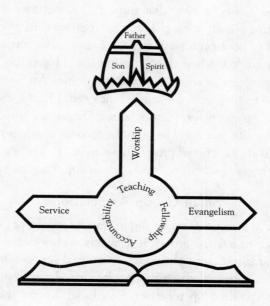

Most of those purposes are somewhat self-explanatory, but there's one that's a real sleeper. When I say "fellowship," I'm not talking of the friendly chit-chat most churches experience for a few minutes following the morning service, nor even of the potluck dinner on special occasions. I'm speaking of real family solidarity, the blood ties of Calvary binding closer even than human blood ties—belonging to one another, providing for one another, companioning with one another, sharing the joys and sorrows of life. God's forever family! But let's return to the six purposes.

Note that all three of the outward-directed purposes could be accomplished alone—worship, witness, and service to the non-church community. All can be accomplished better together with others, of course. But the three inner-directed purposes of the church—teaching, fellowship, and holding accountable—by definition can't be accomplished alone at all. We really do need one another if we are ever to spiral up. How does the church work to accomplish this?

Think about four ways of relating in the church body or congregation: the entire family meeting together, small group associations, one-to-one relationships, and church authority.

The Entire Family Meeting Together

Public worship is directed toward God, bringing Him joy, but it also helps each person who truly participates to spiral upward. Sometimes on Sunday morning, standing with fellow worshipers, I find myself on automatic pilot, mouthing familiar words to a familiar tune. But sometimes my heart is quickened with a spiritual exhilaration I don't experience in my private singing. That's worship! I never hear a sermon that doesn't enrich me. No matter how inept or even misguided, when the Scripture is read and the preacher talks of God, I can find nuggets of truth to make me richer. And when God's people gather on purpose to intercede for some great need, I find a surge of faith in my soul that rarely visits me when praying alone. These are some of the ways the Spirit energizes my life through His church: corporate worship, prayer, and the preached word. And that's no surprise. Those are three major purposes the Spirit had in creating church—worship, family fellowship, and teaching/learning.

Small Group Associations

There are special benefits for meeting in smaller groups of God's people, benefits not available to a large group. If a Sunday school class or a Bible study group is small and interactive, there can be mutual support and even accountability. The study course on which this book is based was designed for just such a relationship of spiraling up together. People who grow through relating in such groups say things like, "They know me personally, where I'm coming from" or "I've gotten personal encouragement" or "The instruction fitted my personal circumstances" or "It's neat seeing that others wrestle with the same problems I do."

People often say, "It's not like church." That's strange—it *is* church! It's not the church gathered in a large group for formal Sunday worship, to be sure, but it is church gathered in a small group for fellowship and accountability. Both are needed. The inner-directed purposes of the church seem best fulfilled in the smaller group: (1) family fellowship, a sense of belonging and even intimacy, (2) teaching and learning, and (3) accountability.

One-to-One Relationships

One-to-one relationships can be personalized even more than the small group. Perhaps you have a regular "prayer buddy" or partner with whom you can share freely. I can't get along without that. A prayer partner is the most common one-to-one relationship in the family, perhaps, but many people have chosen to go even deeper: they have an accountability partner.

Larry was a college professor and lay preacher who wanted someone to hold him accountable so he could grow spiritually. He asked me to meet with him once a week. I was startled at our first meeting when he gave me a list of very pointed and personal questions he wanted me to ask him every week. Here's his list:

~ Ask me about my time each day with God—the content of my prayers, the truths I've learned from Scripture, the amount of time spent.

~ Ask me how eating habits have changed and what specific goals I have reached in losing weight. Did I snack between meals? What size helpings did I take?

~ Ask me to list the amount of time spent with TV and what specific programs I've watched.

~ Ask about how much time I spent with my wife, my sons.

~ Ask about what I've done to combat sexual temptation; probe to see if I have done anything to feed an unhealthy sexual appetite. Ask about my relationship with the attractive girl who works with me.

~ Ask me about my motives in work: what drives me to accept so many responsibilities, what I have said "no" to this week, why I said "yes" to any new responsibilities I accepted.

That's accountability! Larry was serious about "spiraling up." Are you? If you have an accountability partner or if you were to have one, what questions would you propose for them to ask you? Would the questions be honest and open, uncovering the well-springs of your motives, attitudes, and activities, or would they be selective or somewhat opaque, shielding from view the embarrassing truths you'd like to keep hidden? To be of any value, we must be very honest and very thorough in sharing with a true accountability partner. This may be too threatening even to consider, but if you're serious about spiritual advance, why not ask God if this is one way He would have you obey the command "confess your sins to one another, and pray for one another" (James 5:16, NASB)? Even if you're not ready to begin such a relationship, it might be helpful to write out the questions you would ask if you had such a partner, questions that would probe everything you want to become as you spiral up. All the purposes of the church can be strongly advanced in partnership with another person, but especially the inner-directed purposes are taken to a deeper level in such a relationship: fellowship, teaching/learning, and accountability.

As we have seen, there are many ways "church" helps me grow or spiral up: Sunday church service, small group gatherings, a personal relationship with another believer. Some call it "body life." But there is a crucial difference between personal relationships within the family of God and church as church.

Church Authority: Discipline

The New Testament is clear on the role of the church in the individual member's life: the organized church is responsible for each member, has spiritual authority over every member. If I sin and refuse to repent or if I teach false doctrine, it's the responsibility of the church to discipline me, to bring me back into line. Paul rebuked the church in Corinth for failure to discipline a sinning member (1 Cor. 5). Many churches, like Corinth, are defiled and weak because they don't do the hard thing: discipline those who are sinning, first by counsel and rebuke, and ultimately by separating them from the fellowship if the gentler methods don't work. "If your brother sins against you, go and show him his fault, just between the two of you. If he listens to you, you have won your brother over. But if he will not listen, take one or two others along, so that 'every matter may be established by the testimony of two or three witnesses.' If he refuses to listen to them, tell it to the church, and if he refuses to listen even to the church, treat him as you would a pagan or a tax collector" (Matt. 18:15–17).

Method of Church Discipline

Let's apply Christ's formula. You've just discovered that someone in church is having an affair. What do you do? Here are some of the things church people do:

- Nothing—it's none of your business
- Tell a close friend
- Tell the pastor
- Bring it up in church business meeting
- Share it as a prayer request in your small group
- Go to the person alone and seek his or her repentance
- Start a campaign among the members to deal with the matter ("political action committee")
- Have nothing to do with the person in any way that would validate him or her as a fellow Christian

The more common approaches in that list of options violate Christ's command and harm both the offender and the church. Jesus says that we are to go first to the offending person alone, one-to-one—not to anyone else! Then, should there be a rejection of your approach, go with spiritual leaders, seeking to persuade the person to change his or her sinful behavior. If that appeal doesn't work, it is to become an official matter for church discipline.

Purposes of Church Discipline

There are many purposes for church discipline in Scripture, but it must never be to seek retribution: "Vengeance is mine," says the Lord (Rom. 12:19, KJV). The paramount reason is to restore the one who failed. That's a critical way church is needed for us to grow spiritually, to get the person who has stumbled back on the upward spiral.

Church Authority: Guidance

There's another way in which the church as church assists each member: guidance. It was to the church at Antioch meeting together in prayer that the Holy Spirit revealed his missionary purpose for their senior pastor, Barnabas, and one of his assistants, Paul (Acts 13). The Spirit didn't speak directly to Paul, but to the church about Paul. It was hard for me to learn this lesson.

In the first ministry for which I was responsible, a Christian school, the board did not always agree with me on the direction we should go. Gradually, through painful experience, I began to have more confidence in the leading of the Holy Spirit through our responsible body than through my own independent judgment. It became a life principle for me. Sometimes the body is dysfunctional, of course, a rebel church abandoned by the Spirit, the kind of church whose guidance shouldn't be sought or accepted. But normally our ministry choices should be made in the context of church.

Christ said, "I will build my church," and that is what we must be doing. The church, then, in turn, will build us. Very few have survived spiritually, let alone prospered in faith, without active participation in church life. God doesn't save us and put us on a lonely pilgrimage. The Holy Spirit is our constant companion, but He provides touchable companions too. And we neglect those intimate relationships to our own spiritual peril.

The more gregarious or outgoing among us may like the "church" tool of the Spirit even more than the private tools, prayer and the Bible. But few of us would ever choose the fourth "tool" if we could avoid it—adversity. Yet when we work with the Spirit in harnessing our adversities to power spiritual advance, we may discover the fast track on the spiral upward. We turn now to discover how that can be.

Chapter 21

Stormy Weather: Adversity Fast Track

Colin Green greeted me with a big smile and a cheery "Praise the Lord!" Praise the Lord? For what? Here she was, cooped up in the hospital room with that giant of a man she'd lived with for decades, now incoherent, uncooperative, belligerent, far down the terrifying road into Alzheimer's.

"Why so happy?" I asked. She told me the story of how she found a despondent woman wandering in the hospital corridor, a mother who had traveled from a distant city to watch her son die. Colin, forgetting her own woes, became a friend to her, and led that distraught mother to find hope in Christ. Both were inundated with unexpected happiness as they embraced and mingled their tears.

But what about Colin? Bit by piece I dragged from her the story. Last week her husband broke down the door of their small home to get out of his "prison." Halfway across the front yard he stumbled to the ground and couldn't get up. Colin couldn't lift him, but she was reluctant to call 911 lest they find her beloved in his pitiable condition. He was incontinent and his clothes totally soiled. Colin pulled off his clothes, cleaned him up, and redressed him as he lay there, helpless. Then she called for help.

She spent the night with her man in the hospital, protecting the nurses from his irrational behavior. The next morning, Sunday, her ne'er-do-well son arrived with bad news: "Mom, your house is going up in flames!" A few hours later I entered that bleak scene, received a warm embrace from that courageous little black lady who called me her "white family" and whispered in my ear, "Praise the Lord!"

Why Trouble Destroys People

Not everyone responds to trouble like Colin Green. Some emerge from the storm better people, some worse. Why? Various answers have been given:

- ~ Some people inherit a stronger temperament than others
- ~ Some people have traumatic childhoods while others have a nurturing home background
- ~ Some people face more tragic events than others
- ~ Some people have more faith than others
- ~ Some people have a stronger support network of loving people

Which would you choose? Perhaps *all* of them contribute. The crucial factor, however, is not the circumstances, but my response to them. Faith in God keeps the circumstances outside, pressing me ever closer to God, and I become a stronger, better person, more like Jesus. Unbelief, on the other hand, lets the circumstances come inside and put a wedge between God and me, and I become a weaker person, less like Jesus than before, perhaps discouraged, despondent, even bitter, or at least a miserable, complaining person. Remember, though, it's not the quantity or even the quality of our faith, but the object of our faith—a trustworthy God—who is able to transform our trouble into strength and beauty.

Where Does Trouble Come From?

Sometimes it's quite clear who caused me pain, but often it can be frustrating trying to figure out who's to blame. The effort can be self-destructive, besides. Some people forever blame others for their troubles—they are victims of others' malice or stupidity. It may be a misguided or evil parent or spouse, a society stacked against them, or the devil himself. Of course there are others who tend to blame themselves for everything, guilty or not. Have you ever fallen into the "blame-it" trap? The strange thing is this: even if my blame-laying is on target, that truth has little power to deliver me from my problem. Indeed, the blame hunt itself may make me a worse person, less like Jesus.

But there is a way out. No matter where the problem may seem to come from, it always originates in one source. And, surprise—that one source of all trouble is God! "Being predestined according to the purpose of Him who works all things according to the counsel of His will" (Eph. 1:11, NKJV; see also Deut. 32:39; Job 1:12; 2:6; 2 Cor. 12:7; Amos 3:6; Isa. 45:7; Prov. 16:4).

Of course, the awful tragedy in your life that came as the result of someone's sin is not at God's initiation, at least not normally. He didn't send it. But He did permit it. And one thing is certain, no harm can touch the child of God unless it passes through the nail-scarred hands of Jesus. To know that God is behind every grief of mine may create some other problems, but at least it simplifies the search!

Once we understand that basic truth concerning suffering, we no longer need to devote our energies to determining the guilty party and making them pay for it. We can give our attention more to understanding the reason or purpose God has in our suffering. To discover the purpose in the suffering relieves the deepest agony of it. For meaningless suffering is the greatest torment of all, and that is the distress of every person who doesn't know God.

The Purposes of Pain

Consider some major adversity in your life and reflect on God's purpose in sending it or permitting it. Here are some possibilities:

1. Punishment for sin (Jer. 11:10–11; 1 Cor. 11:30–32; 2 Sam. 12:13–14; John 5:14). No believer will face punishment for sin in eternity, but while still here on earth Christians may suffer as a result of sin. In former days when tragedy struck, people asked, "For which of my many sins is God judging me?" Today we tend to ask, "What's wrong with God? Why me who deserves so much better?" In searching for the purpose in my grief, it doesn't hurt to ask the former question because God does still punish sin.

2. Chastisement indicates the chief purpose of punishment, to bring erring children back to the right way (Ps. 119:67, 71; Heb. 12:5–11).

3. Warning—God may punish an erring child as a warning or example to others to be careful (1 Cor. 10:11).

4. Guidance—sometimes God allows hard times to get us to go somewhere or do something we otherwise might not consider (Acts 8:1, 4; Matt. 10:23).

5. Comfort—suffering prepares a person to help others (2 Cor. 1:3–4). Sometimes it's difficult to be truly comforted by one who has not suffered. Suffering is God's great tenderizer.

If you have difficulty in deciding what purpose God has in mind for sending or permitting a particular adversity, it may be because I left out the most important purposes in suffering. Those I listed are sometimes God's reason, but often those purposes are difficult to sort out, as you may have discovered. There are two purposes, however, that are always present in every trial. It is simpler to concentrate on those!

Stormy Weather: Adversity Fast Track

God's Glory

When I respond to trouble with childlike confidence in God, people see it and give God the credit, whether they see a miraculous deliverance (John 9:2–3) or miraculous strength in the midst of suffering (2 Cor. 12:7–10) as we saw in Colin Green. Suffering always has that purpose—the glory of God (Ezek. 20:9, 14, 22, 33, 39).

My Growth

Suffering also has the purpose of growing me up into Christ's own likeness—the fast track on the spiral up. By the time we met Colin Green she seemed to live only for others. Every circumstance in my life is designed to make me more like Jesus: "The Spirit . . . pleads for God's own people in God's own way; and in everything, as we know, he co-operates for good with those who love God and are called according to his purpose. For God knew his own before ever they were, and also ordained that they should be shaped to the likeness of his Son." (Rom. 8:27–29, NEB).

Talk about a powerful spiral up! The Holy Spirit uses everything in the life of believers for the purpose He had all along: shaping them into the likeness of the Son. That includes, especially, the pain (see also 2 Cor. 12:7; Phil. 3:10; Heb. 12:4–13; John 15:2–4; Rom. 5:3–4; Ps. 119:67, 71).

How do I make sure the adversity actually brings glory to God and growth to me? Watch the spiral carefully: "When all kinds of trials and temptations crowd into your lives . . . don't resent them as intruders, but welcome them as friends! Realize that they come to test your faith and to produce in you the quality of endurance. But let the process go on until that endurance is fully developed, and you will find you have become mature in character, people of integrity with no weak spots" (James 1:2–4, author's paraphrase).

Faith is the key! When I pass the faith test I become tougher in endurance, and that leads to maturity, which, in turn produces, more and more, the character of Christ in me. On the other hand, if I doubt that God is big enough to handle my problem, that He is smart enough to know what's best for me, or that He cares enough to see me through, I spiral down—I crumple in self-pity and give up, or grow hard and cynical or even mean-spirited and hostile. But faith will transform that same trouble from a stumbling block into a stepping stone, God's fast track to spiritual growth. Without the testing we would remain spiritually flabby and quite unlike the One who "learned obedience from what he suffered" (Heb. 5:8). When we respond with childlike trust in a loving Father, we can join Colin in trusting God with a mate's Alzheimer's, a ramshackle little house that just burned down, an only son who never panned out. And I can say from the heart, "Praise God!"

I don't always respond that way. Remember how to strengthen faith?

~ Faith begins with an unconditional "yes" to God's will in the matter
~ Surges forward on the wings of praise
~ Is reinforced through Bible promises
~ And the help of fellow pilgrims.

All those ways of growing faith are essential. Leave off even one of them and you're stalled at the starting gate. Faith—the alchemy that transforms the most bitter pain into a life-giving elixir. The adversity that can poison your whole life is the very thing the Spirit can use to bring God high praise and put you on the fast growth track.

It almost seems like we should be grateful for trouble! Well, we are to give thanks always for everything (Eph. 5:20), not just for the pleasant things. That doesn't mean, of course, that we must be grateful for the pain itself. It may be evil incarnate that you resist and seek deliverance from. But in the meantime, we trust the all-wise, all-powerful, all-loving God to bring about His purposes through it. And what clearer expression of faith than thanksgiving and praise? So pause before we move any further, name your greatest heartaches and problems to the Savior, and thank Him that He will use that adversity to bring great glory to Himself and growth in your own likeness to Jesus.

O Love divine, that stooped to share
Our sharpest pang, our bitterest tear,
On Thee we cast each earth-born care;
We smile at pain while Thou art near.

Though long the weary way we tread,
And sorrow crown each lingering year,
No path we shun, no darkness dread,
Our hearts still whispering, "Thou art near!"

When drooping pleasure turns to grief,
And trembling faith is changed to fear,
The murmuring wind, the quivering leaf
Shall softly tell us Thou art near!

On Thee we fling our burdening woe,
O Love divine, forever dear,
Content to suffer while we know,
Living and dying, Thou art near!

—Oliver Wendell Holmes (1809–1894)

Chapter 22

My Spiral

> But we all, with unveiled face, beholding as in a mirror the glory of the
> Lord, are being transformed into the same image from glory to glory, just as by
> the Spirit of the Lord.
>
> 2 Corinthians 3:18, NKJV

*S*ince this is the theme verse of *Life in the Spirit*, let's pause for a moment
to analyze it. The promise of transformation by the Spirit is not for everyone.
When Paul says, "We all are being transformed," he doesn't mean all people on
planet earth. Notice he puts two qualifiers on whom he means by "we." (1)
"We all" are those whose "faces" are "unveiled." (2) "All" includes those who
"behold as in a mirror" the glory of the Lord. Both descriptions are in picture
language and a bit enigmatic. What does he mean literally? This is very important to know as we surely want to be part of the "all" Paul has in mind!

In the verses immediately preceding, Paul speaks of how a veil of sin blocks
off our "hearts" and "minds" from understanding the truth of Scripture even if
we do hear it (vv. 14–15). Notice he uses heart, mind, and face interchangeably—it's the core me that's blocked off by sin from knowing God. But when
we make the big turnaround, repent, and trust the Lord (v. 16), the Spirit
removes the veil (vv. 16–17). The other qualification is "beholding." The term
could be translated either "looking," or "reflecting," as some contemporary
translations have it. I think "looking" fits the context better, though "looking"
is too tame and "beholding" is archaic. To get a better understanding of the
term consider the parallel passage in Hebrews: "We must throw off every

encumbrance, every sin to which we cling, and run with resolution the race for which we are entered, our eyes fixed on Jesus, on whom faith depends from start to finish" (Heb. 12:1–2, NEB).

There's the idea—the steady focus of faith on Jesus. To successfully run the race of the Christian life it's necessary to stay disentangled from sin and keep a steady focus on Jesus. Then, Paul tells us in our theme verse, the Spirit of God will do His mighty transforming work. Here's my paraphrase of the passage: "All of us who have the sin barrier removed and who keep a steady faith-focus on Jesus are being transformed from one level of His glorious likeness to another by the power of the Spirit."

Sometimes it helps to see an example, so let me tell you how this, my life theme, has worked out in my own life.

I mentioned my turnaround at age twelve. But I must not have turned 180 degrees because the growth didn't follow. Why? As we saw earlier, the possible reasons are ignorance, disobedience, or unbelief. Consider each of those barriers.

Reason 1. Ignorance: *Learning Who I Am, Who God Is, and How I Can Be What He Wants Me To Be*

I was sincere enough—I proved that by never going back on my commitment to God. But I was ignorant of what "yield" means. I was also ignorant of what was needed to advance up the spiral. Jesus was dear to me but the Holy Spirit was a stranger. Ignorance blocks progress.

Reason 2. Unyieldedness: *Settling the Sin Question*

At age eighteen I became restless about my Christian life. I had a list of items for daily prayer and on that list I noted "T & T." I put it in code in case my college roommate snooped! T & T stood for tongue and temper. I had the same problem Matsuyama had. What changed imperceptibly in those days was the completion of that original turnaround. To yield to God in biblical terms is not just a passive cry of "uncle"—"I quit, God, you win." It's positive, aggressive, an active desire for God and good, an attitude of going for the gold of likeness to Jesus. This desire became an obsession with me. I had completed the turnaround, was headed up. But I didn't seem to be making very rapid progress. Enter the preacher . . .

Reason 3. Unbelief: *Making the Trust Connection*

The man in the pulpit said something so simple I wondered how I, a grown man of twenty years, could have missed it so long. "The key to the victorious Christian life," he said, "is surrender and faith." I hadn't been at all sure I could make it spiritually or that God would enable me. But, sitting there on the pew, the confidence began to surge that God would make me into a different person. And that's the meaning of the word in 2 Corinthians 3:18, *metamorphosis*: a transformation of nature. I began to believe it really could happen in me; I tightened the trust connection.

Once those inhibitors of growth are identified and removed—ignorance, unyieldedness, unbelief—the Spirit is free to move in transforming power. But He doesn't do it to a passive me. He expects me to participate in the process through using the "tools" He provides: prayer, Scripture, church, adversity. We introduced those tools in the last three chapters, but let me illustrate how each of these worked in changing me from a short-fused, shoot-from-the-lip person into something more like Jesus.

I was praying, reading my Bible, and attending church faithfully. But these activities weren't focused on growth, especially growth out of my occasional outbursts of bad temper. Now that the turnaround was complete and I was "going for it," those "tools" began to work.

~ The Word preached enlightened me and gave me confidence of what could be.

~ My daily prayer focused on a desperate cry for deliverance from my personal quagmire of spiritual failure.

~ The church? The preaching enlightened and got me started, but at that point I didn't know about small group accountability and I didn't have a spiritual "buddy." My father, however, was "church" to me. I wouldn't have made it on my own. He instructed me, was always gently available, and, above all, lived the life I longed for. That kind of close-up view will give a person assurance about the reality and possibility of a life of "victory."

~ Those three tools became an indispensable part of my upward spiral, but to answer my prayer for mouth-control and a patient spirit, God used the circumstances of life—adversity. Forty years and counting! They were God's severe mercies, designed to make me like Jesus. Paul calls suffering a grace (Phil. 1:29)—the same word used of salvation—an unearned gift for our welfare, a "means of grace." Watch the spiral. "We . . . rejoice in our sufferings, because we know that suffering produces perseverance; perseverance, character; and character, hope" (Rom. 5:3–4). "God disciplines us for our good, that we may share in his holiness. No discipline seems pleasant at the time, but painful. Later on, however, it produces a harvest of righteousness and peace for those who have been trained by it" (Heb. 12:10–11).

In high school I sometimes settled disagreements with my fists. In college, when I got desperate for godliness, that never happened. But sometimes, my tongue hurt people and I began to feel the pain. That's why the first "T" was on my list—tongue.

God had used the Word and His people (the church) to dispel my ignorance about the evil in my life and His ability to change me, and He used prayer to link me up with the Spirit's power. But He also used adversity. At just the time I began to get serious about "spiraling up," I met the most delightful creature God ever created. Muriel and I heard all the horror stories of marriage wars and we were determined not to follow the pattern. If Jesus were central to both of us, how could we fight? And we kept our vows—no controversy for three or four years! If one of us got contrary, the other stayed cool and it does take two to make a fight. Remember this is the "T & T" man we're talking about. A walking miracle.

But then came the first child, Mardi, and something wholly unexpected emerged in our marriage. Muriel and I had never discussed child discipline and now discovered we differed radically. When little Mardi was about three years old, we reached a crisis. I began to seethe inside and pulled down the shades. Communication shutdown. Oh, I was civil, said "good morning," and such. But bubbly, outgoing Muriel knew something was wrong. I boiled for three days until finally I could stand it no longer. As I drove down the highway, thinking of how dead wrong Muriel was and how she wouldn't change, the Holy Spirit made me so miserable I pulled over to the side of the road, crumpled over the steering wheel and pled with God for two things: forgive me and deliver me.

But it happened again. And again. Three days of seething anger, finally repentance and restoration. Three or four times it happened in our first ten years of marriage. Finally, when I was in Christian ministry—a missionary, in fact—I decided this could not go on. I went away into the mountains alone for three days of fasting and prayer. With tears I cried to God for deliverance. In desperation, I said, "Lord, if you don't deliver me, I quit. What message do I have for these lost Japanese if it doesn't even redeem me from an evil temper?" I meant it. And so did God. It never happened again. Do you see what was happening to me? I didn't, but now I can trace it—spiraling up from physical violence to verbal abuse to internal anger and finally, to deliverance. From one degree of His glorious likeness to another, through the means of grace—all of them. By the Spirit of the Lord.

But that wasn't the end of it. As the children came along, with them came the old temptations—to punish them in anger, to speak harsh words. I remember the day I realized it was OK for a father to apologize to a little person and with tears I knelt by Jan's bed and told her I was sorry for what I had said.

As the children grew older and began to leave home, God brought other circumstances to shape me. There was long-term betrayal in the ministry. By then I wasn't tempted to fight with words or even to feel rage within. But it took me years to truly forgive. Finally, reading Christ's words from the cross, it dawned on me that I should ask God to forgive my "Judas," the ring leader of that conspiracy. I was startled at the residue of feeling inside. "Oh, no, Lord!" I said. "I've forgiven him, never held all that garbage against him anyway, never tried to get back or make him pay for it. But I don't want *You* to forgive him. Isn't there any justice?" But the persistent Holy Spirit worked on me day and night. Finally I was able to pray from the heart, "Father, it's OK. You can forgive him, too. Treat him as if it had all never happened." And once again God put me on the track of spiraling upward into greater strength of will, inner tranquility, and love for friends who behave like enemies.

And now? God must have taken those "T & T" prayers of my youth seriously, for He seems to have put me in a post-graduate program in patience, caring for a dear one whose needs change daily. For twenty years. So far.

What is the Spirit of God up to? He will, if we let Him, make us into working models of Jesus to attract people to Himself. How has He been doing that in your life? Look back at your own life, or at the recent past if you have become serious about your faith only recently. Matsuyama had only a couple of years to grow before he fell to his death from a utility pole. How his wife and children rejoiced that he had changed so radically! Or perhaps you count your spiral in decades like I must. How have you changed from impatience toward inner tranquility, from lust toward purity, from gluttony toward self-control, from materialism toward contentment and generosity, from egocentric thinking toward preoccupation with the concerns of others, from doubt toward confidence in God's promises? Or maybe it's been something else God has been working on . . .

The Spirit wants to spiral you up, but He won't force you forward. So it may be time to reconnect. If we are to get disentangled from the web of sinful attitudes or actions, we must be very honest about it, both with ourselves and with the Lord. If you can't truthfully see any progress toward Christlikeness, it may be time for the U-turn, the unconditional surrender. It's either "yes" to God with no fine print in the contract, or it's "no." You don't grow into a right relationship with God, much less drift into it. You must deliberately step into it. Are you ready to make the great turnaround? Do it now!

But to spiral upward toward ever greater likeness to Jesus takes more than surrender, it takes trust in Him, it's "by faith from start to finish." I must focus my confidence on God to do in me what I can't do for myself, change me in my core being. But, unlike surrender, trust may not come in an instant. We grow in confidence in God's wisdom, power, and love as we companion with the Spirit and use His tools. Trust grows as we grow in knowledge of a person, so perhaps to reconnect or tighten your connection, you need to pray with the father of the demon-possessed child, "Lord, I do believe. Help my unbelief!"

Well, that's the story of my spiral. What's your story?

All of us who have the sin barrier removed and who keep a steady faith-focus on Jesus are being transformed from one level of His glorious likeness to another by the power of the Spirit.

Chapter 23

Expectations

*M*arguerite had high expectations. She had been so miserable with her failure to measure up that in desperation she turned to Jesus and invited Him into her life. She thought, "Tomorrow everything will be different. I won't get angry with Robertson any more."

When she told me her story, I responded, "And I gave you plenty of cause to be angry."

Marguerite, my older sister, said, "No, not just you. I was mad at lots of people."

Why did she think her temptation to get angry—and all those other miserable temptations that held her in their grip—would disappear? Because they seemed to have disappeared for her father.

Our father preached all over the world about the victorious Christian life. He wrote about it in articles and books read by tens of thousands, but he did more. He lived that life right before us in the home. To outward appearances he led a flawless life full of love, joy, peace, and all the fruit of the Spirit. How was Marguerite to know she was comparing a babe in Christ to a mature Christian?

Marguerite awoke to great disappointment the morning after her conversion. As she put it, I "smart-mouthed" her, and she blew up just as she always had. In addition, none of her other temptations or failures disappeared. "I was so disappointed," she said. "At first I struggled and fought the temptations, just like I always had. Finally, I gave up. For me the Christian life didn't work." For years

Marguerite settled for spiritual defeat. She struggled to be good with sometimes modest success, often with failure to be and do what she longed for.

When were Marguerite's expectations of her Christian life too high? When were they too low?

After several years overseas, I returned home to discover a beautiful person, one of the most godly people I've known. Under the most bitter of circumstances, she lived a life of quiet patience and tireless service for others. What had she found?

Whatever it was, that's what I want, don't you? But what expectations of my Christian life are valid—can I actually move with Marguerite beyond her earlier experience of daily defeat? Let's search out that fundamental puzzle of life in the Spirit.

Our Goal: What We Can Become

The Holy Spirit is in the business of taking sinners and making saints of them—all are agreed on that. But on the outcome of His activity there is strong disagreement. Here are examples of some leading ideas about what we can expect:

~ Marguerite was transformed into a radically different kind of person and experienced consistent victory over her old temptations.

~ Jason is quite certain that both he and all Christians sin consciously and deliberately every day.

~ Virginia says she was baptized by the Spirit last year, her sin nature was expunged, and she no longer sins.

~ Mary has given up on any miracle deliverance from her many woes and relies on her therapist to help her cope. Prozac helps too.

~ Evan claims that he's composed of two natures, an old one that can't improve and a new one that can't sin. His vote determines which will win out, so last night, watching TV, he voted for the new nature, which actually is Christ living in him, and Christ won out in the battle with lust. That time.

Various Christians fervently stick with each of those positions and just as fervently deny the others; so how can we know for sure? Let's try to sort it out. Did you notice there's a tendency to go to one extreme or its opposite, to expect absolute, sinless perfection instantly, or not to expect much of anything? It's always our temptation to take a biblical teaching and so emphasize it that we neglect balancing truths, end up with a lopsided view, and suffer the consequences.

A best-selling author alludes in virtually every book he writes to the teaching of his childhood church—and especially to the teaching of his mother—that perfection is not only possible but that they were experiencing it. As a youth he was painfully aware of how far short of perfection they fell. Not only is he scarred deeply by this experience; he feels it destroyed his brother. On the other hand, I sat for some years under a pastor who was a constant proponent of "grace." But after a time I realized he didn't believe in much grace between justification and glorification! He would lead us in weekly confession of deliberately and constantly sinning. As a result, the handful of godly seekers after holiness in the congregation were left without hope and the rest were lulled into spiritual complacency by the assurance that their pastor was as wicked as they. But there must be some middle way, some liberating yet realistic biblical expectation.

In search for the central biblical truth, let's look first at the distortions we must guard against. In this chapter we'll note how the Bible cancels out the extremes at both ends of the spectrum. Then we'll look more carefully at the results of settling for too little; and finally we'll examine the danger in expecting more than God intends.

Listen to some of the things Paul says about our potential:

~ Thanks be to God! He gives us the victory through our Lord Jesus Christ. (1 Cor. 15:57)
~ In all these things we are more than conquerors through him who loved us. (Rom. 8:37)
~ But thanks be to God, who in Christ always leads us in triumph. (2 Cor. 2:14, RSV)
~ For if you live according to the sinful nature, you will die; but if by the Spirit you put to death the misdeeds of the body, you will live. (Rom. 8:13)

These are just samples of a basic theme of the New Testament from Christ who commanded us to be perfect (Matt. 5:48) to Peter who teaches that if we aren't godly we are "shortsighted, even to blindness" (2 Pet. 1:9, NKJV) and John who assures us that if we live sinful lives we aren't children of God at all (1 John 3:6–10). No, we're not condemned as human beings to a life of spiritual failure. Hallelujah!

But if we resist those who would push us back into the bog of struggling failure, what of those who hold out the hope of perfection? Anyone who testifies of reaching perfection sure has got Paul beat! Listen to him: "It is not to be thought that I have already achieved all this. I have not yet reached perfection, but I press on, hoping to take hold of that for which Christ once took hold of me. My friends, I do not reckon myself to have got hold of it yet" (Phil. 3:12–13, NEB).

John spells it out clearly: "If we claim to be without sin, we deceive ourselves and the truth is not in us . . . If we claim we have not sinned, we make him out to be a liar and his word has no place in our lives" (1 John 1:8, 10).

If the Bible is truly our authority, we will resist the temptation to do the easy thing, taking one emphasis and pushing it to a seemingly logical conclusion, beyond what Scripture teaches.

The Means: God's Role and Mine

Our expectations are warped not only about the goal of what can be achieved in the Christian life. We're tempted to distort the means by which we achieve the goal, thinking it's all up to us or concluding that God does it all.

Note the following descriptions of how some people feel the Spirit makes us successful in our Christian walk:

~ It's a hand-and-glove relationship. The Spirit is the hand, you're the glove: so "let go and let God" do His thing in and through you.

~ It's a relationship in which you are invited to companion with God, and the closer you stick with Him the more He empowers you.

~ It's the substituted life—just as Christ died as your substitute, now let Him live as your substitute.

~ It's pretty much up to you—your will power, determination, hard work. God will assist you, but don't count on any miracles. ("God helps those who help themselves" is the slogan eighty-five percent of Americans identify as the best known verse in the Bible, even though it nowhere appears in Scripture!)

~ You'll know it when the Spirit comes—you'll experience a surge of spiritual energy like you've never had before and, if you'll let Him, He'll keep you on that high plane from now on, free from struggle and failure.

~ You have your part in the process—the Holy Spirit puts tools in your hands so you can cooperate with Him in the remodeling of your life.

Though most of those approaches have an element of truth in them, all but the two we considered in recent chapters—the second and last options above—have dangerously misleading elements. We'll see that more clearly in the chapters that follow.

We can miss the way by having false expectations about our goal, what we can achieve spiritually. And we can miss the way by having false expectations about the means, especially what part God plays in reaching whatever goal we may set. But we can also stumble by misunderstanding our own part.

Remember that faith is the uplink to connect us with Holy Spirit power. We can fail through trying to live by self-effort rather than by faith. But another way we can stumble through false expectations is by a misguided understanding of faith itself. There are some counterfeit forms of faith, ideas or attitudes that masquerade as faith, that will never connect with Holy Spirit energy.

What the Faith Connection Really Is

At the two extremes of this "masquerade ball" are resignation and presumption. I'm more tempted to the resignation end of things. Actually, to be resigned to whatever may come to pass can be a form of genuine faith, even if it tends toward fatalism—"whatever will be will be." But by definition there's no joyful expectancy in it. It isn't the kind of living faith that trusts God to hear and answer prayer, to give me the victory over my circumstances. Don't settle for resignation.

The other extreme of counterfeit faith is presumption—believing God will do something He never promised. Many of those lovely lakes scattered across Wisconsin hide the wreckage of the trucks and cars of owners with misplaced faith. No matter how confident the driver was in that ice, no matter how often during the winter he'd saved time in getting to his favorite fishing spot, his faith ended in loss. So with our faith. Churches hide the wreckage of those who firmly believed God would do something He never promised to do, victims of presumption, not beneficiaries of faith.

In the next chapters we want to discover the solid biblical ground between resignation and presumption, not expecting too little of our life in the Spirit, and not expecting too much. But in this chapter we've sought to identify the not-so-biblical views of what we can expect from our life in the Spirit in the three basic elements of life as God intended it:

1. Our goal, what we can become
2. The means, how the Spirit changes us
3. Our responsibility, what the faith connection really is

At this point in our study, I found a prayer welling up in my spirit. Maybe it expresses your desire, too:

> Father, it can be confusing to hear sincere people fervently pressing on us expectations that are so contradictory. I want to know Your way, so please guide me as I study to show myself approved of God, a worker who has no need to be ashamed. When we sort through the various options and reach some conclusions, I don't want to become arrogant about being right and others being wrong, but I do want to have clear light on the pathway before me. Thank You that You sent the Spirit to guide us into all truth and that He will do it. I ask this light for my own sake, but in reality it is for Jesus' sake, that He may be pleased by my life. Amen.

Chapter 24

How's Your Aim: Too Low? Too High?

We confess, Lord," the man in the pulpit prayed, "that we Your people turn our backs on You, shake our fist in Your face every day of our lives." Would you say the "amen" to that pastoral prayer or do you think he's aiming too low? A recent book is entitled *Less Than Conquerors*, and the author's point is just that: the best we can expect in the Christian life is struggle and failure, and anyone who claims more is deluded or hypocritical.

Here are a couple of statements that are true, but dangerous. They're often used by those who settle for too little of the Christian life:

~ Nobody's perfect and God understands that I, too, am weak and flawed.

~ God loves me unconditionally and accepts me just the way I am.

I'm a little uneasy about these common statements and maybe you are too. Perhaps it's because the thought is incomplete and we worry about what conclusion the person draws from the statement. Perhaps we hear, "Nobody's perfect," but what is left unsaid is "So don't bug me about changing for the better." To be biblical a person would need to say, "Nobody's perfect but I want to be on the upward spiral toward that goal." Again, it's true that I'm invited to come to God "just as I am without one plea." But if by saying, "He accepts me just the way I am," we mean, "He approves of me the way I am," or "God accepts me, so don't you be a judgmental hypocrite," we have missed the whole point of salvation. He accepts me as I am to transform me into what He designed me to be. He loves me too much to leave me just the way I am. That would be far too low an expectation.

~ It is God who saved us and chose us *to live a holy life* (2 Tim. 1:9, NLT, italics added).

~ For we are God's masterpiece. He has created us anew in Christ Jesus, *so that* we can do the good things he planned for us long ago (Eph. 2:10, NLT, italics added).

The purpose of our salvation, from the beginning, was to make us what we're not: holy!

Broken Choosers

Some people have too low expectations for theological reasons, as we have seen. They just don't believe God will change human beings that much. But there are others who have low expectations for psychological reasons. They believe few people have the ability to choose God's way—most have been disabled by circumstances. I met someone who based his ministry on that assumption.

I was talking with Gregg, a full-time counselor on the staff of a large Midwestern church. "My counselor friend, Buck," I said, "tells me that some people can't respond to God in obedience or faith because, as he puts it, their 'chooser' is broken. They *can't* choose God's way. They need therapy first so they can begin to follow Scripture. What do you think of that theory?"

"Oh, I agree completely."

"In your church, about what percent of the people don't have the ability to make godly choices?" I asked.

"I'd say about ninety to ninety-five percent."

I didn't tell him that Buck had said five to ten percent.

And then there's Al, head of a large counseling staff in a megachurch. I asked him the same question. "We operate on the basis that everyone has the ability to make choices," he said, "unless a person has mental problems of an organic nature. The Bible assumes that people can, with divine assistance, respond to God's commands and are responsible to do so. We build our therapy on that biblical assumption."

Who's right, biblically—Gregg, Buck, or Al? The truth is the church is full of hurting people, some battered more than others. And when people are blind to their own sinful behavior, or their "chooser" is so bunged up it can't function, or their "truster" is so violated they can't get through to God, a trained counselor, using some of the tools of the profession, may be able to help them see themselves, others, and God in clearer perspective. Then they can begin to trust God and choose God's alternatives.

133

But ninety to ninety-five percent? Gregg and Al have widely different expectations of the Christian life. A lowered expectation of what the Holy Spirit can do without professional intervention may come from making the therapy model the rule rather than the exception, as Gregg does. It's easy to see where lowered expectations of Holy Spirit generated possibilities come from. As mentioned earlier, Americans in general believe less and less in sin and guilt, more and more in a battered psyche that needs healing. We are no longer guilty sinners needing salvation; we are victims of someone else's hurtful behavior and we need to have a healthy self-image restored, by therapy if necessary. We could picture the difference in viewpoint this way:

Bible idea of the human predicament and the way out:

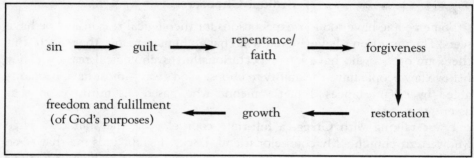

Modern idea of the human predicament and the way out:

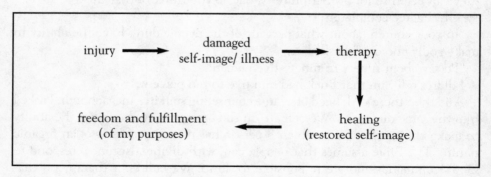

If a therapist buys into the modern way of seeing things rather than the biblical view, he may lock a person off from God because the view of self as a hurting person, damaged by wrongs inflicted by others, often leads to a person's not feeling responsible for his feelings or even actions. Gradually he is into denial about his own guilt and personal responsibility to choose the right. And that's a box with no exits.

How's Your Aim: Too Low? Too High?

There are two major ways, then, to lower expectancies: theological and psychological. If I've been led to believe there is no hope for me to be an overcomer, to experience miracle intervention by the Spirit of God, surely the theory, theological or psychological, will prove self-fulfilling.

In contrast, Scripture bases its promise of salvation and power-filled Christian living on the assumption that we can respond to God in faith, we can choose His way. Some of us may need more help from the outside than others and the church should provide that help. But let us never underestimate the power of the Holy Spirit to give us "the will and the way" so that we can indeed "work out [our] own salvation with fear and trembling" (Phil. 2:12).

To counter the rat-a-tat-tat drumbeat of low expectancies, perhaps you would like to pause for a few minutes and examine how Paul describes Holy Spirit potential in the life of every believer, reading the eighth chapter of Romans slowly and letting your spirit bathe in the glory of what God promises for your Christian experience. This passage is the peak of all Bible teaching on the Holy Spirit, His name appearing almost twenty times! Pause and let the Holy Spirit through Paul suffuse your spirit with expectancy—legitimate expectancy, because realistic—but also exciting and very satisfying.

Romans 8 isn't the whole of it, however. Let's review again some of the other key passages on the rightful legacy of every believer, beginning with Paul's great proclamation of emancipation: Sin shall not have dominion over you! (Rom. 6:14). Paul gives thanks to God who always causes us to triumph (2 Cor. 2:14) and exults in the assurance that we are more than conquerors (Rom. 8:37). "Thanks be to God," Paul says, "who gives us the victory through our Lord Jesus Christ" (1 Cor. 15:57). Incredibly, he promises a life filled by the Spirit so powerfully the only way to express it is to say we're "filled to . . . all the fullness of God" (Eph. 3:19), "to the measure of the stature of the fullness of Christ" (Eph. 4:13, NKJV)!

These are not isolated proof texts but rather reflect the mood of the entire New Testament from the promise by Jesus Himself of abundant life (John 10:10) and a bumper crop of Christlike characteristics (John 15) to the promise of Peter that we can escape from the world's corruption and experience abounding godliness (2 Pet. 1) and to John's assurance that we must (and can) live out life in the moral light (1 John 1). John even draws the curtain on the final act: "He who overcomes shall inherit all things, and I will be his God and he shall be My son" (Rev. 21:7, NKJV). Such is the destiny of the overcomer. Hallelujah!

Aiming Too High

We've seen some of the dangers of aiming too low in our Christian life. But the opposite can derail us, too, as we'll soon see. Some see the grand promises we've just discovered and think they mean we can become sinlessly perfect in this life, perhaps even instantaneously, through a post-conversion experience.

Boris was that way. He enrolled in our graduate program and wanted me to experience what he had experienced years before when God had supposedly eliminated his sin nature. Since then he had preached in mighty power all over the world. I'm not altogether sure why he enrolled in a school in which, he assured me, none of the teachers had experienced such a transforming encounter with God.

In contrast, another preacher who turned the world upside down testified that he had not yet attained perfection (Phil. 3:12). Paul struggled with temptation and weakness. He was sometimes filled with fear, for example, and had more than one squabble with his colleagues. How do we read the same Book and come up with such different answers? By the way you define "sin" or "perfect."

Defining Sin

Sin has been defined in various ways:

A sin is an action that violates God's law—feelings don't count. An action that violates God's law is certainly sinful, but "feelings don't count"? Christ carefully designated wrong attitudes as sin (Matt. 5:21–30) as well as the outward acts. Some say anger or sexual desire is wrong only if you act it out, that emotions are morally neutral. But Jesus said wrongful anger itself and lustful thoughts themselves are sinful.

Sin is transgression of the law. We have to agree with that definition because it's a biblical statement! (1 John 3:4). But it was not intended as an exhaustive definition of sin—there are other attitudes and actions which don't actively transgress the law but which fall short, such as "sins of omission" or failing to think or do what I ought.

Sin is any falling short of the moral character of God. Here's one that is thoroughly biblical because God's standard is to be just like Him morally (Matt. 5:48) and yet "all have sinned and are falling short of the glorious character of God" (Rom. 3:23, author's paraphrase). Who is as good as God? As contented, courageous, clean as Jesus? Acts always in love toward others? We're all falling short, Paul says.

To sin is to knowingly violate God's revealed will: involuntary attitudes and misbehavior I don't know to be wrong are part of my finite human nature, not sin. Though to sin knowingly is indeed sin, it is nevertheless sinful to have attitudes or actions that are not like Christ, whether I am aware of them or not. "Sins of ignorance" we call them, and we are not innocent when we sin in ignorance. As Paul said, "My conscience is clear, but that does not make me innocent" (1 Cor. 4:4).

How's Your Aim: Too Low? Too High?

If we lower the standard, then it's easier to reach it. If I'm guilty of sin only when I deliberately violate the known will of God, maybe it is possible to live a life relatively free of "sin." So one reason Christians differ on "perfection" is because they differ on the definition of sin.

Defining Perfect

Linked to one's definition of sin is the definition of *perfect*. We use "perfect" in many different ways.

- ~ The Smith's new baby is perfect.
- ~ Gifts of ministry enable God's people to grow up into perfection. (Eph. 4:13)
- ~ Be perfect as God is perfect. (Matt. 5:48)
- ~ This ice cream is perfect.

There would be no problem among us if people who teach the possibility of perfection in this life meant healthy (like the Smith's new baby) or mature (as in Eph. 4:13) or outstanding, really good (like the ice cream). The Bible uses the term "perfect" in all these ways. The problem comes when some speak of sinless perfection meaning "without flaw in the moral realm." As we have seen, Scripture says a person who says he is without sin is self-deceived or, worse, makes a liar of God. The only way a person can do this is to redefine sin, to make it something less than any falling short of God's moral perfection. Thus when people speak of sinless perfection, the difference is often semantic; the term "sin" is defined with limitations. If I'm promised a life free of deliberately choosing to break the known will of God, for example, maybe perfection is within reach. But if I promise a flawless life, free from all wrong attitudes and actions, full of God's perfections, my expectancy is too high.

Of course, it's no doubt better to aim too high and fall short than to aim too low and hit the target! In fact, Paul prays for the perfection of the Christians in Corinth and tells them to aim for it! (2 Cor. 13:9, 11).

Results of Unrealistic Expectations

What is the result of unrealistic expectancies? Boris said that he alone on our campus was perfect. But don't ask any of the secretaries about that evaluation—they feared his explosive rage that could be ignited by the slightest thing that didn't go his way. What was his problem? Was he self-deceived? He no doubt considered his anger "righteous indignation" and thus remained "perfect." That result comes from a difference in definitions and can lead to self-deception. Of course, there may be some who know they've not reached their standard of perfection, yet who still talk like they had. They would be in danger of hypocrisy—not self-deceived but seeking to deceive others.

For many, however, the danger is the opposite of self-deception: discouragement—discouragement in not being able to achieve or maintain what is expected. Many become so discouraged as to drop out altogether. Such are the hazards of unrealistic expectations:

~ Self-deception, especially by redefining "sin" or a particular sin
~ Hypocrisy, knowing I fall short but professing otherwise
~ Discouragement from expecting perfection and falling short

We've spoken of too low expectations and too high expectations, but there's a strange combination of the two, not in any church's formal doctrine but common in Christian practice. "I don't do half the bad stuff most people do," people say and feel that's good enough. Another variety of the same syndrome: the Christian who prays, "forgive us of our many sins," but doesn't pause to think of any specific wrong he needs to right. Both may be jealous of a fellow worker or critical in spirit, for example, but quite satisfied with their level of achievement. Their expectations are too low by biblical standards, but their evaluation of themselves is way too high! They too qualify as misguided in expectations, and they too may be self-deceived or hypocritical. They don't have the third bad result, however. They're not in danger of becoming discouraged about falling short!

We've looked at some of the results of holding unrealistic expectations about our potential for life in the Spirit. Surely this chapter is not the most exciting point in our study of life in the Spirit. But before pressing on to "lay hold on all for which Christ laid hold of me," I need to accept the biblical limitations on my expectancy. I'll never in this life be absolutely perfect as God is, without sin, though when I see Jesus I shall be like Him (1 John 3:2). Hallelujah for that!

How can we praise God for the bad news of limited expectations? Here's my response:

Thank You, blessed Spirit, for releasing me from the drivenness and disappointment of unrealistic expectations. Help me to accept my own limitations and those of others. And please, please don't let me swing to the other extreme and settle for less than You intend. I want to be all a redeemed human being can be. And that's for Jesus' sake—not just for mine. Amen.

Chapter 25

Two Kinds of Sin, Two Kinds of Victory

*I*f the expectancy of some is too low and of others too high, what is the biblical vision of a Spirit-filled life? Somehow our expectancy of spiritual success seems linked to our view of sin, so let's examine that more closely.

Two Varieties of Sin

When I first saw the biblical distinction among sins, it became a liberating truth that gave birth to hope for my personal life in the Spirit. "The priest is to make atonement before the LORD for the one who erred by sinning unintentionally, and when atonement has been made for him, he will be forgiven . . . But anyone who sins defiantly, whether native-born or alien . . . that person must be cut off from his people. Because he has despised the LORD's word and broken his commands, that person must surely be cut off; his guilt remains on him" (Num. 15:28, 30–31).

Scripture clearly distinguishes between unintentional sin and defiant, or intentional, sin. When I think of "unintentional," several synonyms come to mind: unknown, unconscious, involuntary, unpremeditated, unthinking. For "defiant" or "intentional," I think of deliberate, knowing, willful.

This distinction between two varieties of sin may help solve the mystery of two passages in the New Testament:

~ If we claim to be without sin, we deceive ourselves and the truth is not in us.

~ He who does what is sinful is of the devil . . . No one who is born of God will continue to sin.

Those two teachings can hardly be viewed as contradictory because they're by the same author only a few verses apart (1 John 1:8; 3:8–9). The apostle didn't slip up—he meant both basic truths. But how do they fit together? It might help to understand John if we recognize the two kinds of sinning Moses just distinguished for us. In chapter 1, John is talking about any and all varieties of sin, including any falling short of God's glorious character, intentional or not. If you claim to be without any kind of sin whatsoever, you're badly deceived, he says. But in the third chapter he uses a continuous action verb (not clear in some English translations), "if anyone keeps on sinning," he says. If you deliberately choose to violate the known will of God and stick at it, John says, you're not a Christian at all. And Paul says the same thing:

~ Do not be deceived: Neither the sexually immoral nor idolaters nor adulterers nor male prostitutes nor homosexual offenders nor thieves nor the greedy nor drunkards nor slanderers nor swindlers will inherit the kingdom of God. (1 Cor. 6:9–10)

~ The acts of the sinful nature are obvious: sexual immorality, impurity and debauchery; idolatry and witchcraft; hatred, discord, jealousy, fits of rage, selfish ambition, dissensions, factions and envy; drunkenness, orgies, and the like. I warn you, as I did before, that those who live like this will not inherit the kingdom of God. (Gal. 5:19–21)

Two Kinds of Victory

Thus it would seem that for deliberate sin the Bible offers complete victory by the power of a new nature and the indwelling Spirit of God. Hubert thought so. In our Sunday school class we were discussing our failures when old Hubert finally spoke up: "Well, fellers, whenever I'se borned agin, I quit sinnin'." Every head whipped around toward Hubert. We knew he was a godly man, the best among us, perhaps, but quit sinning altogether? He continued: "After I wuz borned agin, I'd *never* deliberately choose to do wrong." Hubert had a limited view of what sin is, but he had the right theology of post-conversion behavior: a Christian doesn't deliberately choose to do wrong. The unconverted can do right but can't consistently choose to do right. The truly converted can choose to do wrong but can't consistently choose to do wrong. For that, God offers total victory. And expects it!

But what does the Bible offer for victory over the other kinds of sin, the unintentional? Sometimes there is instant deliverance from that kind of sin, too, like Muriel and her worry. And when we find ourselves in any kind of spiritual failure, we should do like Muriel and cry out for total deliverance. But sometimes it doesn't happen that way, like Matsuyama's temper or my impatience. For us there was a pattern of growth.

I was speaking to a skeptical audience. The 400 preachers and missionaries had a theology that permitted them to believe we all sin deliberately every day and they were suspicious that I believed in sinless perfection. "For me, the Westminster catechism, 'We sin daily in thought, word, and deed' should be revised," I said. Their worst fears about the guest speaker were confirmed. Palpable tension turned to stony-faced glares. I continued, "For me, it should read, 'I sin uninterruptedly in thought, word, and deed.'" You could hear a corporate sigh of relief. Their speaker was as sinful as they!

I continued, "Never for a moment do I love as Christ loved. I never—and never shall in this life—have His level of courage, of purity, of contentment, of faith. Yet that's my goal. I intend to move in that direction." So far, we were reading from the same page of Scripture, 1 John 1! When I moved into chapter 3, however, I left some of them behind. "But notice," I said, "that I don't get up in the morning and say, 'Today I'm going to get irritated four times, lust six times, covet my friend's new house, worry for ten minutes, and grouse about certain things that keep bugging me.' I don't intend to do those things, I don't choose to do them. And when I find myself thinking that way, when my falling short of Christlikeness rises to the conscious level, I immediately cry for help and, by God's grace, quit."

I went on to explain the deliberate kind of sin that calls for total victory: the new believer doesn't cut down his bank robberies from ten to two a year, he doesn't try to seduce fewer women than he used to, she doesn't quit cheating on state income tax while still fudging a little on the feds, quarrel only with those fellow church members who are totally unreasonable, talk about people hurtfully now only when it's true. We join Hubert and "quit sinnin'." The 1 John 3 variety of sin doesn't call for growth! But the 1 John 1 variety—that's a different story.

Victory as Growth

The consistent teaching of the New Testament about the Christian life is growth, as we saw in chapter 18 on spiraling up. We are to grow in all ways, but Peter commands us to grow in two specific things that help with unintentional sin: "But grow in the grace and knowledge of our Lord and Savior Jesus Christ" (2 Pet. 3:18).

Grace

A grace is a gift given to one who hasn't earned it. It's something you can't get no matter how hard you work, like salvation. When we grow "in grace" we receive more and more Holy Spirit power for godly living. "Let us then approach the throne of grace with confidence, so that we may . . . find grace to help us in our time of need" (Heb. 4:16). The Spirit's bank of grace is infinite, to be sure, but my capacity to receive His gifts is limited. I need to grow in appropriating more and more the resources the Spirit makes available. For example, when I diligently use the weapons the Spirit provides through prayer, Scripture, and the church, the Spirit's power is released and focused through those channels He provides and energizes. That's grace! In fact, those "weapons" are called by theologians, "the means of grace." We'll study how that works in chapters 30–33.

Knowledge

We're also commanded to grow in "the knowledge of our Lord Jesus Christ." I must grow in understanding what the will of God is. For example, when Ben dominates his wife, claiming biblical sanction ("Wives, be subject to your own husbands," Eph. 5:22, NASB), he needs his knowledge greatly expanded to understand what his relationship was intended to be. He needs to read the rest of the passage—loving her "as Christ loved the church" (v. 25).

Sin can be unintentional, then, for two distinct reasons: weakness or ignorance. I know well enough it's wrong to be impatient and I don't plan to "lose it." But suddenly I find myself upset over the way that jerk cuts in front of me in rush-hour traffic. I need God's enabling grace. On the other hand, I keep discovering racial prejudices that are buried so deep I had no idea they were there. I need knowledge—of myself and of God's view of right and wrong.

The idea that there are two kinds of sin and two kinds of victory has been a transforming concept for me:

~ Deliberate sin? There's potential in the new me and my powerful inside partner to consistently say "no" to the enemy, "yes" to God.

~ Unintentional sin? There's potential for growth by the empowering Spirit as I learn more perfectly His ways, yield to His will, and trust Him to do what He promises.

But not everyone agrees. Some don't find that teaching in Scripture, and I freely admit it's not like most of the teaching in this book, clearly taught in the Bible. But for me, there's sufficient biblical evidence, and I've certainly found it liberating and empowering. Then why would some disagree? Perhaps because there are attitudes and behavior that seem to fall between the two, or don't seem to fit unequivocally into either category.

Two Kinds of Sin, Two Kinds of Victory

The Twilight Zone

Break-Through to Consciousness

Some say it's possible to live free from all known sin, meaning all conscious sin. I don't find that in Scripture. By "unintentional" I don't mean I'm unaware of it. I'm painfully aware of falling short of Christ's kind of love. But I don't intend to, I don't want to. And more—I can grow toward that goal, more loving this year than last, this decade than last.

In the same way, when I speak words that aren't Spirit-inspired and turn out to be hurtful, I may not be aware of it. When I start glowing in the praise someone heaps on me, thinking how well-deserved it is, I may not be conscious of the God-dishonoring pride that lurks in the shadows. How then do I distinguish between "unconscious" and "deliberate"? I can only do so when the sin I'm not aware of rises to the point of consciousness. At that point, for the first time, I can make a choice. At that point the true bent of my spirit will stand revealed. Do I instantly agree with God about the sinfulness of it and call on the Spirit to overcome it, to change me? If not, the sin becomes deliberate. Perhaps I can't control the lustful thought that flashes through my mind when I see a lust-inducing picture or an attractive woman, but continuing to turn the pages, leaving the TV on that channel, continuing the mental fantasy—that's deliberate, that's a choice. What do I do about it? That reveals the true bent of the soul.

But how do I get at the attitudes and actions that are "falling short of the glory of God" if I'm not even aware of them? Three ways: the Bible, prayer, and true friends.

1. I stay sensitive in my daily reading of the Word of God so I can hear Him when He wants to alert me to something I've been blind to or insensitive about. And I stay open when the Bible is taught by others, not getting defensive when the preacher hits home.
2. I pray, asking the Spirit to reveal my true self to me. When I do, I'm sometimes surprised how quickly the events and people in my life begin to direct my attention to that characteristic the Spirit wants me to acknowledge and begin to change. We must stay sensitive to hear His whisper when our attitudes or motives hurt Him.
3. A true friend will help me see things I was blind to. That's what an accountability partner is for. Periodically I have asked family and those who work closely with me, "If there was one thing about me you could change, what would it be?" Look out! It might hurt. But what a means of growth it has been for me!

143

Rationalization Hazard

This is my big one. I suppress the activity of the Spirit when He raises my need to the conscious level. The instant I'm conscious of some attitude that might be considered wrong, I figure out a way to justify it, to make it acceptable or at least to make the motive clean. Is it a TV program that doesn't pass the 4:8 test? "Whatever is true, noble, just, pure, lovely" (Phil. 4:8, author's paraphrase). "Well, but I'm so tired," I sigh. "I need a little relaxation; it's not *that* bad. Besides, I need to know what the people I minister to are being exposed to." You see, I'm pretty good at rationalization!

What's the solution? Eternal vigilance with a good dose of skepticism about my own purity of motive. Most of all, sensitivity to the still, small Voice. There's a practical approach I've often found helpful. When a debate starts up in my mind about whether something is right or wrong, I'll cut short the debate by deciding to treat it as wrong whether or not it actually is, since I'll rarely suffer harm that way and I may well suffer damage if I go with the self-justification.

Compulsive/Addictive Behavior

The person in bondage to alcohol or drugs may finally come to the place of recognizing it as a bondage. At that point, for the first time, deliverance becomes possible. Yet it's anything but certain! Still, in seeking victory, the addiction seems to be a twilight zone. When they continue in the destructive behavior, it seems neither "unconscious" on the one hand, nor "deliberate" on the other. Certainly they're painfully conscious of it and don't really choose to do it. It's compulsive, almost involuntary, perhaps. I confess that the model in this chapter may not be that helpful to those with compulsive behavior. Still, there's good news and bad news.

The good news is that the same approach to seeking victory has proven effective in this kind of bondage, too. For some there has been instant deliverance when a person turns in faith and makes an unconditional commitment to God, as in the case of deliberate, voluntary sin. After all, the beginning stages of addiction were deliberate choices. But for most addicts deliverance comes through the growth pattern for overcoming unintentional sins. So we can really by-pass the question of which category it fits. Furthermore, the strategy for overcoming temptation outlined in chapters 30–33 will prove effective for compulsive/addictive behavior as well as more common temptations. If you are currently battling an addiction, you may want to skip over to those chapters now!

The bad news is that nowadays virtually any behavior is dumped into the discard bin of "addiction." Sex, consumerism, anger, lying—you name it! If it's habitual and difficult to root out, define it as an addiction. Isn't that true of all strong temptation, though? Sin is powerfully addictive! I call it the "discard bin" because, by blaming our behavior on an uncontrollable addiction, we deflect the blame from ourselves. After all, we're powerless to overcome. If I'm a victim, I'm not quite as responsible for the personal choices as I once was. That's why, when we look for deliverance from a pattern of bad behavior, I resist the pressure to create a special category and call it compulsive or irresistible. I think it more appropriate to reserve the category of "addiction" for some kind of chemical dependency. Otherwise, any kind of habitual behavior can be put in a category that shields us from the responsibility to engage the sin-bully in our lives with the fire-power of the Spirit.

In any event, there are two things to remember—

~ I am responsible for my attitudes and actions.
~ God can deliver me from any sin.

And the weapons of our warfare are the same for this kind of enemy as well, and our responsibility is to grasp those weapons with courage and fortitude, expecting our all-powerful inside partner to win out!

It's all-out war, however, and for that we don't need a "touch of the Spirit," we need the Spirit full strength! That fullness and how to experience it is our next theme.

But for now, I hope you're as excited as I am with the realization that you can have total success in saying "yes" to God and "no" to sin whenever given the choice, and you can expect to "spiral up" in every way in which you unintentionally fall short of Christ's likeness. If you are grateful, why not tell Him so now?

Activity Six

Filling

Chapter 26

Filled Full

Do you remember me?" The bright-eyed teen looked at me eagerly. I couldn't bring myself to say "no," so I stalled: "Are you from Birmingham?" I knew there was a large group from Birmingham at the youth conference, and the leader had told me a remarkable story of how God had moved in the local high school all year long. The whole campus was transformed, starting with a couple of girls in an early morning prayer meeting. Dozens had come to Christ.

The seventeen-year-old must have decided to let me off the hook when she heard "Birmingham," so she continued, "Do you remember last year, the night after that last meeting of the conference when we sat on that stone wall over there?" It all came back to me. "Oh, yes, Debbie, I remember."

That night she had talked despondently of a failed Christian life. "I didn't respond to the invitation to consecrate my life to the Lord," she'd said, "because I'm sick and tired of doing it over and over. Nothing ever comes of it. I go forward in a meeting and everything changes. It's really great—for two weeks. Then it's boom, back to the same miserable failure again. What's wrong with me?"

"I really don't know, Debbie. Tell me, who's in the driver's seat of your life?"

"Jesus is—" she paused, and then added, "most of the time."

"Oh, no," I said. "It doesn't work that way. You don't let Him drive down the road to the first intersection and then grab the wheel when you think He's turning the wrong direction. I think this is what you're saying." On a piece of paper I wrote two words: "No" and "Lord."

"Well, yes, sometimes I do say that."

"But you can't," I said.

Debbie bristled a little, "But I *do!*"

"But you can't," I insisted. "What does 'Lord' mean?"

"Savior?" she asked.

"The Savior is Lord, but what does the word *Lord* mean?"

A few more guesses and she gave up. "Well," I tried again, "How about 'king'? What does 'king' mean?"

"That's easy. A king is the big boss."

"Do you say 'no' to the king?"

"Well, it wouldn't be healthy."

"Right," I said. "And Jesus is King of all kings, Lord of all lords. You can't say 'no' to Him! It's either 'yes, Lord' or 'no, Jesus.' 'No' cancels out the meaning of 'Lord.'" I tore the paper in half, with 'no' on one piece and 'Lord' on the other. "Which will it be?" I asked. "'No' or 'Lord'?" She dropped her head and her long hair covered her face as she wrestled with the choice. Minutes passed. Finally she threw her head back, tears streaming down her face. She reached out to take the paper with 'Lord' written on it, but I pulled it away.

"How long do you want Him to be Lord, Debbie?" I asked.

"Oh," she said, "I want Him to be Lord forever!" In that moment she was filled with the Spirit of God. And then He began to overflow into the lives of those around her until a whole high school was transformed.

Being filled with the Spirit isn't optional; as Debbie discovered, it's commanded: "Be filled with the Spirit" (Eph. 5:18). But what does it mean to be "filled" with the Spirit? After all, He isn't a liquid or impersonal force. Do you sometimes wish the Bible didn't use so much picture language, that it would just tell you straight out what it means? When you get right down to it, what does it look like to be "filled with the Spirit"? What actually happens? What does it feel like? The Bible never defines it for us. It just points out people who are said to be filled full of the Spirit: John the Baptist, even as a baby (Luke 1:15), Stephen in the face of death (Acts 7:55), Zechariah when he sang (Luke 1:67), and Bezalel for crafting the tabernacle (Exod. 31:3). We may not be able to describe "full" precisely, but it's a wonderful picture word. There's excitement in it, a completeness, a satisfaction. And a mystery.

Part of the mystery is that we use the word "full" in many different ways:

- ～ John is full of whisky.
- ～ That kid is full of mischief.
- ～ Judas was full of the devil.
- ～ Betsy is crazy full of John.
- ～ The book of Philippians is full of joy.
- ～ He opened the jet full throttle.

~ We've got a full tank of gas.
~ The people were filled with fear.

As we saw in our overview (chapter 2), when Scripture speaks of being filled with the Spirit, the term is used in three different ways. So if you asked me if I'm filled with the Spirit, I'd have to respond, "Yes" or "You tell me," or "Sometimes," depending on the definition you had in mind.

Definitions: Three Kinds of "Full"

In the list above there might be a parallel between Spirit-fulness and Judas's being full of the devil, an unholy spirit (see John 13:2). The chief idea seems to be that he was under the devil's control. Although the devil "entered in" to Judas and the Spirit "indwells" our bodies, the idea of being filled is not physical like a tank of gas. We're talking about a relationship between two persons, and in that relationship one might allow the other to dominate. That kind of "full"—full control—is the first meaning of being filled with the Holy Spirit. If you asked me whether I'm filled with the Spirit and you have that in mind, I'd have to say, "Yes, so far as I know my own heart, I'm unconditionally yielded to the will of God."

But there's another meaning. When a child is said to be full of mischief or Betsy to be full of John, we mean that those characteristics are highly visible. Everyone is aware of the mischief or the infatuation. Most of the Scripture references to being full of the Spirit indicate some evidence, some outcome of that filling. Not just an illness healed or miraculous speaking in an unknown language, however. When the disciples acted courageously instead of fearfully, preached with life-transforming power, sang while chained in a filthy dungeon, met a crisis with faith, people saw that unexpected—even miraculous—behavior and concluded, "The only way to explain that is to recognize Holy Spirit power at work." So, if that's what you mean when you ask if I'm Spirit-filled, I'd have to say, "You tell me!" You never have people in Scripture claiming to be Spirit-filled. Rather, it's always "they, filled with the Spirit," or "he, filled with the Spirit."

But there's a mystery to being filled that defies analysis. It has something to do with an inner surge of feeling. Joy is often associated with being filled with the Spirit, for example (Acts 13:52). That's what some people have in mind when they speak of being filled: an ecstatic inner sense of God's presence. If that's what you have in mind when you ask, I'd have to respond, "Sometimes."

From the list above you may have chosen the first option, "John is full of whisky." That's a good choice because Paul tells us not to get drunk on wine but on the Spirit! Well, at least he tells us to fill up on the Spirit: "Do not get drunk on wine, which leads to debauchery. Instead, be filled with the Spirit" (Eph. 5:18).

What happens to a tippler? "Under the influence," we say, and the change of control is clearly evident to everyone. He doesn't have to tell you he's drunk. Not if he's full of it. His talk tips you off; his walk proves it. Besides, it feels so good, I'm told. Isn't that parallel to what happens to one filled with the Spirit?

~ You are under the controlling influence of another
~ So that influence is very evident, it's the dominant characteristic, something others are aware of
~ And it creates powerful feelings

What Can I Claim?

Notice something about these three meanings. Whether or not I'm fully yielded to the Spirit, whether He is or I am in control is something only I may know for sure. The same is true of any feelings resulting from that relationship. But the outward evidence, the result of the Spirit's full control, is something others are best able to evaluate.

The First Meaning of "Full": Controlling Influence

Since this first meaning of "full" refers to a relationship between two persons, it's quite possible for the relationship to change, as we saw with Debbie. When she refused to let God have the steering wheel of her life, she felt the anguish of a failed relationship. If we can turn control over to Him, we can take it back! The Bible uses another word to describe that, the opposite picture of "full": we can quench the Spirit, we can put out the fire. Paul says, "Don't do that!" (1 Thess. 5:19, author's paraphrase).

Putting Out the Fire

The Spirit of God is a gentleman. He won't force His way on you. So any kind of "no" will "quench" the Spirit, put out the fire of passion, stop the flow of power. Whenever I take back control of my life, I'm shutting off His free flow of life. How can you tell? He seems more distant, close companionship seems to have slipped away, service for God lacks power, temptations begin to win out, I'm beginning to spiral down. Here are some ways I've "quenched" the Spirit:

~ Neglect my devotional life
~ Watch a typical TV drama, sitcom, talk show
~ Rationalize some failure instead of acknowledging it
~ Refuse to forgive someone who hurt me
~ Flip through a magazine with sexy pictures
~ Say "yes" to too many people and get overloaded
~ Nurse my bruised ego, self-pity

~ Let my mind dwell on how someone else has it better than I

~ Listen to a song that promotes this-worldly values

And of course, choosing against God's will, saying "no" to anything He wants you to do or to stop doing, will cause the fire of the Spirit to die back instantly.

Making God Sad

There's another expression used of our relationship to the Spirit. The Holy Spirit is a person with feelings—it's quite possible to make Him sad. "Do not grieve the Holy Spirit of God," Paul says (Eph. 4:30). Then he tells us exactly the kind of thing that will make the Spirit sad: unwholesome talk, bitterness, rage and anger, brawling, slander, malice (vv. 29–32).

The first meaning of being filled with the Spirit, then, is to yield full control to Him. Are you a Spirit-filled Christian in that sense? There's no place else to begin. Yet that's far from exhausting the meaning of this vivid word, so in the next chapter we'll consider the other meanings of being filled. But for now, let's be sure our unconditional "yes" to the Spirit is up-to-the-minute current in our relationship. Here's how I responded to this challenge:

Holy Spirit of God, thank You, thank You for allowing me to have a personal relationship with You. I really do want You to be the controlling partner in that relationship and I reaffirm today that You are indeed Lord of my life. I'm truly sorry for the ways I've made You sad. Please forgive me. And give me strength to always say "yes" to You in the small things as well as the major choices I make. Let me ever be filled with Your presence and power.

Chapter 27

What "Full" Looks Like

When I was twelve I was "filled" with the Spirit in the sense of turning over full control of my life to Him. But the results weren't all that visible. I wasn't "filled" in the sense of being a showcase for Jesus' characteristics. There was "fruit," the result and evidence of God's indwelling presence, but it wasn't so abundant people would notice it and say, "That young man is so Christlike!" I went to work for the Lord, too, which none of my teen friends did. But no one would have said, "The only way to explain what happens through that boy is that God's Spirit is at work!"

And what about the "full" feeling, the excitement that bubbles over from a heart intoxicated with the very presence of God? Oh, I had a rush sometimes when someone sang a wonderful song I'd never heard before, but mostly my inner state was quite predictable—no more than what the circumstances of my life and the state of my health would dictate. I was not exactly filled in any sense you could feel. Let's turn now to consider what it looks like to be truly filled with the Spirit in every sense of the term.

The first—and most important—outward evidence of filling up on the Spirit is to produce Spirit fruit. But what does the picture-word "fruit" of the Spirit mean literally?

Seeing the Evidence: A Bumper Crop of Jesus Fruit

Fruit, of course, is the product of a plant or tree, but it also is the evidence of what is inside, what kind of plant or tree it is. A peach tree, if living and healthy, will produce fruit, and if you see a peach, you know what kind of tree

153

it came from. So in human life. If we have become "Jesus plants," and are alive and healthy, we'll produce Jesus fruit. Everyone in my life is a fruit inspector: they can tell what's on the inside by what comes out. "By their fruit ye shall know them," said Jesus (Matt. 7:20, KJV).

And Jesus never intended us to have a few little shriveled "fruits," just enough to prove we're alive and what kind of "tree" we are. He promises a bumper crop—a lot of Jesus' characteristics. You might call it a "full" crop. He told us about it Himself in Scripture's most complete chapter on fruit, John 15. We find there characteristics that only the Holy Spirit can produce:

~ You discover in that passage a lot of love-fruit (vv. 9–10, 12–13, 17). That's appropriate, for love is at the head of Paul's list of the fruit of the Spirit too (Gal. 5:22–23) and Jesus tells us love is in first place. In fact, He said that the whole Bible depends on this fruit (Matt. 22:37–40).

~ Joy is found in this fruit passage too (John 15:11). And there you find the word *full* again—He's teaching us about fruit-bearing for the specific purpose that our joy will fill to the brim.

~ Obedience is a sort of summary of Jesus-fruit. He speaks in many different ways of obeying His commandments—all of them! (For example, vv. 10, 14.) That points to all the fruit there could be. Jesus says we must allow His words to take up residence inside us (v. 7). Don't you get the image of a vine or tree so heavily loaded that the fruit is pervasive, not just visible evidence but the dominant characteristic? Everyone can tell! (Except maybe the person himself.) There is so much Jesus fruit that people will be drawn to Jesus, either to embrace Him or to crucify Him.

Paul gives a more complete list of Spirit-produced fruit in Galatians 5:22–23: love, joy, peace, patience, kindness, goodness, faithfulness, gentleness, self-control. If these characteristics are the product of the Spirit's activity, they can't be explained by the influence of a person's early environment or present circumstances. That kind of love, joy, or peace, though desirable and beautiful, would be quite natural, not supernatural.

For example, Pastor Kim attended the trial of a young man accused of killing his two sons in a communist insurrection. He asked the judge to pardon the murderer and turn the young man over to him to train to take the place of his sons in serving God. Only the Spirit of God can produce that kind of "fruit." But there's another way to describe what it means to be Spirit-filled.

What "Full" Looks Like

Seeing the Evidence: Titles of the Spirit

One way to identify the evidence of the Spirit's activity is to examine the titles given the Spirit. He is called the Spirit of truth (John 14:17; 16:13). He is also a willing Spirit—you don't have to coax or coerce Him into action (Ps. 51:12). He is called the Spirit of grace (Zech. 12:10) because He is actually the dispenser of all of God's free gifts. There's a marvelous passage in Isaiah that gives many characteristics of the Spirit which He would produce in the coming Messiah: "The Spirit of the LORD will rest on him—the Spirit of wisdom and of understanding, the Spirit of counsel and of power, the Spirit of knowledge and of the fear of the LORD" (11:2).

Nine characteristics in one two-line verse! But still he didn't mention the most important of all. The Spirit's title throughout Scripture is "holy." Above all, He is holy, set apart from all moral pollution, clean and pure. And His objective is to make holy people.

Seeing the Evidence: A Fruit Inspector

There's one sure-fire way to know what your crop looks like. Do you have an accountability partner? Remember, Christlikeness is the one meaning of "full" only others know for sure. You need a fruit inspector! Here's a plan you may want to follow. Show your partner, or someone you can trust to be honest about it, the three lists of possible fruit noted above (Jesus' description of fruit, Paul's list, and the titles given the Spirit) and ask for an evaluation: "Is my life obviously full of any of these characteristics? Are there others you have to search for to find?" It would help to write down your partner's answers, perhaps in your spiritual journal.

Notice that I sometimes suggest it would be appropriate to pause and pray about what you've just read. I think this is one of those times. If you were truly full of the Spirit, are there attitudes, actions, or responses you want to have more consistently, more often, more fully? First, reflect slowly on the three lists above. Circle the three "fruits" you most want to grow in. Choose personal characteristics that don't remind people of Jesus. In fact, they're your own product, coming right out of your circumstances and temperament. Now ask the Holy Spirit to grow you in each of those qualities. If you keep on praying about those daily, it won't be long until people will exclaim, "She sure reminds me of Jesus!" or "Now there's a *real* Christian!" What they mean is, "There's a Spirit-filled Christian." And even a blind man can see it!

Power-Filled Ministry

Another evidence of being filled with the Spirit is some result in our work for God we can't account for by a person's natural abilities or training. Every believer has at least one God-given ability to serve Him: "There are different kinds of gifts, but the same Spirit . . . Now to each one the visible evidence of the Spirit is given for the common good . . . All these are the work of one and the same Spirit, and he gives them to each one" (1 Cor. 12:4, 7, 11, author's paraphrase).

The gifts are so important we'll devote several chapters to considering that activity of the Spirit, but in this chapter we'll focus on how a Spirit-given ability can be evidence of whether a person is Spirit-filled. Later we'll note all the gifts, but now we'll use a few of the gifts Paul lists (Rom. 12; 1 Cor. 12; Eph. 4) to introduce the subject and focus on being filled—the difference between merely having a Spirit-given ability and having maximum impact with that ability.

Minimum Evidence

The Bible doesn't tell us how to distinguish spiritual gifts from natural gifts. But it's fairly easy to tell. Is the outcome supernatural? The Corinthians said Paul was an unpolished pulpiteer, in fact a sorry communicator. And he didn't dispute their judgment. But when Paul taught the Bible, lives were transformed. There's the touch of the Spirit! The congregation may go wild over a guest soloist and indeed her ability is outstanding. But is there a spiritual impact? Are lives changed? That's the touch of the Spirit. But we're left in the dark on how natural abilities and Spirit-giftedness relate. So maybe we should look rather at the tasks that need to be done and trust God to give us the right combination of natural and supernatural ability to fulfill that role.

For example, what is your current role in the church or in other service to God? How can you tell if you have the touch of the Spirit to accomplish the goals? Let me suggest a few possible indicators of the touch of the Spirit on a ministry.

- ~ Teaching: in response, someone yields His life to God
- ~ Preaching: after the sermon, someone trusts God to change his life
- ~ Hospitality: someone is drawn to the church through gracious hospitality
- ~ Evangelizing: someone is saved
- ~ Missionizing: churches actually come into being
- ~ Counseling: someone not only experiences healing but begins to become more like Jesus
- ~ Leading: the church begins to move together toward biblical goals
- ~ Helping the poor: someone is drawn toward Christ through the assistance received
- ~ Encouraging: someone begins to draw strength from God

You may want to check that list to see if any relate to responsibilities you have or would like to have. As you reflect on the effectiveness of your role or ministry, remember that "effectiveness" means some Holy Spirit effect, some outcome that can't be fully explained in terms of your natural abilities, training, or experience.

Maximum Impact

We've been describing the minimal evidence of Spirit giftedness, but what is the maximal? If God so empowered you that whatever gift you had was greatly used so that everyone could plainly tell the origin of your success, maybe that could be called "full." Actually that's the way the Bible seems to use the term most often. The apostles were filled with the Spirit on the day of Pentecost and 3,000 people were converted (Acts 2:41), not just "someone," which would have been evidence enough of the Spirit's presence. I'd call 3,000 responses really full. Yet a few weeks later they had a special need—their leaders had been arrested. So they did the only thing they knew to do, they called a prayer meeting. Once again they were filled with the Spirit (Acts 4:31) and as a result proclaimed the word with boldness. Amazing! Spirit-filled men were filled! It's common throughout Acts—Spirit-filled people are said to be filled. How can that be?

Remember, it's a picture word. I get the picture of a great schooner plowing through the Atlantic with sails full of wind when suddenly a gust of wind sweeps down and the schooner surges ahead under really *full* sail. So it is with the wind of the Spirit (the Hebrew and Greek words for "spirit" are "breath" or "wind"). There is a sort of overdrive surge of power, as when a car appears from nowhere, heading toward you, and you put the pedal to the floor to get out of there. Perhaps you've had such an experience:

- Your boss wants you to lie, threatens you if you don't; you ask God for help and suddenly have a surge of courage to do right.
- Someone makes fun of the church and you don't know where the ideas come from but Scriptural truth just flows and the attack fails.
- You haven't been able to give a clear explanation of the gospel to your neighbor, you plead with God for help, and you're astounded to hear yourself give a winsome, clear presentation.
- As you teach your Sunday school class, suddenly a hush falls over the group and several tell you later their lives have changed.
- The meeting is deadlocked, no solution can be found, so you suggest a time-out for prayer. The Spirit moves, brings unity and a clear vision of where to go.
- You're naturally a timid person, so ushering isn't easy, but you pray about it ahead of time, and your wife is astounded at the way you are so outgoing and helpful with new people.

My responsibility is to preach and write. Before I preach I always remind the Lord that though I've been at it a long time and can explain Scripture and tell stories and people will listen and say nice things, if He doesn't act, nothing of eternal value will happen. Then I watch in wonder as God transforms lives. Sometimes there's a mighty "wind" of God and many are moved. Other times, I watch in vain for some small sign of the Spirit at work and my heart is wounded, sometimes broken. I need to be filled up once again.

When I write, people buy the books or tell me of how their lives were changed through a magazine article and I'm grateful to note the "fruit" God has given. But once in a while the words flow almost uninvited out of my computer and it's like they're on fire. When published they seem to take on a life of their own. When I read it later, I say, "Where'd that come from? Did I write that?" The Spirit had been blowing that day, and it wasn't just my hard work. I wish it happened always—how I long to be ever filled up with the Spirit so that people will know for sure it's God and give Him the credit.

Do you have some gift at a minimal level—you can tell God is at work through you, but it's not full-throttle, other people can't tell for sure whether it's God or just you? Now's the time to ask Him to fill you up. Open your heart to the wind of the Spirit and trust Him to do His thing. And begin the habit of asking Him, at the time of special opportunity or challenge, to put it on overdrive and fill you *really* full!

To be full of the Spirit, then, is to live a miracle quality of life that others can see the "fruit" and the "gift." There'll be a bumper crop of Jesus fruit, attitudes and actions that are produced by God-power. And there'll be Holy Spirit power clearly seen in the ministry God gives. That's a small glimpse of what "full" looks like. But what does it feel like?

Chapter 28

What "Full" Feels Like

As we've seen, in Scripture there seem to be three different emphases of the picture word *full*. First, a person is full when, in his or her relationship with the Spirit, the Spirit is in full control. Second, a person is full when there is plenty of evidence of the Spirit at work—a miracle quality of life or a miracle impact in ministry. People can see it. The third emphasis is more illusive, as feelings always are. Do I *feel* full?

A Mystery: Like a Good Marriage

"Full" speaks of a personal relationship, and that kind of thing defies scientific analysis. It is like a good marriage. The outward evidence—children, for example—may be obvious, but there's a mystery about the feelings. There are moments of shared ecstasy and times of shared agony, a deep and constant sense of well-being and surges of passionate love. So with the Spirit and me.

If I'm filled with the Spirit, I'll have joy, for example, or confidence, or peace when there's no earthly reason to have any peace at all. There'll be a passion in my affection for God, an excited sense of anticipation when I pause to worship Him, a rush of pleasure when I think about His love for me. It may not be a sustained emotional high, but there are moments of uninhibited ecstasy, especially in those devotional times alone with Him. But also, unexpectedly in the midst of a busy day, the wind of the Spirit may blow in gale strength. I can't explain it, but I can feel it. That's to be "full"!

Have you recently had such a surge of affection or some other emotional response to God's presence? If you can't remember anything out of the ordinary

159

in your relationship with God and you're thirsty for a full surge of God-consciousness, why not pause right now and tell Him so? But don't leave it there. Tell Him how much you love Him, how grateful you are for Him, for His constant companionship, and for all the wonderful blessings He floods into your life. And ask Him to fill you up with Himself. "And I pray that you, being rooted and established in love, may have power . . . to grasp how wide and long and high and deep is the love of Christ, and to know this love that surpasses knowledge—that you may be filled to the measure of all the fullness of God" (Eph. 3:17–19).

Downers and Uppers

To sort out the objective and subjective meanings of being full, think about the fruit of the Spirit as Paul lists them:

> But the fruit of the Spirit is love, joy, peace, patience, kindness, goodness, faithfulness, gentleness and self-control. (Gal. 5:22–23a)

Circle or in some way identify all the "fruits" that have an emotional aspect. I circled all but faithfulness, though even the steadfast spirit indicated by the term surely has a subjective element. Furthermore, not one of them is purely or even primarily subjective—all have an objective outworking. To love, for example, is to act lovingly no matter how I feel. Maybe that's why God seems to expect us to have these qualities steady-state—all the fruit all the time. Their presence is evidence of the Spirit at work. That's how "full" looks, as we saw in chapter 27. But the emotions may not be surging all the time.

Perhaps God intends the fruit—the visible outworking of the Spirit's inner working—to be constant and the surges of feeling to be special gifts? Jesus was a man of sorrows and acquainted with grief. He agonized in the garden, for example, but there were also times of surging joy: "At that time," Luke tells us, "Jesus, full of joy through the Holy Spirit . . ." (Luke 10:21). David, the joy-filled singer for the ages, often experienced dry times, times when God seemed distant, when he would cry out in alarm, "Don't take your Holy Spirit from me!" (Ps. 51:11, author's paraphrase). Even Paul had times of fear and called on friends to pray for the Spirit-gift of boldness (2 Cor. 7:5; Eph. 6:19–20). It seems that the inner sense of fullness is not a constant but a periodic gift. At least for the people I know that's the way it is.

In my own life I can count on having a truly exalted experience of God when I go away for my annual time of fasting and prayer. So much so, I can remember many of those occasions, even decades later. But only occasionally do I have that rushing sense of God's presence in my daily quiet time; even less often unexpectedly in the midst of a busy day. How I long, sometimes ache, to have those experiences often, yes, daily. But such has eluded me.

I'd say, "It's OK. No one does." But I'm not so sure. The mystics through the ages give testimony of such a walk with God. It is so with my son, Kent, who lives among the slum dwellers of Calcutta, surely the nearest place to hell on earth. Kent keeps so in step with the Spirit that those highs seem to come daily, right in the midst of agonizing squalor. He doesn't say so, but he is so pained when he doesn't experience God that way, I wonder if the rest of the time he may not join the mystics in a daily fulltide of the Spirit. For myself, I'll keep exulting in the sporadic winds that blow and stay on the alert for a more constant walk on the highest plane—however God defines that for me.

Fullness, then, in the sense of an inner feeling, is not subject to analysis, but it can be a glorious experience, and the Holy Spirit will give it to those who love and stay tight with Him.

Measuring the Three Kinds of Fullness

If full feelings are illusive, the other meanings of "full" are not. Here are some examples of fullness that can be known for sure, examples we have already discovered:

1. A spirit of yieldedness:
   - Debbie, the teen from Birmingham, chose "Lord" rather than "no."
   - "Only I know for sure if I'm 'full'" (in the sense of full control).
   - Hubert said, "If'n I knowed it was wrong, I'd never deliberately choose to do it."
2. A miracle quality of life:
   - My father was the most victorious Christian I ever knew.
   - I would never claim for myself to be "full" (in the sense of abundant outward evidence).
   - Widow Smith is dying of cancer, but she's always so joyful; and it's not put on.
3. A miracle quality of ministry:
   - Billy Graham wins thousands to Christ.
   - Bill, like Paul, isn't the greatest communicator, but when he teaches the Bible, lives are transformed.
   - Many in that church are spiritually gifted.

Those are contemporary illustrations, but what evidence is there in Scripture of what "full" might look like to others? Here are some Bible illustrations of being filled with the Spirit:

   - All of them were filled with the Holy Spirit and began to speak in other tongues. (Acts 2:4)
   - The disciples were filled with joy and with the Holy Spirit. (Acts 13:52)

~ Then Peter, filled with the Holy Spirit, said . . . (Acts 4:8)

~ Enable your servants to speak your word with great boldness . . . And they were all filled with the Holy Spirit and spoke the word of God boldly. (Acts 4:29, 31)

~ Choose seven men from among you who are known to be full of the Spirit and wisdom. (Acts 6:3)

~ He was a good man, full of the Holy Spirit and faith, and a great number of people were brought to the Lord. (Acts 11:24)

~ Then . . . Paul, filled with the Holy Spirit, looked straight at Elymas and said . . . (Acts 13:9)

Those are most of the places in the New Testament where the context tells us the evidence of being filled with the Spirit. Note that most of them have to do with power in ministry. That's why we'll devote several chapters to considering ministry in the power of the Spirit. But there are some subjective evidences here. I found joy, boldness, and faith. Note, however, that the boldness and faith are both related directly to ministry! So, in biblical example, the subjective element which we so emphasize today is not prominent.

While my relationship with the Spirit, letting Him take charge, is clear enough to me, and my fruit and gifts—or the absence of them—may be clear to others, the inner sense of fullness may not be so clear. It's difficult to analyze something that is beyond our understanding, yet God promises, in filling us with Himself, to give us love that is beyond comprehension (Eph. 3:19). And we can't even fathom the kind of peace that stands guard at our mind's gate. But, says Paul, we can experience it (Phil. 4:7). How exciting to feel the surge of the Spirit!

Steady-State Fullness

"Be very careful, then, how you live—not as unwise but as wise, making the most of every opportunity, because the days are evil. Therefore do not be foolish, but understand what the Lord's will is. Do not get drunk on wine, which leads to debauchery. Instead, be filled with the Spirit. Speak to one another with psalms, hymns and spiritual songs. Sing and make music in your heart to the Lord, always giving thanks to God the Father for everything, in the name of our Lord Jesus Christ." (Eph. 5:15–20)

The verb commanding fullness is unusual in that it is a command—something I must do—but it's in the passive form, something the Spirit does to me. "Be being filled" would be an awkward translation but gets at the meaning. So how do I obey if He is the one who does it? I take the initiative and deliberately yield control and then I keep on praying and expecting Him to produce the fruit of godliness: "Be very careful, then, how you live . . . understand what the Lord's will is." I expect Him to empower for ministry: "making the most of every opportunity." He even indicates the inner state of those who are filled:

"Sing and make music in your heart to the Lord, always giving thanks to God the Father for everything."

Notice another thing about the command. It's a continuous action verb: "Keep on being filled with the Spirit." It's a constant in that sense, an abiding relationship. Steady-state filled, you might call it. If I stay tight with Him, He'll continually fill me with power to live and serve and to have a singing heart. It won't be like being filled with wine, the counterfeit filling. That's only a temporary high and doesn't change anything for the better. No, no, Paul says, let the Spirit fill you always as a way of life.

Baptism of the Spirit

A transforming encounter with the Holy Spirit that happens when an unyielded or doubting believer comes back under the control of the Spirit is sometimes called "the baptism of the Spirit." Some use the expression as synonymous with being "filled with the Spirit" and mean a one-time experience of the Spirit subsequent to initial regeneration. I have avoided those controversial issues in order to focus on the central theme that all agree on: God provides a supernatural quality of life by His Spirit to all who yield control to Him and trust Him to do what He promises. Such a turnaround in relationship to God is necessary for all unbelievers (repentance and faith) and seems to be needed by most believers at one time or another (yield and trust), because most of us, through drift or rebellion, get out of phase with God. We're no longer "filled with the Spirit" and need a fresh filling.

This "filling" is not the same kind of filling the disciples received at Pentecost nor the super-charging of those same Spirit-filled disciples a few weeks later when they needed extra help and were "filled." Rather, this "filling" is a renewal of the original relationship. That original relationship is the only way the Bible speaks of being baptized by the Spirit.

> For we were all baptized by one Spirit into one body—whether Jews or Greeks, slave or free—and we were all given the one Spirit to drink. (1 Cor. 12:13)

Some who believe in a "second work of grace" needed by all believers subsequent to salvation agree that Paul here speaks of the initial regenerating work of the Spirit, but point to Luke's use of the term as baptism "in" rather than "by" and thus conclude that Luke speaks of a different kind of "baptism," one that points to baptism of the Spirit as a second work of grace. Again, some use the term to mean a special "anointing" for service. It isn't my purpose to try to resolve those differences of understanding but rather to invite those who hold such positions to join me in recognizing that many Christians need a fresh filling of the Spirit and can have it by bringing their relationship to Him back into alignment through surrender and faith.

The reason Paul uses baptism to refer to initial regeneration by the Spirit is that the term "baptism" was commonly used to mean "initiation" or "act of joining." It could also mean "to be suffused with," as in a baptism by fire, or an overwhelming experience like the crucifixion—"I have a baptism to be baptized with," said Jesus. So for people to use the term to describe an overwhelming experience is legitimate. But since the Bible seems never to use "baptism" to describe a necessary second stage of Christian experience, it may be confusing to use it that way. In any event, that's why I've avoided using it, choosing rather to describe in biblical terminology exactly what we can expect in our Christian experience.

True, the term "filled" is, like baptism, a picture word and therefore capable of conflicting interpretations. But it is the picture word the Scripture uses throughout, rather than "baptism," to indicate what our relationship to the Spirit should be. So in these chapters we have concentrated on the theme of being filled with the Spirit, seeking to work through the basic meanings on which we can find agreement.

The permanent relationship God wants every believer to have can best be described as "full"—fully yielded to the Spirit's control, giving evidence in a life and ministry charged with His own power, and an inner sense of joy in His presence. Then, from time to time, of His grace, He'll blow into your life with gale force and fan the embers into an all-consuming fire of the Spirit's own making. When that happens, you'll be really full! And when that happens simultaneously to a lot of people, we might call it "revival." That will be our topic in the next chapter.

Chapter 29

Revival

*T*hus far, we've talked of being filled with the Spirit on a very personal level. But can you imagine the power that is unleashed when a group of Christians simultaneously yields total control to the Spirit, so much so that His work is plainly seen by everyone? What would a worship service be like with such a group? How would their prayer meetings be? What kind of impact would they make on unbelievers and, indeed, on the whole community? Do you ever long to be part of such a Holy Spirit outpouring? You might call it revival.

But, interestingly enough, the Bible doesn't use the term "revival." Why, then, have Christian people always talked of revival? Because the Bible repeatedly describes great movings of the Spirit, and the church has experienced such movings periodically through its history. Naturally we've called those times "revival"—*re* means "again" and *vival* means "life." So we speak of a renewal of life that once was or ought to have been. With all that experience and the plain meaning of the term itself, however, revival doesn't seem to mean the same thing to everyone. Here are some of the experiences people have called revival:

~ In the midst of the speaker's message students began to stand all across the college chapel and confess their sins, often with tears. The meeting went on until midnight and the movement continued on for days in the dorms and across the campus, with changed lives and spontaneous eruptions of joyful singing.

~ At the revival meetings at Bent Creek Church an alcoholic, a businessman and his wife, three teens, and a prostitute were saved.

165

~ The "Evangelical Awakening," powerfully advanced by John Wesley, transformed the entire British social structure, leading directly to the abolition of slavery, for example, and revitalized the Christian community so that the modern Protestant missionary movement was launched.

~ When the invitation was given, the leading deacon in the church came to the front of the church, asked for the microphone and, with tears, confessed that his opposition to the pastor had caused grief in the church. He asked the pastor's and the church's forgiveness. Then a stream of people came forward or went to others in the congregation, asking forgiveness, embracing, weeping and laughing. Healing of old wounds began.

~ Jan studied *Life in the Spirit*, sensed that something in her life was lacking and turned her life over unconditionally to the Spirit's control. There was such a surge of His life-force that she found herself spiraling up toward greater likeness to Christ, began to see spiritual results from her work for God, and sensed God's own loving companionship. She was puzzled that not everyone in the church seemed interested in her great discovery.

All of those examples could be called "revival," but they're so different, instead of helping us understand the term, they may confuse. So let's try a few definitions I've gleaned from various sources.

1. Revival is a powerful activity of the Spirit in large numbers of people at the same time.

2. Revival is a quickening of believers to extraordinary levels of praise and prayer, of powerful witness, of loving concern for others.

3. Revival is a renewal of God's people in which lives are reclaimed and the dying embers of spiritual life are fanned back into a flame. It's a visitation of life where there had been signs of death.

4. Revival is an evangelistic campaign.

5. Revival is an outpouring of miraculous signs and extraordinary emotional upheaval.

6. Revival is a time when the spiritual becomes the pressing and absorbing concern of many.

7. Revival is a time when Christians are restored to their first love for Christ, when sham and hypocrisy are exposed; when bitterness and strife which exist in the body of Christ are revealed and repented of under the pressure of the Holy Spirit's convicting power; a time when such changes are effected in the lives of Christians that sinners are brought to Christ in great numbers.

8. Revival is a sovereign act of God that cannot be anticipated, let alone brought about by human effort.

Among these definitions I like number 7 best, though each touches on some aspect of what has been called "revival." Since the Bible doesn't use the term, but does report movements of spiritual renewal of various kinds, perhaps we are safest not to prescribe the details of what must happen to qualify as true revival. We can, however, discern some common features among these examples and definitions:

1. Revival is the work of the Holy Spirit.
2. He revitalizes or renews what already partakes of His life.
3. This renewed spiritual vitality is visible to others and leads to change in them also, seen both in a spreading renewal among believers and a turning to Christ among unbelievers.

This last characteristic would seem to rule out the idea of a "personal revival," which some use to mean a fresh encounter with God. Anyone can experience that renewal at any time they are prepared to acknowledge a need, yield to God's control, and trust Him for revitalization. But since "revival" has normally been used of renewal among many of God's people simultaneously, it may be better to refer to personal renewal by other terms like the theme of the last chapters, being filled with the Spirit. But it is encouraging to know that I can experience the fullness of God's blessing whether or not others participate.

Does your church need revival? To help answer that question, here are some signs of revival:

~ There is excitement in our times of worship, both for young and old.

~ People often find Christ through our church; baptisms of new believers are common.

~ There is a feeling of family closeness among our people, a loving spirit of care for one another; criticism is virtually unknown.

~ The people in our community who don't join us still know something is going on and have to admit we're alive; they can't spot many hypocrites, hard as they may try.

~ When one member fails, the others reach out in love and restore the person; repentance, confession, reconciliation are common.

~ Prayer meetings are vital, God is answering prayer for important requests like changed lives, and people often spontaneously cluster with others to pray.

~ Our church has a heart to reach the whole world for Christ; most members could be called "world Christians," and missions is strong in our prayer, giving, and the sending of our sons and daughters into missionary service.

If you can't find more than two or three of those typical evidences of spiritual vitality in your church, how do you feel about it? Are you resigned to the status quo or hopeful of "showers of blessing" from the Spirit? Vern Strom was a wheat farmer in western Canada who tells of the "dirty thirties" when they planted 1,000 bushels of precious seed and reaped barely 1,000 bushels in return. On 1,000 acres, that's a bushel an acre! As with many a church—hard, hard work for a "survival" harvest. But in 1942 the rains came, and they averaged a crop of fifty-five bushels an acre! The silos and barns and garages wouldn't hold it all, so they stored it in piles outside, 12,000 bushels to a pile. That's the kind of harvest when God sends rain. Wouldn't that be great for your church? What can you do about the drought, if that's what you're experiencing? Two things:

1. Be sure that you personally are experiencing the fullness of the Spirit as a continuing pattern of life and
2. Pray diligently for revival, recruiting others to join you in prayer. "If my people, who are called by my name, will humble themselves and pray and seek my face and turn from their wicked ways, then will I hear from heaven and will forgive their sin and will heal their land" (2 Chron. 7:14).

"We cannot legislate spiritual awakening, but we can set our sails to catch the wind," said G. Campbell Morgan. My son Bob and I were trying to cross a large lake on the boundary between the United States and Canada, but the wind kept driving us toward the shore long before we reached the end of the lake. We paddled our canoe with all the energy we could muster, like the poor remnant in a church that stays faithful and tries to move things forward. Also, like that remnant, we wore out, went with the wind and beached our canoe. After a rest we started out again but made little progress. Then Bob, the veteran canoer, told me to tie his poncho between two paddles, sit in the prow and hoist my "sail" to the wind while he would relax in the stern and navigate. Amazing! We began to skim across the lake under full sail, much to the astonishment of other canoeists struggling vainly to make progress. So it is when the mighty Wind of God blows through His people with renewing power.

So let us set our sails, let's covenant to pray and keep on praying until revival comes—in your church—in the whole church of Christ. In the meantime, until God chooses to unleash a widespread renewal, each of us can make very sure that we personally are eligible for revival and thus no barrier to what God would do. That's the first meaning of being filled with the Spirit: unconditional yieldedness to His will, making sure each day that He is the one in charge.

> O Holy Ghost, revival comes from thee,
> Send a revival, start the work in me.

Revival

In recent chapters we've seen that by keeping a close connection with the Spirit we can be sure of a full harvest of godly characteristics and powerful service, and at least a periodic inner sense of God-intoxication. We can do what Paul says and keep on being filled with the Spirit! And as He "pours in," we will be truly filled full or, as they say, fulfilled. Enough to overflow into the lives of all about us. On top of that—as if that were not exciting enough—by daily obeying the command to keep on being filled, we set up the whole church for joining us in that filling and experience a "chain revival," leaping on from one degree of glory to another. Hallelujah!

At the beginning of the third millennium I sense fresh breezes of the Spirit blowing through His church here and there, cleansing and empowering. I've seen it in pastors and lay leaders, weeping and confessing to the Spirit their sin of neglecting Him. I see it in the vast prayer movement circling the earth, far wider—if not deeper—than anything known in the history of the church. And certainly the advance of the gospel is at flood tide—new believers coming to Christ in Asia, Africa, and Latin America on a scale the church has never seen. The Wind of God is blowing. Hoist your sail and catch the Wind!

Activity Seven
Overcoming

Chapter 30

Preparation for Battle

$\mathcal{D}$iane had been a Christian for two years, open and eager for all the Spirit was teaching, spiraling up. Then she made a discovery. She took a class I taught on the Christian life where the assignment was to write a paper on developing a battle plan for overcoming temptation. The paper wasn't to be theoretical, overcoming just any temptation. The assignment was very personal: a strategy for overcoming my own strongest temptation. Diane should have known about temptation—even Jesus had to slug it out with the devil! But in the exuberance of her new found faith, she missed it. She added a note to her paper:

> As a "toddler" Christian, I have had very little knowledge about Satan and his tactics. Because I lacked knowledge and understanding, I have never felt plagued by temptation and consequently did not feel I needed to devise a plan to overcome temptation.
>
> After researching this paper, life isn't as comfortable. I now realize the devil's working in my life and I see the temptations that beset me. But how great! I've already defeated Satan in one way because I'm no longer ignorant of and oblivious to his attacks in my life.

Students really got into the project, some writing almost book-length theses, many testifying that the project was life-transforming. "My life has been radically changed. For the first time I'm beginning to see progress toward victory." Once in a while I get a letter from a former student, "Remember the assignment on developing a strategy to overcome temptation? That was the turning point in my Christian experience." The same thing happened with the study course on which this book is based—people write me of how the unit on "Battle Plan" was the most life-changing of all. Each of these students discovered that being filled with the Spirit doesn't lift one beyond temptation. In fact, the battle may be hotter! Too many sincere, growing Christians are caught off guard by this, falling before they know what hit them. And others know full well they are being tempted, but don't know how to defend themselves and so go down in defeat.

Each of the papers I received from students was unique, a different approach to overcoming temptation. But the temptations were similar. As often as not, the men wrote of sexual temptation. "I love my wife and kids dearly, but that cute girl at the office obviously likes me. . . . How can I control my imaginings? My eyes, even?"

Often the women spoke of emotional struggles. Like:

1. Sandra who's thirty-eight and still unmarried, worried she'll never get married. An unsaved guy keeps asking her out and she knows she can't marry an unbeliever, but . . .
2. Mirabelle has lots going for her and she knows it. It's hard not to feel a little smug when she sees a bumbling plain Jane. Even weak Christians are fair game for her condescension, if you can believe it. She hates herself when these attitudes erupt.
3. The church is in the middle of a real cat fight. Again. Tearing God's family apart. Jocelyn wonders how she can squelch her judgmental feeling and steer clear of anger at the "opposition," even if she does reject the temptation to gossip and politic.

Perhaps you, too, need to develop a personal battle strategy for partnering with the Spirit in winning the victory over those temptations that assault us daily. Here's the Bible passage we'll use to develop such a plan: "I beseech you therefore, brothers, by the mercies of God, that you present your bodies a living sacrifice, holy, acceptable to God, which is your reasonable service. And do not be conformed to this world, but be transformed by the renewing of your mind, that you may prove what is that good and acceptable and perfect will of God" (Rom. 12:1–2, NKJV).

Rest or Wrestle?

People like those students who developed a personal battle strategy found they could win out against the enemy and do it consistently. On the other hand, once or twice in every batch of 150 papers I'd find a "paper" that was one sentence long: "I have no strategy; the Holy Spirit lives in me and that's all the strategy I need." Which will it be? Do I get out of the way and let God do His thing in my life or do I personally slug it out with the enemy? We may be tempted to go to one extreme or the other, opt for a spectator role and leave it up to God or, on the other hand, go with most Christians and develop a do-it-yourself mind set.

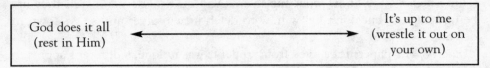

The truth is, the Bible teaches both a faith that rests and a faith that wrestles. We trust the Spirit to do the work of remaking us or it won't be done. But we must also use the weapons He provides and fight the evil in our lives. If we concentrate solely on what He does, we may slip into complacency or presumption and get ambushed by the enemy. If we concentrate exclusively on our responsibility to "fight the good fight," we may become battle-weary and discouraged. We may even give up the battle. The extremes pictured above have results to match:

In the past month, toward which end have you found yourself—so preoccupied with the truth of Christ's indwelling or the Spirit's power you've tended to neglect your own responsibility, or concentrating so much on your own efforts you've tended to forget the resources of the Spirit? Since we've examined the Spirit's role in some detail in previous chapters, now it's time to examine our role in the spiritual battle. In preparation for the war, we've got to develop a war mentality.

> Be strong with the Lord's mighty power. Put on all of God's armor so that you will be able to stand firm against all strategies and tricks of the Devil. For we are not fighting against people made of flesh and blood, but against the evil rulers and authorities of the unseen world, against those mighty powers of darkness who rule this world, and against wicked spirits in the heavenly realms. Use every piece of God's armor to resist the enemy in the time of evil, so that after the battle you will still be standing firm. (Eph. 6:10–13, NLT)

Surrender Is Victory

Strange, isn't it? When faced with temptation, the only way for Sandra, Maribelle, or Jocelyn to win out is to give up! Not to the enemy, the temptation, of course, but to the Victor. "I plead with you," says Paul, "to make a grand presentation of yourself to God." That's where victory begins. If I refuse unconditional surrender to God, defeat before the temptation is all I can hope for.

So the first step in winning the spiritual war is the Big Surrender, the Grand Presentation, the Living Sacrifice. That can be painful, of course—that's what "sacrifice" meant in ancient Israel. To give up a friend who deflects you from God's highest and best, to give up the ambition that is really an ego trip, to give up that fun thing that eats up the time you should be spending on God's business, to give up a purchase so that the hungry of the world may eat—that could hurt.

But the grand presentation He demands is more than those bits and pieces of you—it's all of you, a "living sacrifice." That's where victory begins. That alone sets you on the way to holiness and that alone is acceptable to God, says Paul. But it's only reasonable in the light of all God has done for you. So our theme verse identifies the first step to victory—give yourself over unconditionally to God. But that's only the beginning.

Identify the Enemy

The next step in our battle plan is to identify where temptation comes from. Here are some of the sources of temptation identified in Scripture:

~ Satan
~ Inner desires, impulses
~ Other people
~ Things, circumstances
~ God

One of those is out of place, isn't it? Or is it? In our theme passage, Paul emphasizes the pressure of "the world"—other people, things, circumstances, perhaps. People can cause us to stumble (Matt. 18:6–7), making us angry, seducing us, or making sin look attractive. Also, things and circumstances like poverty or riches (Prov. 30:8–9) can put pressure on us. External sources. Paul also identifies minds that need renovation—our inner desires and impulses. Ultimately it isn't the people or circumstances; it's our response to them that's the source of our temptation. We've given ground already in our minds— "Every man is tempted, when he is drawn away of his own lust, and enticed" (James 1:14, KJV). Of course, though we don't see him in our theme passage, Satan is the original source of all temptation and he still is on the prowl, ever ready to pounce on the unwary (1 Pet. 5:8). We should be ever on guard (Eph. 6:11), never give ground (Eph. 4:27), always fight back (James 4:7), stay alert to his stratagems (2 Cor. 2:11).

All those in the list above can be sources of temptation except one: God. He tempts no one (James 1:13). How then does the Bible sometimes finger the same tempting circumstances as coming from both Satan and God? (See, for example, 2 Sam. 24:1 and 1 Chron. 21:1.) It's the motive. Satan uses people or circumstances to bring us down whereas God uses those same circumstances to build our strength or to test us, to prove our allegiance. Since God is behind everything that touches my life—either sending it or permitting it—and since I'm the one responsible for yielding to temptation or resisting it, there's no need wasting a lot of time trying to figure out someone or something else to blame.

Identify Temptation When You See It, Whatever the Source

Have you ever stopped to analyze just what temptation is? It doesn't look bad, it looks good; otherwise it wouldn't tempt. And actually God is the one who designed our desires in the first place. Enticement to sin is actually the temptation to abuse a God-given desire. God created us to enjoy our bodies, to possess things, to amount to something. But we are forever trying to fulfill those desires in the wrong way. And that's sin. So the next step in our strategy is to identify the enemy, discriminate between what is temptation and what isn't. If I don't even recognize my enemy, how can I fight successfully? Notice in the following list the progression from innocent, God-given desires through temptation to sin and, finally, to a pattern of life.

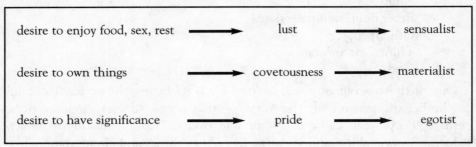

Some hold that all sin is found in one or another of these categories—lust (abuse of our desire to enjoy food or sex), covetousness (desire to possess something not mine or not in God's will for me), and pride (taking credit for some achievement of God). But I think there is another variety of sin that may not be any of those: unbelief. Some say it's the source of all the rest! Eve certainly fell before temptations to lust, covet, and act arrogantly because she doubted God's Word, so maybe unbelief is the taproot sin. At any rate, it helps to identify the enemy precisely so I can fight it successfully.

For example, if I'm tempted to cheat on my income tax return and think the problem is simple covetousness, I may remain vulnerable to the real temptation—wanting more money in order to appear successful, the sin of pride. I need to uncover the roots of my temptations in order to confront them. Look for a moment at the three root sins.

~ Eve fell to the temptation to enjoy the tasty fruit which God had forbidden, Christ resisted the temptation to use His power to create bread from stones. What temptation do you have currently to fulfill some bodily appetite in a way God forbids?

~ Eve fell to the temptation to get something very pleasant to see, and Jesus resisted the temptation to get in a wrongful way the world which was rightfully His. Is your temptation to desire something not yours or not in the will of God for you?

~ Eve reached for that which the Liar said would give her the very wisdom of God and lost everything. If the crowds in the temple courtyard saw angels intercept Jesus' free fall, the applause would have thundered to the heavens. He chose rather to hang on a tree in humiliation. What is your temptation to be recognized?

As in the garden and the desert, temptation always masquerades—it looks so appealing, promises so much good. That's why it's a temptation. If it wore its own face, it would be so ugly we'd run! So the first task is to unmask the temptation, identify it for exactly what it is: lust, covetousness, pride, or unbelief. Such enemies—they could destroy you! And even if you don't go that far, how sad it makes the Holy Spirit.

Watch Out for Deception

Sometimes it's not easy to distinguish between legitimate desires and the bad stuff. Is this new TV a legitimate need or coveting what God doesn't intend? Is this obnoxious guy squeezing righteous indignation out of me or sinful anger? Is the pain I feel justifiable or am I so unhappy because my ego took a heavy hit? People tend to decide on the legitimacy of a desire in one or more of the following ways:

~ Trust the Holy Spirit to show me what's right
~ Recall Bible teaching on the subject
~ Quote a Bible command I've memorized
~ Listen to my conscience

All of those are provided to help us know right from wrong, but the first and last are tricky. None of them will work without the first one, the Holy Spirit. But we mustn't run to the other extreme and assume that the Holy Spirit within is all we need. He deliberately provided the other means of knowing His will, so we'll surely go down in defeat if we neglect any of them. He's no substitute for the others—He's their energizer.

Then there's that last one: conscience.

Conscience: Caution Light of the Soul

"Let your conscience be your guide"—is the old cliche true? Maybe. We are all born with the ability to judge right and wrong and we have called that ability "conscience" (Rom. 2:14–15). It's part of our image—one way we resemble God.

But conscience is not a special computer chip that monitors our behavior, OK-ing some things and bleeping out others. It's simply our judgment in the moral realm, and Paul teaches that it's built in. That is, unlike the animals, people all know, intuitively, that some things are good and some bad. But our judgment has been messed up. We judge things increasingly along the lines our parents, teachers, entertainers have taught us, not to mention the influence of our own sinful inclinations. So the moral alarm system is unreliable. It begins to sound off when something isn't really sinful in God's sight and to remain silent when poisonous ideas fill our minds. So even Christians need their conscience reprogrammed. God does this by the Word and the Spirit. As the Spirit helps me understand and I work diligently to know God's will revealed in the Bible, my moral judgment becomes more and more reliable.

The Spirit daily convicts the believer of shortcomings and sins because daily we fall short. But note that the enemy works also, and when he fails to block out the conviction, to grow hard callouses on our soul, he seeks to push us over the other side and bring condemnation, convincing us we're guilty when actually we're not.

False Guilt

We can have a sense of guilt when we are actually innocent and that is destructive, too, as any break with reality is. Some people are trapped in a prison of inappropriate guilt feelings. If they confess and forsake their "sin," they are carrying an extra load God did not intend. If, on the other hand, they continue to practice what they feel is wrong, they are living in violation of their conscience and the innocent activity actually becomes sin to them—the sin of rejecting God's (presumed) will. On this subject, Paul says, ". . . everything that does not come from faith is sin" (Rom. 14:23; see also 1 Cor. 8). But more often we have no sense of guilt when we should. Guilty feelings when not guilty and innocent feelings when we are not—such is our perversity!

As a result, we seem to have infinite capacity to con ourselves into believing what we want to believe. But the person who has been transformed into a new creation by the Spirit, who has regularly disciplined his or her judgment by Scripture, who keeps tuned in to the Spirit, and who has developed judgment by long and careful use can be trusted more and more to make godly decisions. In the previous sentence I listed four essentials needed to "true" a conscience. Which are strong in your daily experience? Which are missing?

Preparation for Battle

Ready, Aim, Fire!

In developing your "war mentality" and battle plan, you began with unconditional surrender to the will of God, the Grand Presentation. You've made your beachhead! That gets you out of a dangerous no man's land or out from behind enemy lines and solidly on God's side. Now you're ready. The next step was to take aim, identify the enemy—who or what's behind this? That way you can plan a strategy to avoid hanging around the person or place, the circumstances or patterns of thought that lead to your downfall. But sometimes the source may not be that easy to spot for sure, so you may bypass that step and identify the temptation itself—is it lust, covetousness, pride, or unbelief? That isn't always easy, either, since temptation fights dirty, always slips up incognito. But you can spot any disguised temptation by focusing Scripture on your situation, especially the clear-cut laws of Scripture, allowing the Holy Spirit to illuminate your mind. Then, finally, to release His fire-power, you make your choice about that temptation. Choose right and grow stronger, choose wrong and grow weaker.

Being honest with yourself, identifying the enemy, and yielding control to the Spirit puts you in a winning position. So the battle itself should be fun war games? Not at all! It's hot, hand-to-hand, mind-to-mind deadly combat to the death, either of the temptation, or of your spiritual vitality. How we win that battle is what we'll examine next.

Chapter 31

Defensive Strategy

E very battle plan needs defensive strategies and offensive strategies. First, let's look at ways to defend, to ward off temptation even before it strikes. In the next chapter we'll take the offensive, developing strategies to defeat the enemy at the time of temptation.

I had just returned from a twelve-year famine of TV. In Japan we rarely watched TV and understood little of what we did see. Besides, at that time Japanese TV was very tame by American standards. I visited friends and was astounded to hear them guffawing over illicit sexual situations in the popular sit-com M*A*S*H*. "They put garbage like that on television?" I remonstrated—to no avail.

Twenty years passed. I hadn't watched TV much, but enough to get a feel for things. Suddenly I woke up to an astonishing change in me. For a year or more I'd been periodically watching M*A*S*H* reruns, grateful for an oasis of good family fare in the moral badlands of network television. What had happened? I'd been molded by my world into its way of thinking. And Paul says, "Stop!" Our verse might be literally translated: "Resist the conforming influences of your environment and keep on resisting." Who will deny that popular media is hell-bent (literally) on cultivating lust, covetousness, and pride? And I was let-ting it happen to me. In fact, I recently made a covenant with myself to stop surfing the channels because when I finally got honest with myself and God I had to admit what I was actually looking for—and it wasn't purity, content-ment, and humility! Sometimes it was just to relax and unwind after a hard day, but it ate up priceless time and—worse—was subtly molding me into a different kind of person. Paul says to resist and keep it up—eternal vigilance is the price of spiritual freedom.

To take this proactive stance, having gotten into the warfare mentality, decided firmly on whose side I really am, and having identified my major enemies, I need to take hold of my weapons and go for it. Let's consider Bible, prayer, and the church as our front-line defensive strategy—familiar weapons but used in a strategic way.

The Bible: Stockpiling Your Ammunition

> How can a young man keep
> his way pure?
> By living according to your word.
> I have hidden your word in
> my heart
> that I might not sin against you
>   Psalm 119:9, 11

Do you recall the war stories recorded in Genesis 3:1–6 and Matthew 4:1–11? Here we have deadly battles: first between Satan and Eve, then between Satan and Jesus—the welfare of billions depending on the outcome of each battle. Eve met the enemy with a background of a perfect heredity and a perfect environment; Jesus had a dubious human heredity and environment. But Eve lost, Jesus won. As you review the stories, think about who quoted God's Word.

Eve did, but she wasn't all that committed to the authority of God's Word and quickly abandoned her only defense, accepting the Enemy's word over God's. In the wilderness with Jesus, Satan cynically used Bible quotes to push his ungodly ends. Only Jesus used the Word of God as His weapon. And He won! You will, too. But you must stockpile your ammunition or you won't have it available at the time of testing. Jesus knew His Bible.

There are two ways we can stockpile ammunition: regular reading and selective study. For example, I may be blind to the discontent in my life that is choking out the growth of joy and peace. As I read the Word in my time alone with the Lord each day, I see how great God is, how much He cares about me. Then I begin to realize how sinful my discontent really is, how stupid it is in the light of His greatness. The Word has spotlighted a temptation I didn't even know existed, has alerted me to a hidden enemy.

Selective study, on the other hand, is to search out all the Bible teaches about some personal temptation. Those passages can then be used as a weapon in the moment of temptation, as in the case with Jesus. For example, growth may be choked out by things, the stuff I have or the stuff I don't have but want. If the regular reading of Scripture doesn't raise consciousness about a materialistic lifestyle, a study of what the Bible says about covetousness may help. I would find, for example, that covetousness is a slick con artist—it beguiles (Mark 4:19). If I really want something or want to hang on to something, covetousness quickly provides the rationale on why it's OK. Further, I'd find the Bible calls covetousness "idolatry" (Eph. 5:5; Col. 3:5). Why, I'm no better than the savage bowing before his little stone god. And when I find that covetous people are classified along with adulterers and murderers, having no part in God's Kingdom (1 Cor. 6:9–12)—well, I might just be prepared to recognize covetousness as a mortal foe and face down the enemy the next time temptation strikes.

Once you've identified what your major temptation is and what the root sin that entices, it's time to stockpile your ammunition—if you're serious about winning, that is. Check out the cross-references, if you have that kind of study Bible or, even better, get a concordance (an index to the whole Bible) and search out what the Spirit has said about your temptation. Then memorize a key passage or two to use in the day of battle. Let the living Word of God mold your way of thinking.

Prayer: Strategic Bombardment

"Watch and pray so that you will not fall into temptation." (Matt. 26:41)
"Lead us not into temptation, but deliver us from the evil one." (Matt. 6:13)

Remember the story of how I put in my prayer notebook "T & T"? Every day I would pinpoint the enemies of a renegade tongue and an explosive temper. I didn't wait until the enemy loomed on the horizon and started his barrage of temptations; I started out the day with a plea for the Holy Spirit to send in His "troops" and knock out the enemy in my life. He knew in advance what I'd face that day and I asked Him to prepare me, to give me strength to win out, to alert me to ambushes I wouldn't even see.

I didn't pray, "Lord help me be good today." Or, "Lord make me victorious today." I prayed about the specific sins that were winning out in my life, my Big Enemy: "Lord, I've got a loose tongue and a short fuse. Please keep me from temptation today, as you taught us to pray (Luke 11:4). If, however, for your good purposes you permit them into my life, I know it won't be an experience uncommon to your people (1 Cor. 10:13). But remember, you promised to provide a way of escape. Please, in that moment, deliver me from evil."

That's the way we prepare ahead of time—every day—for the ambush the enemy is sure to set.

3. The Church: Building a Defense Team

"All of you stand shoulder to shoulder, becoming one in heart . . . put together your strength and fight." (Phil. 1:27–28, Japanese back-translation by author)

The defensive use of the local congregation is primarily to build a support network of people who grow strong together in studying the Word, uniting in prayer, exhorting one another and setting the example for one another. Together we build spiritual muscle in preparation for the battle in a way we never could on our own.

But there's more. A high-ranking Air Force officer sat by me on the plane. Though American planes over North Vietnam took an average of one hit every twelve sorties, he came through more than 300 flights unscathed. "What a great pilot!" I exclaimed. "No," he responded, "What a great partner! You always go in pairs and you're responsible to watch the tail of your partner. Your job is to warn him when the missile is coming. If you fail, there's no hope for your partner. By the time he sees the missile it's too late." So it is in spiritual warfare—you need a faithful partner to watch your tail!

That's where an accountability partner comes in, someone you can share with openly about your temptations, your victories, your defeats, and with whom you can stand heart-to-heart in prayer for victory. A word of caution: it's not usually wise to share with a partner who is vulnerable to the same temptation you are fighting. A drowning man doesn't need another drowning man to come to the rescue! Steer clear of the weak and disabled when building your defense.

If you can't find a spiritually growing "partner" for mutual support, it's better to find a mature "mentor" who can hold you accountable. One of the greatest defenses against the world, the flesh, and the devil is a buddy in the battle, an accountability partner to pray with you about that besetting temptation and hold you accountable to change, to grow, to spiral up.

We've considered a defensive strategy that uses the weapons of the Spirit to prepare for battle. Only thus can we build a defense around our minds to block out the ideas of the world and counter the onslaughts of the enemy. "Reject and keep on resisting the conforming influences of your environment," says Paul, and this we will do with the Word, with prayer, and with our fellow soldiers. In the next chapter we'll take the offensive.

Chapter 32

Offensive Strategy

$\mathcal{T}$o win in the battle against temptation we need an offensive strategy to go along with the defense we've already been building. To bring this into focus, let's revisit our theme passage. "I beseech you therefore, brethren, by the mercies of God, that you present your bodies a living sacrifice, holy, acceptable to God, which is your reasonable service. And do not be conformed to this world, but be transformed by the renewing of your mind, that you may prove what is that good and acceptable and perfect will of God" (Rom. 12:1–2, NKJV).

Notice a couple of things about Paul's command. The word for "transform" in Greek is *metamorphosis*. Consider how we use that term—the little earth-bound fuzzy worm metamorphosed into a gorgeous creature of the skies! That's what Paul says we're to work at—it's not simply the external behavior but the core self that's to be transformed. Furthermore, he tells us what that "core self" is. Paul designates the mind as the battle ground because that's where spiritual battles are won or lost. Of course, the Spirit doesn't restrict the change to our intellect, leaving our feelings and choices untouched. "Mind" here is a comprehensive category—all of you, what you think about things, how you feel about things, what you choose. All the activities of your mind are to be changed, your entire mind-set transformed.

Another thing. Though the form of the verb is passive, meaning to have this done to you (by the Holy Spirit), it's still a command, indicating some initiative on your part, too. You must participate with the Spirit. One further thing. Though the Grand Presentation (v. 1) is a "point action" verb, speaking of a decisive turning point, the transformation (v. 2) is a "continuous action" verb, speaking of a process—you have to keep working at it.

For this process to be successful, we've seen how a strong defense is needed to resist the conforming influences of this world. But we need an offensive strategy, too, a strategy for winning out against temptation at the time of encounter. And when that encounter comes, there's no need to be apprehensive about the outcome—we have a wonderful promise about that! "No temptation has seized you except what is common to man. And God is faithful; he will not let you be tempted beyond what you can bear. But when you are tempted, he will also provide a way out so that you can stand up under it" (1 Cor. 10:13).

Interestingly enough, the weapons the Spirit provides for that encounter are the same we used for our defense. The strategy, however—the way we use those weapons—differs.

The Bible: Offensive Weapon

Here's how it worked in my life today. Last night I felt an excitement about today—I'd get to write this chapter on winning the victory over temptation! About 4:00 A.M. I woke to the persistent ringing of the phone. My heart jumped—which of my children is in an emergency? The voice said, "Is this Mr. McQuilkin?" "Yes . . . ," I responded as a dread settled in. *Oh, no, not again,* I thought. Three months ago my car had been stolen from the backyard. While the police officer talked, I looked out the back window and, sure enough, it was gone again. And once again, the police had found it, torn up as before.

I was angry. I'd like to put a booby trap on that car. Guess what would happen to the next person who touches it! And I was afraid. Was it the same people? Will our house be next? Maybe we should move out of this inner city neighborhood we deliberately chose to live in . . . . Here are some of the emotions I had this morning. Are any of them acceptable to God?

~ I'm angry.
~ I'll booby trap that car.
~ I'm afraid of what will happen next.
~ I'm outa here—forget this evil neighborhood.
~ Why did God let this happen? I asked Him only last night to protect my car, since the police certainly couldn't.

A couple of those are clearly bad—vengeful (booby trap strategy) and disobedient, leaving my calling to live for God in this neighborhood. Anger and fear are not necessarily sinful—it depends at whom they're directed and why. The last item could have been sinful if I had gone beyond puzzlement—it won't do to get angry with God, nor to conclude He doesn't care for me.

Clearly a battle was raging in my mind. No use to go back to bed—I was too agitated. So I turned to Scripture for an earlier-than-usual devotional time. I was in Hebrews 10, but couldn't concentrate. It was irrelevant to my crisis so I decided to quit halfway through. "I'll pick it up here tomorrow," I told myself. Then, listlessly, I decided to read on. The next words hit me like a bolt from heaven: "You cheerfully accepted the seizure of your possessions, knowing that you possessed something better and more lasting" (Heb. 10:34, NEB).

The word of God was a sword to annihilate those evil temptations that had been winning out in my mind. Cheerful? Hardly. Better and more lasting? A few verses later the Spirit clarified that unlikely reassurance: "Be content with what you have; for God himself has said, 'I will never leave you or desert you'; and so we can take courage and say, 'The Lord is my helper, I will not fear; what can man do to me?'" (13:5–6, NEB).

God is my better and lasting possession! Thus the Bible is not only our defensive weapon, as we stockpile its truth against the hour of temptation; it's our offensive weapon at the moment of temptation. Like Jesus in the wilderness, we wield the sword of the Spirit against temptation and like Jesus, we rout the enemy. My agitated mind settled down in a miraculous calm, and cheerfulness actually began to bubble up as I thought about all the good things:

~ Though it was all the transportation I had, it wasn't much.
~ They broke into my car, not my house.
~ They took my car, not my life.
~ They were the thieves, not I.
~ They can take my stuff but they can't take my God, my permanent, real possession.

I was tempted, but the Spirit delivered me—through the Word. Hallelujah! Now let's suppose you're the one facing temptation. Your arsenal may be stocked with other "swords of the Spirit" from the Word of God, but by way of example let me suggest one sword you might want to try in each of the following tests:

~ Your boss didn't give you the raise you deserved and you're tempted not to work as diligently as you used to. But . . . "Be kind . . . to one another, forgiving each other, just as in Christ God forgave you" (Eph. 4:32). Or try this sword: "Bondservants, obey in all things your masters according to the flesh, not with eyeservice, as men-pleasers, but in sincerity of heart, fearing God. And whatever you do, do it heartily, as to the Lord and not to men, knowing that from the Lord you will receive the reward of the inheritance; for you serve the Lord Christ" (Col. 3:22–24, NKJV).

~ You just heard an unbelievable story about your pastor; you reach for the phone to call your best friend about it. But . . . "Do not receive an accusation against an elder except from two or three witnesses" (1 Tim. 5:19, NKJV).

~ You noticed Jerome didn't speak to you in church Sunday. "He must be mad at me," you concluded. "Wouldn't be surprised, he's such a moody person." But . . . "Do not judge, or you too will be judged" (Matt. 7:1).

~ You have your rights; you're not going to give in to your spouse one more time. But . . . "If anyone would be my disciple let him say 'no' to himself and take up his cross daily" (Matt. 16:24, author's paraphrase).

~ The guys at work are going golfing Sunday. To fit in, maybe you'll just skip church this time. But . . . "Remember the [Rest] day, to keep it holy" (Exod. 20:8, KJV). And, "Don't skip church as some do" (Heb. 10:25, author's paraphrase).

What mighty weapons we have right in our hands! Of course, we have to program those power words into our memory banks if we're to have them when temptation strikes. Don't worry, though, if you don't have just the right weapon for the attack you're under, your arsenal does! Just dash to your weaponry and discover the "sword" you need. Remember when my car was stolen? I didn't draw my sword—it drew me! Or rather, God graciously led me miraculously to the very weapons I needed.

Prayer: Offensive Weapon

"They cried out to God during the battle and he answered their prayer." (1 Chron. 5:20, NLT) "Call upon me in the day of trouble; I will deliver you." (Ps. 50:15)

Not only do we pray about our besetting temptation as the day begins, but in preparation for the battle, we also use prayer as a mighty weapon at the time of temptation. Many men have talked with me about their sexual temptations: movies, magazines, TV, coworker, a friend's wife, or the Internet. I always ask, "Do you ask God to help at the moment of temptation?" So far there's never been an exception: if ever they had called on God for help, they would have won the battle. They just never did. "At that point, I didn't want deliverance," men tell me, or, "When the temptation comes, it's too late." That tells me something about their spiritual state. Do they really want the will of God? It's not enough to love the good; we must hate the evil. And we will hate it if we think about what it will do to us in the end and what it does to Jesus right now. Only when I hate the evil will I cry out for help in the moment of temptation.

Let's make it very personal. That most ominous temptation in your life—the one that wins out so often—do you pray for deliverance at the moment of temptation? If not, why not? If so, did God fail to give the victory?

Another secret to victory through prayer is to confess sin immediately. "If we confess our sins, He is faithful and just to forgive us our sins and to cleanse us from all unrighteousness" (1 John 1:9, NKJV).

Here's the test of where my heart truly is: Do I immediately turn to God in agreement that the failure was sin (not just a mistake or inappropriate behavior)? If I'm yielded and honestly want only God's will in my life, the moment I realize I've failed, I'll eagerly repent. I'll tell Him how sorry I am and ask for deliverance and strength to overcome the next time. When I feel the enemy overpowering me, if I admit it's sin and ask God for help, the Spirit intervenes and delivers. That happened to me yesterday when I was bogging down in serious fretting about my lack of time. Suddenly I realized it was sinful worry, doubting God's ability to handle my situation. So I confessed it as sin and immediately the worry melted away.

Do you have any unconfessed sin in your life? Flee to Jesus! Make it right! Don't continue this book till you have because that sin breaks the Spirit-connection. It's worse than useless to study about the Christian life and not obey what you know—it just damages the relationship with the Spirit all the more.

The Church: Offensive Weapon

My brother-in-law died two weeks ago. The church stood by through the painful weeks of dying and through the long good-byes. The church stands by us still. It wasn't just the theology of dying and eternal life the church had taught us through the years, important as that preparation is for the crisis time. At the time of testing God's people came to the rescue. And in the longer dying of my beloved—twenty years, now, under the hammer blows of the dread Alzheimer's—what would I do without God's people? Think of all the temptations they deliver me from: discouragement, self-pity, worry, loneliness, fear—the list goes on. Don't ever hesitate to call on your brothers and sisters for help in the time of need. That's what they're there for! "A brother is born for adversity" (Prov. 17:17). Or it might be a sister . . .

Before we were married I wrote Muriel about how we wanted to be one in every sense. "Let's not have any secrets," I wrote. She responded, "Yes, let's be completely one and share everything. But let's not make our home a garbage dump." So it was we covenanted before marriage that we would never say anything that would harm another person. We didn't want a dump of foul-smelling garbage in our home. We haven't kept that vow perfectly, but we worked at it, and we did it by keeping watch on each other. She became my accountability partner. When the enemy launched a rocket, my buddy watched my tail and warned me!

"Honey, I probably shouldn't say this about Holly, but . . ."

"Then don't!" she'd interrupt and head off the enemy attack. Or maybe I'd go ahead and say it. She'd quietly respond, "Honey, we really shouldn't be talking like this, should we?" And she'd gently lead me to repentance. A spiritual buddy will help us win in the hour of attack. That's part of "church," a powerful weapon when facing temptation.

We've studied a defensive strategy of preparation for battle and an offensive strategy for the moment of attack. Both are needed. To build up your defenses against the hour of temptation, use the Bible and prayer every day, the church at least every week. Then, when the enemy strikes, reach for those same weapons to fend him off. You'll win the victory!

Chapter 33

Victory Celebration

A ccording to our theme passage, there's one end toward which we've been studying our defensive weapons and our offensive weapons: experiencing God's will. And since God's purpose for me is to be like Him, no wonder Paul

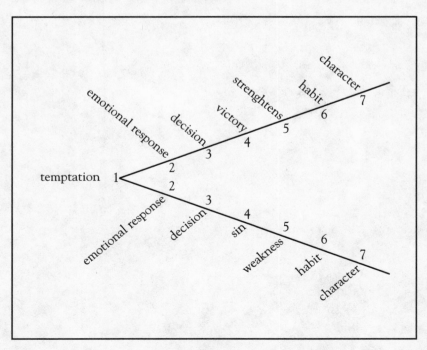

calls His will "good," "acceptable," and "perfect." But what does he mean by "proving" it? When we resist the conforming influences of the world and work with the Spirit in the renovation of our way of thinking, we will increasingly prove to ourselves through personal experience that God's way is best. But the word *prove* may imply more than that. Our victory experience will demonstrate to others also, will actually prove to them, the reality of those excellent qualities of God's will. We will become a showcase for all to see, conclusive evidence that God's will really is good, pleasing, and perfect. Here's how it works:

Step 1. *Temptation* comes, either from without or within. Remember that temptation itself is no sin but merely enticement to sin.

Step 2. *Emotional response:* like or dislike, love or hate

Step 3. *Decision* of will: consent to or reject temptation

Step 4. If I consent, *sin* follows; if I reject the temptation, this is *victory*

Step 5. Failure leads to *weakness* and susceptibility to further failure; success *strengthens* to win future battles

Step 6. *Habit* is formed: pattern of failure or pattern of success

Step 7. *Character* is formed, down or up

To translate the process from general theory to a practical beginning for developing your battle plan, you may want to take your top two or three personal temptations and plot them on the stair-step chart to see where you actually stand in the battle. Each temptation will probably be at a different place, whether up or down, but the important thing is to be very honest about where you are. That kind of integrity is the only place victory can begin.

When, in the battle, you choose right, you put on display or prove for all to see how good, acceptable, and perfect the will of God is, indeed, what God's character is like. Let's take a look at those three words Paul used to describe what you'll look like.

Good

Earlier we discovered that God always has at least two basic purposes for allowing suffering in our lives. By facing suffering in faith we bring praise to God, who either delivers us or enables us to endure, and we bring spiritual growth to ourselves. The purpose of suffering is always growth and glory: our growth, God's glory. Would He have those same purposes for allowing temptation to assault us? Yes and no. Yes, both suffering and temptation are tests (often intertwined) and His purpose in allowing either kind of test is always our growth and His glory. But there's a big difference between suffering and temptation. Sometimes we are to accept suffering as God's will for us, but we can never accept temptation—we fight it!

God's good will is for us to overcome temptation. If we don't, we neither bring credit to Him nor growth to ourselves. When a noted preacher falls to sexual temptation, what bad things happen to God's reputation! When I yield to temptation and throw a "pity party," I grow weaker, less like Jesus, and that's not God's good will. We demonstrate God's good will when we do it. Victory is His good will; defeat is bad and certainly not His will.

Dennis and Brad came to me with a theory they found liberating. They were forever defeated by lustful temptations. "We've decided lust is the cross Jesus is calling us to bear," they said. Some cross! No, God's good will is to nail our evil desires to the cross, not excuse them; to give victory over temptation, not have us giving up in defeat. Dennis and Brad were continually demonstrating for all to see what the will of God is *not* and that's bad. They brought dishonor to the Lord and ever more rapid descent down the spiral for themselves.

But Cubby saw another demonstration that put on display God's good will. He told me of how his business partner, Det, had found Christ and was radically changed. Cubby had been active in church all his life, but he'd never seen anything like this. Det was a big-time political operator and hard-driving businessman, but Cubby watched in amazement as a transformation took place. One day in a particularly difficult confrontation with competitors, Det responded calmly and graciously—not like the old Det. Cubby returned to his office, shut the door, fell to his knees and prayed, "Lord, whatever Det has, I want it!" He had seen God's good will on display in Det, and as a result something very good happened. Cubby was born again. But God's will is not only good, it's . . .

Acceptable

Another word Paul uses to describe God's will is *acceptable*, or as some translations have it, *pleasing*. Success in overcoming temptation is pleasing, all right, but to whom? Who do you think Paul had in mind as being pleased? God? Yourself? Others? Bible scholars may debate which of those Paul had in mind, but I would say all of the above! To overcome temptation and do the good thing brings joy all around. It's a victory celebration! To fail and not do the good will of God is pleasing only to unholy men and unholy spirits. To you and God and all good people, it's distressing.

Perfect

Here are some of the meanings for the term *perfect* in Scripture:

~ flawless, without defect
~ mature, adult, full-grown
~ loyal, sincere, wholehearted obedience to the known will of God
~ ability and readiness to meet all demands, outfitted
~ having reached an appropriate or appointed end, goal, purpose

When I put on display the perfect will of God in my life, I think all those meanings are possible except the first and last. True, our ultimate goal is to be "flawless, without defect" and to have reached our "appointed end, goal, and purpose." Those are just other ways of saying to be like Jesus. And we'll celebrate that level of victory one day. But not now. The other three meanings are more appropriate to describe what we can fulfill in this life—His will is that we demonstrate maturity and obedience. And when we do, what a celebration of the glorious will of God! It's perfect! And that's very pleasing and very good.

A Personal Battle Plan

I've shared with you in these chapters my personal strategy for overcoming the enemies that have most successfully assaulted me. But every battle plan needs to be custom designed for the individual. And it may change for each stage of life, whether the temptations and uncertainties of youth, the frustrations and failed dreams of middle years, or the regrets and anxieties of age. Where are you today in your spiral up toward likeness to Jesus? Are there failures that grieve the Holy Spirit and embarrass you? If so, you may want to pause in your reading—for days, if need be—and develop your own battle plan for winning out. It's an exciting thought—to create a strategic plan you'll use for a lifetime! If you do decide you want to do what has been a help to so many, here are some things to keep in mind:

~ Be honest about whether you really want to be rid of that sin. If you don't deeply desire victory, you might as well hang it up because you've already conceded defeat. When you can say "yes" from your heart, Holy Spirit power is released and you're on your way to victory.

~ If you really want to win that spiritual battle, pause and ask the Holy Spirit to guide you as you think through your strategy. Without His wisdom, nothing's going to work!

~ Choose the temptation you're going to write about.

~ Skim through chapters 30–32 and mark any of the points in my strategy that you think may work for you. Then add other strategies you may have heard about, discovered in Scripture, or learned through experience. Now you're ready to design your own strategy. Here are some questions you may want to consider:

1. Who or what most often causes this temptation?
2. What are the camouflages this enemy uses—how do I tend to rationalize the attitude or behavior?
3. Among lust, covetousness, pride, and unbelief, which is most likely the root cause(s) of my temptation?

4. What is my defensive strategy—how do I plan to use the Bible, prayer, and the church to build up strength to face this particular temptation when it comes?

5. What is my offensive strategy—how do I intend to use the Bible, prayer, and the church at the time of temptation?

If you don't have time to develop your own strategy just now, how about next Sunday afternoon? Last night I was invited to a dinner by a dozen people who had just completed the study course *Life in the Spirit*. They wanted to tell me thank you and provide feedback. They were so excited about the life-change that had taken place. I asked if one part of the study had meant more than others. The first response was "Battle Strategy!" The young woman went on to explain how, as she worked out her personal strategy, her life was transformed. Maybe that could be your experience too.

But don't be misled. It isn't the strategy that wins the victory. It's the Spirit! Never forget that the secret of success in the Christian life, including consistent success in overcoming temptation, does not ultimately depend on a technique, a strategy, or your own activity. No matter how skilled you get in wielding the weapons the Spirit provides as you participate with Him in winning the battles, ultimately it's the Holy Spirit within who is the overcomer.

The indwelling, powerful One doesn't displace your personality with His, however. Rather, He is a personal companion, living in you to . . .

~ strengthen you when you falter
~ remind you of truth from His Word when your focus is blurred
~ point out the enemy when you're about to be blindsided
~ comfort you
~ lift you up when you fall
~ forgive you when you fail and admit it
~ guide you when you're confused
~ sensitize your moral judgment by His Word to discern right from wrong
~ strengthen your will when you waver

What a wonder He is! Our inside companion does all of that all the time! But what He does inside isn't all. He prays for us when our prayers fall short (Rom. 8:26–27), and He engineers all the circumstances of our lives toward the same goal of transforming us into His likeness (vv. 28–29). Furthermore, when it comes to the very weapons we've been studying, It is He who enables us to pray effectively. It is God the Spirit who gave us His Word, and it is He who enables us to understand and appropriate that Word in the face of testing. He is the One who gave us the church too, and He who enables us to live in the kind of relationship with other Christians that will make us overcomers together.

Victory Celebration

Recently I discovered a wonderful hymn that summarizes everything we've been studying about the Holy Spirit. Why, it's almost like Margaret Clarkson had studied *Life in the Spirit* with us!

> For your gift of God the Spirit, pow'r to make our lives anew,
> pledge of life and hope of glory, Savior, we would worship you.
> Crowning gift of resurrection sent from your ascended throne,
> fullness of the very Godhead, come to make your life our own.
>
> He who in creation's dawning brooded on the lifeless deep,
> still across our nature's darkness moves to wake our souls from sleep,
> moves to stir, to draw, to quicken, thrusts us through with sense of sin;
> brings to birth and seals and fills us—saving Advocate within.
>
> He, himself the living Author, wakes to life the sacred Word,
> reads with us its holy pages and reveals our risen Lord.
> He it is who works within us, teaching rebel hearts to pray,
> he whose holy intercessions rise for us both night and day.
>
> He, the mighty God, indwells us; his to strengthen, help, empow'r;
> his to overcome the tempter, ours to call in danger's hour.
> In his strength we dare to battle all the raging hosts of sin,
> and by him alone we conquer foes without and foes within.
>
> Father, grant your Holy Spirit in our hearts may rule today,
> grieved not, quenched not, but unhindered, work in us his sovereign way.
> Fill us with your holy fullness, God the Father, Spirit, son;
> in us, through us, then, forever, shall your perfect will be done.
> —Margaret Clarkson, 1964

Hallelujah! Celebrate!

Activity Eight

Gifting

Chapter 34

What a Gift Is Not

I asked a large group of high school students, "Are all occupations of equal importance?" They were unanimous and vigorous in their affirmation, in good democratic fashion, that all are equal.

"That's an interesting concept," I said, and told them the story of my flight to Norfolk. "On the way here," I said, "I sat by a man who wanted to sell me stock in his company which, he said, was the fastest growing in his industry, and his industry was the fastest growing in the country."

"What's the industry?" I asked.

"Cosmetics," he said.

"In your industry is there some segment that is growing faster than others?" I asked.

"Oh, yes. Male cosmetics."

"Like—what? Deodorant? After shave lotion?"

"Oh, no," he said. "Like last year we sold a quarter million dollars worth of false eyelashes for men."

So I told the students, "There's an occupation—selling false eyelashes for men. But let me tell you about another vocation. My nephew is a skilled surgeon who could make a bundle here in the USA, but chose rather to care for a forgotten people in the heart of Africa. He barely escaped one country as the communist insurgents swept to power, and now, in Kenya, he tells me he does more surgery in a week than he used to do in a year at a renowned hospital in Pennsylvania. Then he adds, with a wry smile, 'and none of it's cosmetic!' There you have it—you can sell false eyelashes for men or you can heal the bodies and souls of thousands for whom you're the only hope. Let's vote again: are all vocations of equal importance?"

That split the crowd and about half wavered. On the front row was a misplaced little girl who didn't belong in the high school crowd. She didn't vote either way.

"What's wrong, Honey," I asked, "not going to vote?"

"No."

"Why not?"

"It's a bad question."

"What's bad about it?"

"You didn't say important for what."

She caught me! Which is more important, a knife, a fork, or a spoon? Well, that might depend on whether you had a bowl of bullion or a steak. So with vocations—important to whom? For what?

Of course, in this chapter our concern isn't with one's calling to a particular occupation, though the Protestant doctrine of vocation is of vital importance. All Christians should do the work in life God designed them for and serve that vocation as to the Lord. But here we consider "gifts," or the enabling God gives each believer to minister in or through the church. This calling of God is for every believer, whether full-time (a few of us) or part-time (most of us). Since each of us has some calling to serve God with that Spirit-gift, we want to examine that calling and see its importance first, for you and me as individuals, second, for the church, and third, for God's purposes in the world. The Spirit confirms His call to service with a gift that enables us to fulfill that calling.

> "To each is given the manifestation of the Spirit for the common good." (1 Cor. 12:7, RSV).

Before we look into the importance of our God-given ability, however, let's get a little orientation on how that gift relates to certain other activities of the Spirit.

Definitions: What the Gift Is Not

A spiritual gift could be defined as a Spirit-given ability to serve God in the church. But so much confusion reigns in the church over the subject of spiritual gifts that many give up and skirt the whole subject. That's a big mistake because the only way church will really work or, for that matter, the only way we'll spiral up into likeness to Jesus, is through each believer's using the abilities the Spirit gives.

> He is the one who gave these gifts to the church . . . to equip God's people to do his work and build up the church, the body of Christ . . . that we will be mature and full grown in the Lord, measuring up to the full stature of Christ . . . becoming more and more in every way like Christ . . . Under his

direction, the whole body is fitted together perfectly. As each part does its own special work, it helps the other parts grow, so that the whole body is healthy and growing and full of love. (Eph. 4:11–16, NLT)

We won't try to settle all the controversy about gifts, but rather we will focus on the basic, clear teaching on which all of us can agree. Even those who think the gifts—or many of them, at least—are no longer given, must agree that unless the Holy Spirit enables us we can never accomplish the tasks He gives the church.

Let's start with what the Spirit's gifts are not: fruit, talents, offices.

Gifts and Fruit

In *Life in the Spirit* so far we've concentrated on the fruit of the Spirit—how the Holy Spirit produces Christlike characteristics in us. So how do the fruit and gifts relate? As we've just seen, the gifts are designed to produce fruit. We don't grow in isolation but as each part contributes his or her special ministry to the rest. Beyond that basic relationship between gifts and fruit, however, questions remain. Several answers suggest themselves, but are they biblical?

1. The more fruit (the more Christlike the character) a person has, the greater the gift they will be given (the more results in ministry)
2. A person could have a godly life while having very little results in public ministry
3. It's more important to have much fruit in our lives than to have a great gift
4. All Christians should have all the fruit but perhaps only one of the gifts

In the most thorough discussion of gifts in the Bible, 1 Corinthians, chapters twelve through fourteen, the first thing that becomes immediately clear is that fruit is more important than a gift (#3 above). Right in the middle of his discussion of gifts, Paul breaks away from his theme to say, "Now I'm going to describe something far more important than all these gifts combined." Then he gives the magnificent "love chapter," 1 Corinthians 13. And what is love but a fruit? In fact, some say it is the summation of all fruit. That's why we devoted thirty-three chapters to fruit! If anything is clear from our study thus far, it is that God intends all His children to be like Him, to bear all the fruit of the Spirit (#4 above).

The gifts are important, too, but the chief point of 1 Corinthians twelve and fourteen seems to be that the Spirit does not give all the gifts to any one person.

"To one is given . . . through the Spirit . . . to another . . . and to another . . . Are all apostles? Are all prophets? Are all teachers?" (12:8–10, 29, NKJV)

200

What a Gift Is Not

It's just as well the Spirit doesn't give all the gifts to one person. What a power-trip that would be! Think of it this way. God wants everyone to be completely like Him in character, to put His beauty on display; and the more like Jesus we become, the more glory to God. But what of likeness to Him in His activity? He never had any intention that anyone be like Him in infinite wisdom or power or other action-capacities. That would make them lust, like Lucifer, to displace God or at least to get along without His help. No one member can be godlike in capacity lest he or she be tempted to act like God in accumulating personal power. But the Spirit does want His church to be empowered, so His plan was to distribute the gifts among all its members.

In summary, fruit: everyone, always; gifts: some one, some another. But the exciting thing is this: every member is given at least one ability to serve God in the church. That includes you!

There's a real conundrum, though, in how the gifts and fruit relate. It's a puzzle because the Bible nowhere spells it out for us. We see a person mightily used of God who may be egotistical or quick-tempered, and we see another who is very godly in character but is not gifted to serve in any conspicuous way (#2 on previous page). How can that be? Here are some possible reasons:

~ God doesn't necessarily evaluate giftedness as we do.
~ "Fruit" is a more certain measure of spirituality than giftedness.
~ Rewards will be based on faithfulness, a fruit of the Spirit, not on the kind or effectiveness of one's gift.
~ Some giftedness can be natural rather than spiritual.

We tend to evaluate people, especially Christian leaders, in terms of their giftedness, but God is the judge and He's already passed judgment: fruit is more important! One reason is that fruit is the more sure measure of our relation to the Spirit and that's why our recognition by Him on the last day will be based on faithfulness, a fruit. Of course, that faithfulness includes faithfulness in fulfilling our calling, using our gifts for kingdom advance, but that will be only one small part of the evaluation. There's another reason conspicuous fruit is more important to God than conspicuous gifting, and that has to do with the relationship between natural and supernatural abilities.

Gifts and Talents

Though my natural ability is a gift from God as well as my Spirit-gift, a natural ability can be used without the Spirit's assistance. And God doesn't usually get the credit for that! So the first thing to note about a natural ability and a spiritual ability is that both are gifts from God. Therefore we must give God credit for whatever ability we have and we must use both natural and supernatural gifts for His glory, not our own. It's a terrible sin to use either kind of giftedness for our own glory, though many do just that. The second thing to note is that the Bible nowhere spells out the relationship between the two.

It's often difficult to tell the difference. For example, a person may have great natural ability to lead or sing or preach or teach or manage money, so great that most of us would be hard put to tell whether the Spirit is at work. Even activity that definitely requires the supernatural touch of God, like evangelizing, healing, and casting out demons can be faked if the person has enough personal charisma, but we're talking here of those who truly lead people to Christ, truly heal the sick, truly exorcise demons. Still, most of the activities of the church can be carried forward on the basis of natural abilities. And that's scary! Who needs the Spirit?

But you *can* tell the difference. Our theme verse for the chapter (1 Cor. 12:7) says the work of the Spirit is "manifest" or made visible. Apparently you can see the evidence and, furthermore, it seems to be our job to do it: "Beloved, do not believe every spirit, but test the spirits, whether they are of God; because many false prophets have gone out into the world" (1 John 4:1, NKJV). John gives the test of orthodoxy: Is the message biblical? But when it comes to gifts of the Spirit, there is a corollary test that should be used along with the test of true words: is there a supernatural touch on the activity, is it clearly *His* activity that is clearly seen ("manifest")? For example, Paul wasn't a world class public speaker—he agreed with the Corinthians in that judgment. But when he taught the Bible, lives were transformed. A popular Christian music group can entertain—a wonderful talent—but are people lifted to heaven in worship? Or do they merely have an emotional high and acclaim such great talent? Do sinners repent and saints consecrate their lives to God when they sing? That's the touch of the Spirit. Does the counselor merely help people change their dysfunctional behavior or adjust their attitude to develop coping strategies, or does he also lead them forward in a supernatural, transformational pattern of life?

Whether God chooses to bypass natural ability/inability or whether the Spirit lifts a natural ability to a higher power we may not always know, but if it's a Spirit-gift, there will be the Spirit's miracle touch. A couple of cautions are needed, however.

~ Some may have "visible evidence" resulting from the work of unholy spirits. For example, the magicians in Pharaoh's court managed to duplicate some of the signs Moses performed (Exod. 7:11) but certainly didn't do them through the power of the Holy Spirit.

~ A person may have been given a gift and still experience a lack of evidence because of adverse circumstances. For example, Ezekiel was God's own prophet, but the people were rebels and wouldn't listen (Ezek. 3). Paul was no doubt the greatest of evangelists, but in Lystra they stoned him out of town (Acts 14).

What a Gift Is Not

In general, however, if no evidence shows the Spirit at work, if the ministry makes no spiritual impact, we need to ask if the ministry is God's. When I fail to see evidence in my own ministry, I don't immediately conclude that I have no gift or that He hasn't called me after all. I ask myself the following diagnostic questions:

1. *Am I harboring unconfessed sin?* When I've preached my heart out and lives aren't changed, I first examine myself to see if something in me blocked the flow of the Spirit. Do I have some unconfessed sin, a wrong motivation (wanting "success" for human praise), unbelief (not trusting God to do what only He can do), or lack of prayer preparation?

2. *Do I need to be persistent?* When I felt called to do missionary work, I kept asking God for the gift of evangelism. People came to Christ through my ministry only sporadically, and I longed for the ability to consistently win people to Christ. I'll tell you the outcome in chapter 39, but I'll give you the principle here. The principle is to keep asking until you see one of two things: "visible evidence" of the gift you long for, or the assurance that God doesn't intend that gift for you. Stop asking only when God shows you the gift is not for you.

3. *Am I in the right place?* In Japan, we discovered we were ministering in a very unresponsive area. We asked God if there should be a change of location to a place or people who would respond. This is what Paul did more than once. (See Acts 13:46, for example.)

4. *Is God vindicating Himself?* Perhaps, on the other hand, God intends a gifted person to stand firm when there is no "fruit" or outward result, as His vindication among an unresponsive people (as in Ezekiel's case). Don't run to this as an excuse, however. The general principle of Scripture is to concentrate one's efforts where there is response.

You can see from the above exceptions that a legitimate gift may be without "visible evidence" in some situations; but ordinarily the touch of the Spirit is the proof of His presence and power.

Gifts and Offices

Just because a person is appointed or elected to an office is no guarantee he or she has the Spirit-given abilities needed for that office. On the other hand, great giftedness in itself doesn't qualify for office.

> Now the overseer must be above reproach, the husband of but one wife, temperate, self-controlled, respectable, hospitable, able to teach, not given to drunkenness, not violent but gentle, not quarrelsome, not a lover of money. He must manage his own family well and see that his children obey him with proper respect. (If anyone does not know how to manage his own family, how can he take care of God's church?) He must not be a recent convert, or he may

become conceited and fall under the same judgment as the devil. He must also have a good reputation with outsiders, so that he will not fall into disgrace and into the devil's trap.

Deacons, likewise, are to be men worthy of respect, sincere, not indulging in much wine, and not pursuing dishonest gain. They must keep hold of the deep truths of the faith with a clear conscience. They must first be tested, and then if there is nothing against them, let them serve as deacons. (1 Tim. 3:2–10)

An elder must be blameless, the husband of but one wife, a man whose children believe and are not open to the charge of being wild and disobedient. Since an overseer is entrusted with God's work, he must be blameless—not overbearing, not quick-tempered, not given to drunkenness, not violent, not pursuing dishonest gain. Rather he must be hospitable, one who loves what is good, who is self-controlled, upright, holy and disciplined. He must hold firmly to the trustworthy message as it has been taught, so that he can encourage others by sound doctrine and refute those who oppose it. (Titus 1:6–9)

Short list on gifts, right? I counted about twenty-five qualifications for holding office in the church and I could find only two that might be considered gifts of the Spirit: the abilities to teach and to manage the affairs of the church. There's another one that might require a spiritual gift, though the spin seems to be more on character than giftedness: hospitality, a fruit surely all Christians should bear. Then there is the requirement of orthodoxy: the officer must be thoroughly committed to biblical truth. Of twenty-five qualifications for office, then, more than twenty are fruits of the Spirit, not gifts. Perhaps *Life in the Spirit* has the right biblical emphasis after all.

But even though the list of gift-qualifications is short, how many churches choose leaders who lack even those? Does your church take seriously these qualifications? And what of those not holding office? Does the church help discover and develop the gifts of each member? For that matter, how about your own gift or gifts? The exciting thing about gifts is that the Holy Spirit intends to give an ability for service to everyone in whom He lives. In the next chapter we'll find out how the church—and you—can discover and develop those gifts.

But for now, remember a gift is not to be confused with the fruit of the Spirit, a natural talent, or an office in the church.

Chapter 35

Defining Gifts

Gifts of the Spirit are distinct from fruit, talents, and offices, but are also somehow interwoven with them. The relationship isn't spelled out in Scripture, however, so it's sometimes less than clear. But what is clear is that the Spirit does give abilities to each believer and that He expects us to know our gifts, develop them, and use them. First, however, we need to know what the gifts are, and there are three ways to find out: biblical lists and examples, tasks to be done, and purposes of the church.

Bible Definitions

Biblical Gift Lists

In the New Testament there are several lists of gifts, or abilities given by the Spirit to do some work for God in the church or in the world.

Some of those are clear in relating what the outcome will be if you have the gift: the name tells you. Others are not that clear; so it's hard to judge whether or not a person has that gift. When it comes right down to it, we don't know for sure what most of those gifts will look like if a person has them. Therefore the meanings are hotly disputed. We will focus here on gifts whose meanings are clear.

Defining the Gifts

Teaching may be clear, but only if we define the outcome as a person so explaining the Bible and spiritual truth that lives are consistently changed.

Romans 12:3–8	1 Corinthians 12	Ephesians 4	1 Peter 4:10–11
prophecy	wisdom	apostleship	various unnamed
service	knowledge	prophecy	speaking
teaching	faith	evangelism	serving
encouraging	healing	pastoring	
giving	miracles	teaching	
leading	prophecy		
showing mercy	discernment of spirits		
	tongues		
	interpretation		
	apostleship		
	teaching		

Healing would seem clear since a sick person would have to get well. I've experienced that. What the doctors described as an incurable disease kept me from becoming a missionary. A friend came and prayed for me and that night my pain left me. Forever! But to my knowledge, that's the only time that friend saw such dramatic results, so he could hardly be said to have the "gift of healing." What would it look like if he did? I get the impression that Jesus and, in the book of Acts, the twelve apostles healed everyone who came to them for healing. Can contemporary healers match that? But even if not, if people are healed often through the prayers of a person I guess we'd have to say they had a gift.

Evangelism. If people often come to Christ through a person's witness, that would be the sign of God at work and such a person could surely be said to have the gift of evangelism.

In all those lists, those three are the only ones that seem to be clearly defined by the term itself. Some would add others, such as tongues or interpretation. They are clearly supernatural, but equally godly and learned people disagree on exactly what those gifts are and how you can tell. So I left them off my list of those in which the exact meaning is evident just by the word used to identify the gift.

There's another one you may be inclined to include—prophecy. If by "prophecy" you mean "prediction," that would be clear and the person with such a gift could be spotted easily—his predictions would consistently come true. But prediction is only one use of the term in Scripture, and, in fact, other uses are more prominent. Basically, prophets were Spirit-ordained spokespersons for God. Sometimes they would foretell future events, but that was not the defining activity. For example, in the Old Testament, musicians, even instrumentalists, were in the order of the prophets: "David . . . separated to the service of the sons of Asaph, and of Heman, and of Jeduthun, who should prophesy with harps, with [stringed instruments], and with cymbals . . . who prophesied . . . to give thanks and to praise the LORD" (1 Chron. 25:1, 3).

How could that be? No prediction there, not even words! But if they officially represented God in leading His people in worship, that was considered "prophecy." If music among God's people leads to true worship, the leader may well have a spiritual gift, perhaps the gift of prophecy.

Thus, what a person was to say in a prophetic word and what the outcome was are not clearly defined by Scripture. I'm sure there are many in our day who are authoritative spokespersons for God, so Spirit-anointed preaching might be one kind of prophecy, for example. But since Scripture is not clear, I'll not be dogmatic about all that "prophecy" might mean.

Importance of Each Gift

Are all the gifts of equal importance or are some more important than others? Remember how the young girl caught me by asking, "Important for what?"

1. *Important for you.* The most important gifts for you or me are those gifts God has given us or would give us if we asked, and the most important thing for us is to find that gift or pattern of gifts and use them to the maximum.

2. *Important for the church.* We might say all of the gifts are important for the church since Paul seems to be saying the Spirit puts into each church all the gifts (or gifted people) needed to accomplish His purposes in and through that church. So the most important thing for the church is for all the members to function in the way the Spirit designs. The problem is that in most churches about fifteen percent of the members try to fulfill the functions of the whole body! No wonder so many church bodies are badly handicapped, or even totally disabled. The Spirit's will for the church is for every member to function as designed because every member is needed to accomplish His purposes. That happens when every member is using fully her or his gifts.

3. *Important to God.* Surely all gifts are of equal importance to Him? Careful! The central purpose of 1 Corinthians twelve through fourteen is to get the church to understand that gifts are not all of equal importance for accomplishing God's will. There are some less important gifts and the church at Corinth was majoring on one of those (speaking in tongues). Furthermore, there are very important gifts which the church at Corinth should have majored on but didn't—gifts like apostle, prophet, teacher.

Paul even numbered them 1, 2, and 3 (1 Cor. 12:28) so they wouldn't miss the point. He doesn't continue his numbering system beyond those three, so they may just be representative. But they give a hint as to what he considers more important: roles which seem to have the greatest impact for God's purposes in the church and in the world. Since Scripture nowhere stops to define those gifts, we're left to study the terms in their use throughout the Bible. After years of doing that, my personal definition of his top three would be pioneer missionary evangelism (apostle), power-filled proclamation or preaching (prophecy), and Spirit-anointed teaching—important tasks, indeed.

Some people read the passage in a hurry and conclude that Paul is contrasting lower gifts with the highest gift, love. But they miss the point. Paul is teaching the people at Corinth about spiritual gifts and having exhorted us to seek the higher ones, he pauses for a mid-course correction. Don't get me wrong, he says, these gifts, even the more important ones, aren't the most important thing. The most important thing is love. Love isn't a "gift" in the sense Paul is teaching about; he calls it a "way." "I'll show you an even better way," he says, better even than the best gift. Elsewhere he describes love as the fruit of the Spirit (Gal. 5:22–23). So let's not confuse fruit with gift. Gifts: Spirit-given ability; fruit: Spirit-given character. So his command in verse thirty-one is to desire Spirit-given abilities to serve God.

Don't misunderstand what we mean by importance. We're not speaking of one gift being more "spiritual" than another. "Spiritual" has to do with fruits of the Spirit, likeness to Jesus, as we've just seen. And we're not talking about greater rewards for greater gifts more greatly used. Reward is based on faithfulness, not outward results.

But to accomplish God's purposes some gifts are of greater importance. For twelve years I was a pioneer missionary evangelist, starting churches. A very high calling, according to Paul. Today I'm a homemaker, primarily, which seems to need more fruit than gifts. My Spirit-gifts have a limited outlet through some writing and speaking. But I'm not arrogant, claiming that my role in life is as important as anyone else's. My calling cannot even compare with Billy Graham's calling in terms of eternal impact, for example. And I'm not jealous of Billy! God expects only that we be faithful to our own calling. Then the whole body can function smoothly, we will find personal fulfillment, and, best of all, God will be pleased.

Although we've learned something about what the gifts are by examining the biblical lists of gifts, apparently the Holy Spirit didn't intend to give a clear-cut list of specific job descriptions. Was He just illustrating the kinds of things the Spirit wants to accomplish through His people? If so, there may be good reason for the imprecision—perhaps He intended flexibility for us to see what needs doing in each situation and trust Him to provide people with the abilities needed to do it.

Task-Related Gift Definitions

We had just finished a faculty workshop on helping students identify their gifts when Kenneth Kantzer, distinguished theologian, seminary leader, and former editor of *Christianity Today*, took the mike. "I've never known what my gift is," he said, to our astonishment. "All my life I've seen a need, been asked to fill it, and trusted the Holy Spirit to enable me to do it." Maybe he's on to something.

As we've worked through possible definitions of spiritual gifts, you may have been frustrated that they are not more precise, especially if there is some favorite gift definition of yours I called into question. I felt that way for years. I read books filled with precise definitions and self-evaluating check-lists, searching, searching, for my personal gift. Could I ever really know my own gift for sure? When it finally came clear to me that the imprecision of Scripture was not by accident, that I should focus rather on the tasks that needed to be done, it was truly liberating. Now all we need do is ask God for the abilities necessary to accomplish what He has clearly told us to do. We can leave the combination of abilities, natural and supernatural, to the Holy Spirit to decide—"as He wills." And we can tell when that custom-designed pattern of gifts is from Him—the supernatural outcome!

There's another reason I've concluded we should focus more on the roles than endlessly debate the meanings of terms the Bible didn't define for us. Each of the biblical lists are quite different, no single gift appearing in all of them. Teaching and prophecy appear in three, apostleship in two, and twenty-two gifts appear only once. So none of the lists is intended to be exhaustive; they're just representative or suggestive.

Perhaps there are other gifts not listed, tasks that need to be done in your church which Paul didn't include in any of his lists. For example, music, a major ministry of the church, isn't on any of the lists. If your church uses drama, you surely don't want your dramatic efforts to be purely human talent. You want the strong anointing of the Spirit to produce eternal outcomes. There are no doubt other contemporary activities or traditional activities that don't clearly fit under any of Paul's categories, like children's work. If we thought it through, however, many of those other activities would be a form of "teaching" or "prophetic proclamation." Writing, for example, might fit under one of those. And what of counseling? It may be on one of those lists.

The Bible doesn't define "pastor," but the word literally means "shepherd." That sounds a little like counseling, doesn't it? Today we use "pastor" as the over-arching identification of the chief church leader, and certainly the shepherd was called to lead the flock. But the original idea was more akin, perhaps, to what today we call discipling, counseling, or nurturing. "Encouragement" in the Romans list of gifts might fit here, too. Many lay people are like Barnabas, good at "coming alongside" and helping others through the tough times. Studies consistently show that such a loving relationship has more healing power than the professionals can provide!

The ancients called counseling the "cure of souls," or, to use the original Greek, the "cure (or healing) of psyches." Professional counselors who have the gift of curing the whole soul, who see supernatural results in life transformation toward likeness to Christ as the outcome of their counseling, might be said to have the gift of "pastor." Others have the gift of pastoring or "curing souls," of course, but if the professional adds to his natural talent and training an anointing of the Spirit, he or she can be especially effective in healing the soul.

There are other possibilities for linking contemporary tasks with biblical gifts. "Leading," "administration," "wisdom," "discernment," or "helps," for example, are capable of wide application. Just be sure not to be too dogmatic in claiming that your understanding of a gift name is the only meaning it could have. And always identify the touch of the Spirit by spiritual outcomes.

Defining Gift by Purpose of the Church

Remember the purposes of the church? (See diagram on page 111.) One vertical—worship; three internal—teaching, fellowship, and accountability; and two reaching out—evangelism and service. I have often asked a group of graduate theology students, drawn from many denominations, to identify which church would come to mind as I mentioned each purpose of the church. It was amazing to see, year after year, how people with varied backgrounds identified every denomination by the strength of one purpose and the weakness or absence of most of the rest. They not only knew their own group; they knew the others as well! That must mean some activity of the Spirit in gifting members is being neglected. How would you rate the strength of each of those purposes in your own congregation? If there are purposes poorly fulfilled, perhaps the need is to "desire earnestly the . . . gift." What gift?

- ∼ It seems to me that the gifts of preaching, leadership, and administration are needed for the fulfillment of every purpose since those are gifts needed to accomplish the over-all purposes of the church. For example, leaders are needed who are gifted to understand the way God wants the church to go and get people to go together in that direction.

- ∼ The ability to lead people to worship in spirit and in truth is needed if the church is to bring God joy and honor Him.

- ∼ The ability to proclaim God's truth with life-changing authority is needed if the pulpit is to be more than an empty symbol.

- The ability to teach the Bible in such a way that lives are changed is needed if godly learning is to take place.
- The ability to discern a person's spiritual need and give wise counsel is needed if people are to be made whole and grow toward ever greater likeness to Christ.
- The fellowship function of the church, the family solidarity, is something that is the responsibility of the whole church, each one caring lovingly for the emotional, physical, material, and spiritual needs of other members of the family. It seems to be fulfilled more by people bearing the fruit of the Spirit than by any particular giftedness. But if the church is to function as a family well cared for, special abilities are needed to help out in practical ways like financial management, feeding people, seeing needs and meeting them.
- The ability to win people to faith is needed if the church is to fulfill Christ's last command and grow as He promised.
- The ability to help the physical and social needs of the community in such a way that people are drawn Godward is needed if the church is to fulfill the mandate of Christ. Actually, this would be a "gift" only for some who may specialize in social helping and healing, perhaps as a full-time ministry. Otherwise it's the responsibility of every member, the fruit of the compassionate Holy Spirit, more than any special gift.

Go for It!

How is it at your church? Are some of those purposes falling short of God's intention? What kind of gifts would the Spirit give to meet those needs? If you have a strong desire to see some of the gifts used more in your church, or even a strong desire to be more used personally, Paul says to "earnestly desire" the higher gifts. That's a command! So if you don't feel strongly about something you'd like to accomplish for God, now's the time to pause and ask God to give you such a holy desire. If you already have a longing for a particular gift, pause now and ask God for it!

In discerning your own gift and those of others we looked at the gifts of the Spirit as listed in Scripture and then at the abilities needed to accomplish certain tasks. You might call that definition by job description. Thinking of tasks leads directly to focusing next on the purposes of the church and the many-splendored mosaic of gifts the Spirit wants to give His church. There are three ways to define gifts. But with all the defining, what about identifying my own gift? After checking out the needs in my church and the desires of my own heart, there's an essential way to identify your gift: try it out! Since that's also the basic way to develop your gift, we'll turn now to consider using your gift.

211

Chapter 36

Developing Your Gift

$\mathcal{U}$sing the ability God gives you has a dual purpose: to prove what the gift is and then to develop it. Though most of this chapter is devoted to developing your gift, let's look first at the confirming-your-gift purpose of getting to work.

Discerning Your Gift by Involvement

The churches we started in Japan were composed of people who had known nothing of the gospel and, of course, nothing of what a church is supposed to be. But we assumed that these newborn Christians would be given abilities to serve God, just as the Spirit promised. So we gave everyone a job. We even gave unconverted regular attenders a job, like cleaning up before and after services or serving tea and rice crackers. From the outset they felt part of us, and people were born into the family serving. That is, they assumed that to be a Christian meant to participate in God's work. At first the assignments were housekeeping, nothing that would test one's spiritual giftedness but would test one's availability and heart for serving the rest of the family. Here is a list of jobs we gave, in the order of spiritual responsibility, beginning with the task requiring the least supernatural enabling.

~ Straightening the shoes or *geta* in the vestibule where they were left upon entry
~ Greeting and seating guests
~ Serving rice crackers and tea

Developing Your Gift

- ~ Playing the electronic organ
- ~ Giving a testimony at an evangelistic meeting
- ~ Leading the meeting
- ~ Preaching to non-Christians
- ~ Teaching a Sunday school class
- ~ Preaching to Christians
- ~ Teaching Sunday school teachers

We would train and coach believers until they seemed ready for the next assignment, stopping when they wanted to stop or the leaders in the church felt they were not yet gifted for the next assignment. There are two reasons for this approach. First, how do you know whether you have a gift or would be given a gift until you try it out? Second, giftedness should be confirmed by the church.

A man once wrote me from across the continent, asking for help. He was an evangelist, he said, but the church wouldn't recognize him. Could I write a letter of endorsement so he could get meetings? Two problems. If a person is truly gifted in evangelism, that is self-evident. But there's a deeper problem. I didn't know the man, his character, how he went about evangelizing, what the results were. He is accountable to his church, not to me. The church must confirm a person's gifts.

Does your church have a systematic plan for helping people discover their gifts? Is every member expected to serve in some capacity? Are people encouraged to try out new roles and use their abilities to the maximum? If not, perhaps it's time for change—change in attitude to raise expectancies, change in structure to make it happen. Not only must the gift be confirmed by the church, it ought to be sought in the context of the church to begin with. If God doesn't intend for me the gift I aim for, the church leadership should help me reach that conclusion.

Once I've identified the gift I have or the gift I'd like to have, or once I've identified the job I'd like to do, I must get to work. I must develop the abilities necessary to do that job effectively. The church's role is to help me identify the role I should pursue, free me to do it, and help me grow in it.

Developing Your Gift

Paul told Timothy, "Do not neglect your gift . . . Be diligent in these matters; give yourself wholly to them, so that everyone may see your progress" (1 Tim. 4:14–15). In our churches in Tsuchiura, Japan, we used all the training methods I'll describe in this chapter, and the result was that we started three churches in five years. We could never do that if the "professional," in this case the missionary, had to do all the important functions of the church. But because the people were freed up to use the abilities the Spirit was distributing and because I concentrated my energies on equipping them for their ministries

(Eph. 4:11–12), we could move forward simultaneously in every outlying community. Here's the strategy we used:

1. Practice

We've seen how getting to work on a job is the one sure way to identify a gift. Don't give up too soon, though. If the kids throw spitwads the first day in class, don't conclude you're not called to teach! Work at it.

Contrary to the proverb, however, practice doesn't always make perfect. In fact it can make very imperfect—consolidating all the bad habits we practice. We need someone who's gone on before and knows how the job should be done to come alongside and help us grow.

2. Apprentice/Mentor

Dan was to be envied. A handsome people-person with a gifted wife, he had just been called to his first assignment after graduation: associate pastorate of a prestigious old church. He was excited because the senior pastor was a remarkably successful leader and Dan intended to learn all he could. So he soon approached his boss, asking the pastor to help him discover and develop his gifts. The pastor, a self-starting, can-do man who had never asked anyone for help, said, "Who do you think I am? The Holy Spirit?" Crushed, Dan limped along for a few months, dropped out, and has been in construction work for the last twenty-five years. I've often wondered, had Dan encountered a true mentor, would he have been building the church all these decades?

If your church has structured it so that everyone has a mentor, or, even if not, if someone has reached out to help you grow in your ministry, how blessed you are! But if not, what can be done? *You* can do the reaching out. Ask for feedback on your performance, for example. Have the best teacher you know sit in on the class you teach and talk with you informally afterwards. You have to really want candid responses and you have to let them know that, or the exercise will be a waste of your time and theirs.

Another way to get feedback is to distribute questionnaires to those who see you in action, the one to whom you are responsible, the students in your class—anyone whose judgment might be helpful. If you don't feel competent to develop an evaluative checklist for the job you're doing, perhaps there's someone in the church who could help you develop such a questionnaire or checklist. In ways like this, you can take the initiative and recruit your own mentor, but the best way is for the church to provide mentors to apprentice everyone who begins a new ministry.

Looking at it from the other end, however, perhaps there is someone you could help in developing his or her gift. Be careful, however, to pray for wisdom on the best way to feel that person out and see whether he or she would like such a relationship. But perhaps God would use you in an even larger role. If you are in a leadership role in the church, consider what steps you could take to get the church into a developing-everyone mode.

3. Literature and Media

In our churches in Japan we gave everyone, along with the job, a page of simple instructions on how to do that job. But in America we are rich in resources: teachers' manuals or how-to books on virtually every job in the church. Be sure the church library has a good book on your job. For some of the key roles there are videos or series of audiotapes produced by people who are the best in the particular role you have. If you don't know how to get at those resources, inquire around to see who does, and if no one in your church knows such things, try the local Christian bookstore.

4. Special Training Classes

We opened a mini-Bible college on Tuesday nights to train people who were serving or wanted to serve in spiritual ministry. Here are some of the courses we taught these new believers: teaching methods, preaching, principles of Bible interpretation, Bible survey, church history, theology, various Bible book studies, principles of Christian ministry, evangelism. We should have taught world missions but didn't. Would any of those be helpful for a training program in your church?

5. Inter-Church Seminars

Our "mini-Bible college" was an inter-church project, and people came from a distance to attend. But one of the most popular means of learning today is the major regional event, seminars on Christian education, counseling, witnessing, apologetics, family life, political action, preaching, prayer, missions—you name it. World famous teachers lecture, specialists offer workshops on every conceivable related topic. Does your church budget include funds for key people to attend such conferences? Have individuals or groups from your church attended such a conference, whether under church auspices or independently? Which kinds of seminars should your church leadership consider for making a major part of the church program?

6. Formal Training

Finally, there is formal training available for those who have grown beyond what the local church offers or who feel the need of intensive study. From our fledgling churches in Japan more than half a dozen went away to prepare for full-time ministry and two have become pastors with a nationwide impact. This from churches which at the time totaled less than one hundred members!

In America today increasing numbers of mature adults are choosing to attend a resident program, when one's life situation permits. Some Bible colleges (undergraduate) and seminaries (for college graduates) have one-year introductory courses to give a broad overview of biblical studies, and the full program is available for those who feel the Spirit's drawing toward full-time vocational Christian ministry. Furthermore, seminaries and Bible colleges offer studies in locations away from their home campuses—perhaps near you—and a few have a highly-developed home study curriculum.

You already knew about most or all the possibilities for developing your gift I've mentioned. I've outlined briefly the possibilities for a specific purpose. I'm hoping that you have identified the gift or gifts you already are using and the gift or pattern of abilities you'd like to have, and that you have a desire to serve God in a particular way beyond what you are now doing. It's time to develop a personal plan for developing that gift. Are there any of the strategies I've suggested, or other methods you know about, that you feel you'd really like to try out? If you don't take those first steps this week, when will it ever happen?

Chapter 37

Desiring the Best

$\mathcal{P}$aul says, "Eagerly desire the greater gifts" (1 Cor. 12:31). In this chapter let's examine three important things about this crucial command. It's an active command, a continuous action command, and a command for the whole church.

An Active Verb

The command to "desire earnestly" is not a description of the feeling you have when you watch a luscious slice of pizza, dripping cheese, move across the TV screen. The word used has the concept of action. "Go for it," we would say, or "get with it!" If you pick up the phone and order that pizza, then you've "desired earnestly."

My mother wanted me to desire earnestly service for God, but I didn't. I'd yielded my life to God, but it was a passive yielding. I wasn't excited about it. "God, you shove and I'll move" was my mode. I didn't add, "But I won't like it, I'm sure," even though that's the way I felt most of the time. I wasn't obeying the command; I wasn't desiring earnestly any gift.

But I was involved. Mother saw to that. That's what Sunday afternoons were for. She arranged (I later learned) to have college students invite me, just a young kid, to go with them in their ministry to housing developments, for example. Flattered by the attention, I went with them. Even helped start a little country church one year—I hauled wood for the pot-bellied stove in that one-room ramshackle schoolhouse. Mother was "church" to me, my incognito mentor, helping me discover my spiritual gifts. But I wasn't desiring anything.

When I was eighteen, however, the desire began to stir. In fact, I began to desire most earnestly that my life should count to the maximum for whatever God designed me for. That meant getting involved. I joined other young men in preaching on the street corner. Folks didn't stop much, so we took up preaching in jail. There no one walked away! I began to obey the command to "get with it" and "go for it."

You may not have desired earnestly the jobs you've held in church; you may have been drafted, in fact, like my mother drafted me. But whether you volunteered or were recruited, think through every job you've held in the church or in ministry outside the church's auspices, and note any that really excited you. Do your effectiveness or excitement about any of those point to the possibility of your being used in a larger way, maybe even some other more important-to-God role? If so, then don't consider it presumption to go for it. Paul says, desire it earnestly, go for it vigorously.

Seek and Keep on Seeking

Taking action, seeking to uncover the latent gifts by getting to work, is important, but obeying the command to "earnestly desire" means first of all to tell God of that desire. Not just a one-time, timid request, either. The form of the verb means to pray earnestly and keep at it, to keep on desiring. Pray persistently until God gives the answer. Here are a few possibilities to check out:

- ~ How many adult baptisms were there in your church last year? Is it growing in numbers, at least five percent a year in baptisms of adult converts? If not, your church may need more people with the gift of evangelism.
- ~ Or perhaps your concern is the lack of spiritual growth. Once a person joins the church, nothing much seems to happen in spiraling up. Many gifts would help, no doubt, but how about Spirit-anointed teachers, counselors, or disciple-makers?
- ~ Is the church harassed with gossip, squabbles, in danger of splitting up? Is it stuck in the rut of some worn-out tradition? Maybe you need a courageous prophet or the dynamism of Spirit-anointed leadership. Are you asking God for that? Earnestly? Persistently?

You can't go for all of the gifts needed, of course; you must discover how God will use you personally. But the Spirit intends to meet all the needs of the church; so this "desiring earnestly" can't be a Lone Ranger, individualistic pursuit. The church as a whole must obey the command.

United Prayer

Actually, the verb Paul uses is in the plural: "You all desire earnestly." If you can't inspire the church as a whole to focus on this kind of praying, some smaller prayer group could include this request on a regular basis. If not, perhaps you and a prayer partner could begin to focus on asking for the gifts the Spirit wants to give. Such a prayer meeting must not be a thinly-veiled invitation to criticism, focusing on the negative. It must spring from earnest desire for God's highest and best. Perhaps it's time to start an action plan to involve others in desiring earnestly the needed gifts.

Heart Trouble

Translators seem to have difficulty getting just the right word in English to translate this command: "eagerly desire" (NIV); "covet earnestly" (KJV); "set your hearts on" (TEV, Phillips); "try your best" (TLB); "be ambitious" (JB); "earnestly desire" (RSV).

There's something emotional about it, a deep longing that moves to action. That's what I began to experience in my late teens. It never left me—a compelling desire to count to the maximum for God. Every possible gift and opportunity the Spirit would give to advance the cause of the gospel—that's what I wanted.

But some people are like me—for years I had heart trouble. I didn't see the needs or opportunities or, seeing them, didn't care that much. Notice that Paul doesn't say, wait around till the desire hits you. It's a command: set your heart on that gift that is so desperately needed by your church or by a dying world. Take the initiative, says Paul. Go for it! If you don't have a desire to be used more in God's service, that may be the place to begin. Instead of asking for a particular ability, as I have often suggested in these chapters, perhaps the request should be for the Spirit to ignite a great flame of desire in your heart. If you've got heart trouble like I did, why not stop now and tell Him about it? And commit to keep on asking Him every day until He lights the fire.

Giftedness is great, but never forget something greater: fruit. How do the two relate? Both are the work of the Spirit. And both represent a part of His intentions for every believer. But remember the major difference between the two: the Spirit longs to give all the fruit to all believers in maximum measure, while the gifts He distributes among believers. Some receive greater gifts, some lesser. Great fruit without great gifts can bring great glory to God, but great gifts without great fruit clouds, perhaps even eclipses, His glory. When a godly person is also gifted, however, what glory to God!

How exciting! The Spirit plans to use you in God's service more than you ever dreamed possible. And what a treasure hunt—to discover the gifts He has for you! What a privilege, too. Do you ever feel the wonder of God's amazing plan—to accomplish His purposes in the world through mere mortals, through you and me? And what about the exhilaration of cooperating with the Spirit in developing and using your gifts to the maximum? Isn't it time to tell God how much you appreciate Him? Do it now!

Activity Nine
Sending

Chapter 38

Seeing Things God's Way

*T*he students at a leading seminary wanted to examine the question of the biblical role of world evangelism in the life of a Christian and in the life of a church. Being seminarians, they staged a debate. They invited the most influential man in world missions at that time, Donald McGavran. I once heard McGavran say, "Missions is a most important purpose of the church." After that meeting I had approached him, "Dr. McGavran, the last time I heard you speak you said it was the most important task of the church. Which is it, *a* or *the?*"

"Well," said the old gentleman, "if it's *the* purpose, that includes a, and some audiences aren't ready to call it *the* purpose of the church." He obviously ranked world evangelism near the top of his agenda of what the church is about.

On the other side of the debate was a leading evangelical theologian. Before the debate began, the theologian said, "Dr. McGavran, before we begin I just want you to know that I believe in missions. It's even in my theological system. It's point number D-12 in my theology." That's not bad, since most theologians don't include it at all—they leave missions to the church history or Christian education departments! That set the stage, for missions was clearly A-1 in McGavran's theology. After the debate the theologian said, "Dr. McGavran, you're very persuasive, and I admire you and your work. But I want you to know that missions is still point number D-12 in my theological system."

Where would you cast your ballot in that debate? For ninety to ninety-five percent of evangelical churches in America, world missions is point D-12 in the church program or off their agenda altogether. What about the handful who are gung-ho for world evangelism? Are they misguided, or are they merely obedient to the Lord of the church?

More important than where you or I stand in that debate on the importance of world evangelism is discovering where God stands. As an initial clue, notice that when the Holy Spirit was given, nothing is said of all the glorious truths we've been studying, how He enables us to spiral up into likeness to Christ, to be free and fulfilled. The Spirit's coming focuses on something outside ourselves: You will be witnesses! "But you will receive power when the Holy Spirit comes on you; and you will be my witnesses in Jerusalem, and in all Judea and Samaria, and to the ends of the earth" (Acts 1:8).

I believe God went to considerable effort to reveal exactly the way He thinks, and if we'll look even casually at that self-revelation, the Bible, we'll discover that world evangelism is indeed central in God's thinking. When we do, I think we'll find that

~ God's character makes world evangelism inevitable;
~ God's activity proves what His heart is like;
~ God's promises assure a successful conclusion to His plan;
~ God's command means we must think the way He thinks, act the way He acts.

In this chapter we want to get the big picture, reviewing Scripture from beginning to end to see the world the way God sees it; we want to discover a biblical theology.

God's Character

What characteristic of God do you like best? Perhaps you agree with John, who said there is a certain characteristic of God so central to His nature you could even say He *is* that. John wanted us to be sure to get the point so he repeated himself a few verses later: "God is love," he insists (1 John 4:8, 16). God didn't create love to give His creatures something to aim at. He's that way Himself by nature, the blessed triunity, bound together in living bonds of love. We met such a God in chapter four, who, from the overflow of His loving nature, desired a being to love Him back. As a result, the Spirit created humans on the pattern of God so that He could love them and be loved of them—the goal of creation.

It was a risky proposition. If He created such a being, that person might not love Him back, might choose to walk away from a loving relationship, might even defy that love. That is just what our first parents did, and every son and daughter of Adam since. But that didn't change God's character. He continued to so love the world that He gave His own Son to buy us back for that love relationship (John 3:16). That's the express purpose for His invasion of our humanity—to seek and to save the lost (Matt. 18:11).

If love was the reason for Jesus' first coming, love is also the reason He hasn't come again. People keep resisting God's loving advances to them, keep perishing, and it breaks His heart. The broken-hearted God delays His coming for one reason, Peter tells us—because He doesn't want anyone to perish (2 Pet. 3:9). Consider the tension in the loving heart of God: longing to return to embrace his bride, the church, and set all the wrongs right in this old sin-cursed world, but, at the same time, distressed over the fact that so many are lost.

How many? Just to say a number doesn't reach our hearts since we don't have the capacity to love each one as God does. But He does love them, even the nine out of ten who don't know Him. Although almost two billion people are called Christians, the vast majority of those are Christian in name only. For example, Europe could be counted almost wholly Christian because people are born into state or dominant churches, but in many nations no more than two percent even attend church. Ever. The most generous estimates are that active, Bible-believing Christians in the world number no more than 600 million. If that estimate by the statisticians of "born-again" believers is anywhere near accurate, it means that more than 5 billion people today are lost. It's difficult to grasp such numbers and even harder to love those faceless multitudes. But God does love each one—they aren't faceless to Him.

It's not merely that so many are out of Christ, however. It's worse than that. Half of those lost people are out of reach of any witnessing church. And it breaks God's heart. Because God is love, world evangelism is central in His thinking. Is it central in yours? What would the people who know you best say is the big thing in your life, the A-1 subject? If what is central in God's thinking turns out to be peripheral in mine, perhaps I have heart trouble. But God doesn't. God is love, so much so that He gave His one and only Son that none might perish.

God's Activity

Someone said, "Every major act of God since the Fall is a missionary act." That's quite a statement. I wonder if it's so. Let's look at some of those acts.

~ Abraham wasn't called by God to shower all His loving attention on his descendants and let the rest of the world go to hell. God favored Abraham in order to bless the whole world though him (Gen. 12:1–2). God needed a people isolated from the moral pollution of the nations so they could receive a revelation of Himself without distortion and be His messengers of God's saving truth.

224

~ The Exodus seems like it was just for Israel—it meant the destruction of Egypt's military power and the subjugation of the people of Palestine. But there was a larger purpose. God was re-establishing His missionary task force which had been in danger of extinction in Egypt.

~ But God's missionary task force itself became corrupt, running after other loves, other gods. So God disciplined them, sending them into captivity in order to purify them. It worked! Never again has Israel been idolatrous. God was creating the spiritual and social context into which He could come Himself and find a foothold.

~ So the next major event was the greatest missionary act in all history—the incarnation, when God's only Son left His homeland to become one of us in order to save us (Matt. 18:11; John 1:14).

~ Then He sent the Spirit at Pentecost for the express purpose of establishing a new method to carry out His saving purpose for the whole world: the New Testament church (Matt. 16:18; Acts 1:8).

Such is God's activity. God's actions prove what His missionary heart is like. Perhaps our actions prove what our hearts are really like, too—what we talk about, what we do with our money, how we involve ourselves in the church's missionary enterprise. Heart monitors.

God's Promises

God's promises, from Genesis to Revelation, assure a successful conclusion to His plan of world evangelization. "I will make you into a great nation and I will bless you; I will make your name great, and you will be a blessing . . . and all peoples on earth will be blessed through you" (Gen. 12:2–3).

That's the reason God blessed Abraham—to make him a conduit of God's blessings to the nations. And why does He prosper us? "May God be gracious to us and bless us and make his face shine upon us . . . that your ways may be known on earth, your salvation among all nations . . . God will bless us, and all the ends of the earth will fear him" (Ps. 67:1–2, 7).

Remarkable! Abraham's blessings and ours are for the same purpose: that God's salvation may reach all people. And it *will* happen, God promises both Abraham and us.

Here are some promises of a coming Messiah. Jews, including Jesus' disciples, expected Messiah to deliver them from Roman bondage and set up a Jewish state. In these two ancient promises of a coming Messiah, note how mistaken they were:

~ *The Father promises the Son:* "Ask of me, and I will make the nations your inheritance, the ends of the earth your possession." (Ps. 2:8)

> ~ *The Father promises the Son:* "It is too small a thing for you to be my servant to restore the tribes of Jacob . . . I will also make you a light for the Gentiles, that you may bring my salvation to the ends of the earth." (Isa. 49:6)

Repeatedly in Old Testament prophecies the coming of Messiah was predicted, but He was not just for Israel. He was coming for all peoples. That's Old Testament. What does the New Testament predict about Christ's second coming?

> ~ *Jesus Himself said:* "And this gospel of the kingdom will be preached in the whole world as a testimony to all nations, and then the end will come." (Matt. 24:14)
> ~ *John draws the curtain on the final act of earth's drama:* "After this I looked and there before me was a great multitude that no one could count, from every nation, tribe, people and language, standing before the throne and in front of the Lamb." (Rev. 7:9)

From Genesis to Revelation, the Bible is full of promises about God's plan of world evangelization. The Spirit has a global plan and He is bringing it to pass in our day as never before. In fact, more people were born into God's family in the last quarter of the twentieth century than in all the previous centuries of church history!

God's promises assure that His salvation purpose will be accomplished. Surely this major theme of Bible promises demands that in my prayer life I reach beyond those glorious promises of personal peace, protection, and provision, constantly reaching out to embrace in prayer the world God loves.

Christ's Command

We often call Christ's command to preach the gospel in all the world the "Great Commission." On how many different occasions after the resurrection do you think Christ gave what might be called a "Great Commission"? I've put that question to dozens of pastors and church leaders in workshops designed to help churches evaluate their Great Commission involvement. Astonishingly, I've never yet received a correct answer!

> ~ On the night of the resurrection, Christ appeared among the disciples in the upper room and said, "As the Father has sent Me, even so I send you" (John 20:21, RSV). With that same heart of love the Father had in sending Me, Jesus said, I'm sending you, and with that same heart of love I want you to go.
> ~ Next we meet them up north in Galilee where He announced, "All authority has been given to Me in heaven and on earth. Go therefore and make disciples of all the nations" (Matt. 28:18–19).

~ Then we find them back in Jerusalem, again in the upper room where He explains to them His intention of world evangelism, showing them from the Old Testament how "repentance and forgiveness of sins will be preached in [My] name to all nations, beginning at Jerusalem. You are witnesses of these things" (Luke 24:47–48).

~ From there, He led them out toward Mount Olivet where He was to be parted from them; they were still thinking about kingdom restoration. He told them that that wasn't their concern and that they weren't ready for what was to be their concern, and so they should wait in Jerusalem until the Holy Spirit would come on them. When that happened, He said, "you will receive power . . . and you will be my witnesses in Jerusalem, and in all Judea and Samaria, and to the ends of the earth" (Acts 1:8).

~ The most well-known "Great Commission" of all is found in Mark 16:15, but the writer doesn't give us enough context to know if it was on one of the other four occasions or on yet a fifth: "Go into all the world and preach the gospel to all creation." Four or five times He gave the command!

For a few weeks following His resurrection Christ appeared among the disciples many times and talked of many things, but there was one theme He returned to on virtually every occasion: what he wanted them to do. We call it the Great Commission. This is what was heavy on Jesus' mind. No wonder. God's character of love demands that world evangelism be central in His thinking, His activity demonstrates what His heart is like, and His promises assure us that it's going to happen. Naturally His commands require that we think the way He thinks and behave the way He behaves: Go! Go! Go! That's the mandate of the church.

So if evangelism is point number D-12 in my life—my prayers pretty self-serving, my talk mostly about earthly things, my personal involvement in missions marginal, my finances focused on time rather than eternity—do I not run the risk of finishing life and looking back, only to discover I played a game of trivial pursuit? If God's program of world evangelism seems pretty far down the list of important things in your life, why not tell Him so now and ask Him to move you up a notch or two toward likeness to Him in His passion for the lost? Surely we need to see the world more nearly through His eyes.

Chapter 39

Jerusalem, Judea, Samaria, the Uttermost Parts

When God commissioned the church as His agent for accomplishing His purpose of world evangelism, He told them to start at home—in Jerusalem. He's concerned about the lost people in your world—where you live, where you work, where you play. And if God's passion is the salvation of people and His method for reaching them is other people, surely the Spirit-given ability to win people to Christ is very important. But what does the gift look like?

The Gift of Evangelism

To help identify the gift, consider which of the following have the gift of evangelism and which are just faithful witnesses:

~ Billy Graham has preached to more people and won more to faith than anyone in history.
~ Dennis shares his faith on the job so that everyone knows he's a Christian, but none of them have come to Christ yet.
~ Denise invites her friends to her home for coffee and talk, which she tries to turn to spiritual things. On special occasions the pastor's wife comes and shares the gospel. Several have come to Christ.
~ Jeb likes to wander around the local college campus looking for lonely students who want to talk. Several have prayed with him to receive Christ.

~ Jill is on a team that calls on visitors who attended her church. Unlike some of the others, she sees someone trust Christ almost every week.

If the Spirit has given a person the gift of evangelism, we would expect to see results, right? So it would seem clear that Billy and Jill have the Spirit-given ability to win people to faith. Jeb and the pastor's wife probably do, too; but what of Dennis and Denise? If the gift of evangelism means the ability to consistently "close the deal," often leading people to acknowledge Christ as Lord and Savior, they don't seem to have the gift. They are faithful witnesses and God uses them as part of an evangelistic team, the church; but they could hardly be said to have demonstrated an ability to consistently win people to faith in Christ. Perhaps there's a difference between the calling to witness and the gift of evangelism?

My ambition was to be a pioneer church-starting missionary among those who had never heard the gospel, but I was a school teacher. So I prayed earnestly for the gift of evangelism. And I went to work, preaching on weekends and during vacation times. Sometimes many would come to Christ, sometimes no one would respond. Did you ever see Billy Graham give an invitation and no one respond? I pled with God, sometimes with tears, to give me the gift. After all, the Spirit had told me through Paul to do that: "Earnestly desire the greater gifts" (1 Cor. 12:31). My problem was, I had the wrong idea of what the gift looked like. I thought of "evangelism" as a public meeting in which the gospel is proclaimed, an invitation given, and people respond. That is evangelism, of course, but, as we have seen, it isn't the only kind. Another thing. I wasn't clearly distinguishing between witnessing and evangelism.

Witness or Evangelist?

A witness is someone who has a personal experience and talks about it. In court, if I've only heard about the crime but haven't seen it, I'm no witness. If I've seen it but won't talk, I'm no witness. In the last of the great commissions (Acts 1:8) all disciples are commissioned as witnesses—they've experienced God personally and they're supposed to tell others the good news that they can too. Every Spirit-filled Christian will be a faithful witness. Not every Spirit-filled Christian, however, is a gifted evangelist (1 Cor. 12:29).

When I agonized over not having the gift of evangelism, my definition of "evangelism" was too limited, as we've seen. Perhaps God heard my prayer, was giving me the gift, and I just wasn't smart enough to recognize it. When we got to Japan we found we could live in a community and love people in Jesus' name and many would come to faith. In a land where the average church has twenty-five members, even after decades of existence, we were baptizing twenty new converts a year. God had answered my prayer for the gift! Or had He? I rarely prayed with someone to receive Christ, and we never gave a public invitation. Then how did they come?

Body Life Reproduction: How the Church Brings to Birth

In Japan we discovered that the church as a body can bring to birth in God's family. If many members are living authentic, Spirit-filled lives and are talking about that life, and if some are gifted at "closing the deal," people will come to faith.

Those who study this sort of thing say that in the typical American community a church should be growing at five percent a year. Not through baptizing its own children, important as that is, and not through transfer growth—baptized believers coming from other churches—as exciting as that may be, but five percent "conversion growth," baptizing people who come to faith. If a church isn't baptizing new believers, something is wrong. Here are some possible reasons:

~ The church may be spiritually ill, incapable of reproducing, in need of revival (as we saw in chapter 29). Members aren't modeling an authentic Christian lifestyle that's attractive to unbelievers. Or perhaps the passion for lost people has died out; united prayer for the lost weak.

~ Not many members may be "gossiping the gospel"—too few are faithful witnesses.

~ Too few members have the gift of evangelism. Some who study this sort of thing say that in most churches which are growing through new believers coming to faith, about ten percent of the members have the gift of evangelism.

~ In some cases the people to be evangelized may be especially unresponsive. For example, a missionary to Muslims in New York City would not likely get rapid growth. The problem with acknowledging this reason for non-growth, however, is that we often use unresponsive people as an excuse. Wherever I am, if people are not being saved, I'm tempted to proclaim it to be "hard soil." Assuming that we aren't rationalizing, unusual hardness in a given community can be a cause of little fruit.

How is it at your church? Are you pleased at the "birth rate"? Do you think God is pleased? To be a little more objective in your evaluation, here's a checklist. Some items are statistical and you may not know the answer. If you think an objective evaluation is worth the effort, you could call the church office or a leader in the church to find out, or you could just make an estimate based on your own experience. Other items are subjective evaluations. We don't want to "play god" and be judgmental, of course, but as spiritual "fruit inspectors" it

Total active membership _____
How many adults were baptized last year? _____
What percent of church membership is that? _____
What percent of members live authentic Christian lives so non-Christians can tell pretty much what Jesus is like just by watching them? _____
What percent of members talk about spiritual things with non-Christians, even seeking opportunity to do so? _____
What percent of members consistently win people to faith? _____
Is there specific group prayer for the lost? _____ How often do they meet? _____
What percent of members attend such a prayer group? _____

wouldn't hurt to make a general estimate. In fact, I think it's very important to be honest in evaluating our own church life as best we can.

If you spot areas of weakness, why not lay plans with others who share your concern on how to become more effective as a church in doing what Christ commissioned us to do—reach our own "Jerusalem"?

Getting Personal

One other thing. How about you? Are you a faithful witness, letting people know what Jesus means to you? Perhaps the Spirit is nudging you to pause now and pray for each person in your life who doesn't know Christ, and especially for yourself that God will give you (1) opportunity, (2) wisdom, (3) boldness, (4) sensitivity, and (5) Holy Spirit power to reach out to them.

Do you have a growing desire to be more than a faithful witness, to have the gift of evangelism? Why not boldly ask the Spirit for that gift? Start today and keep on praying until He gives an answer, a clear-cut "yes" or "no." We've concentrated on the church as a whole in our discussion of witnessing and evangelism, but whatever the church does or doesn't do, you can be all God intended for *you* to be. Go for it!

Judea, Samaria

All are to be witnesses by Holy Spirit enabling, as we have seen, and some are gifted by the same Spirit as effective evangelists to reach their home community, their "Jerusalem." But the church also has a responsibility for the surrounding area, its "Judea." If the evangelistically-gifted person reaches out to start another congregation in a place where there's no gospel witness, Scripture calls him or her an apostle, or, literally, "one who is sent." We would probably call them home missionaries if they are in evangelistic church-starting in surrounding communities.

Paul says apostles rank number one in God's plan of salvation (1 Cor. 12:28). He isn't talking about the twelve apostles in that passage, but the gift of pioneer missionary evangelists, people like Timothy and Barnabas and others on Paul's missionary team who are called "apostles." The extension of the kingdom depends on such gifted people. No wonder Paul says, "first, apostles."

If the apostolic missionary crosses cultural barriers into another ethnic group, we might call that our church's "Samaria." Samaritans lived near those early Christians, but they were a different kind of people—a despised people, actually. The "Samaritans" or ethnically or culturally different people near us, if they don't already have the gospel, also are our responsibility. Few churches survive when their neighborhood changes ethnically. Sad. That's their God-given "Samaria"! And finally, there are the "uttermost parts" or those peoples who live out of reach of present gospel witness.

The Ends of the Earth

Every local church is responsible, not only for its own community, but also to participate fully in reaching "the ends of the earth," especially the dark half of the world where one out of two people on planet Earth live out of reach of gospel witness. But not all churches take that responsibility seriously. In fact, very few do.

Tale of Two Churches

I spoke in two church missions conferences in the same state, the same month. There were many similarities. They were both noted widely for their missions interest; in fact, one was the anchor church for the eastern end of the state, the other for the west. Both were large, vibrant, growing churches. Both had very large budgets for missions, perhaps half their total giving. "East" supported 180 missionaries, but they had 1,800 members; "West" was half the size but supported, partially at least, about 75. There the similarities ended. "East" was only thirty years old, but those 180 missionaries were all their own sons and daughters! "West" was 150 years old but only one of their own had ever gone to the mission field. And she was now retired and present in the conference. "West" paid for others' sons and daughters to go.

Where would your church fit on a continuum between "West" and "East" so far as sending your own members into missionary service?

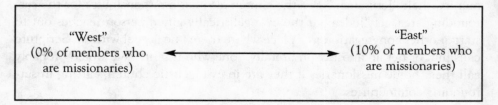

232

But the Need at Home Is So Great

It's true the need at home is great, and furthermore our first responsibility is for those nearby. It's not either/or but both/and. That's why Jesus' command was Jerusalem and Judea, yes, but also Samaria and the ends of the earth. To get a feel for the relative needs of our world, let's look at three places: The slums of Calcutta where my son Kent lives; Columbia, South Carolina, where I live; and your city or county:

	Columbia, South Carolina	Your home city	Calcutta slum dwellers
Population	300,000		5,000,000
Number of churches	600		5
Number of evangelical Christians	100,000*		1,000+-
Christian radio stations	3		0
Christian Bookstores	15		0

*This is an estimate based on the national estimate of twenty percent evangelical Christian. Columbia, South Carolina, may actually have fifty percent or more, rather than the conservative estimate here of thirty percent.

In America one out of five people you do business with or meet at PTA will be Bible-believing Christians; in Calcutta one of 10,000. And how many Bibles are in Columbia, South Carolina? A million? Calcutta may have a few hundred, and for many of the languages in that great city, none at all. I use Calcutta merely as an example of the spiritually dark half of the world where people don't have access to the gospel at all. If someone doesn't go in from the outside—if an apostolic missionary doesn't come—they cannot even hear the gospel. Yes, our first responsibility is for "Jerusalem," but God loves the world. Shouldn't we?

God's Scout

A large church contributed financial support toward seventy-five missionaries, including us. In fact, it was the second largest missions donor church in the nation, of any denomination. One day I walked down the long hallway in which the photographs of the missionaries were displayed, studying the biographies of each. To my astonishment, not one of their missionaries was from that church! They gave lots of money to support other people's sons and daughters. A young businessman noticed the same phenomenon and decided to do something about it. Calling himself "God's scout," Frank volunteered to teach the college-and-career Sunday school class. Within five years eleven members of that church were on the mission field—all from that class! God hadn't called him to go as a missionary, but Frank heard the call to send.

Perhaps God wants you to be His scout. If He did, how might you go about it? Think of the possibilities. Better yet, pray about them! Is there a boy or girl or young adult about whom you think, "That youngster would make a great missionary, so spiritually alive, gifted, and active in service to God"? If so, perhaps God would use you to help them find God's path. Here are some possible approaches:

~ Pray for that person, especially that they will hear if God is calling.
~ Talk with them about their future, their ambitions.
~ Seek for an opportunity to suggest the possibility of full-time ministry, even of missionary vocation.
~ Find a task in the church for them in which their gifts will be challenged, developed, and used.
~ Encourage them often.
~ Like Frank, teach a class in which you seek to inspire members with a clear, strong vision of God's purposes in the world and their responsibility to participate with Him in achieving that purpose.

"Here Am I, Send Me"

In the past, only young people who had not yet launched into some other vocation were considered potential candidates for missionary service. But no longer. Many missionaries today have joined the task force in mid-life, leaving other vocations. Most Americans change careers several times anyway. Perhaps God would give you the high privilege of being His ambassador to a people who have had no chance to hear the gospel.

When I was eighteen, I began to ask God for the gift of apostleship. I wanted my life to count to the maximum for what God was up to in the world, and gradually I found the same ambition Paul spoke of burning in my spirit—to proclaim Christ where He had never been named (Rom. 15:20). I entered the field of education—teaching and administration, but still the ambition burned to go. Yet there were many obstacles: I didn't think I had the gift of evangelism, I had an illness which the doctors said was incurable, others didn't think we should go because "God is blessing you where you are" (a strange logic!), we had four children (several mission boards didn't like that), and finally, after we boarded ship for Japan, my daughter was injured and we had to disembark. But we kept on obeying the command to "desire earnestly"; we kept asking God to send us and use us. I'm so glad we did, for there is surely no joy quite like living among a people who have never heard the good news and watching the Holy Spirit work in giving hope to the hopeless, healing broken lives, and forming a church where there was no witness before.

Perhaps God would give you that high privilege. At any rate, isn't the possibility worthy of a moment's reflection? If the passion burns, at least He might want to use you as a sender. Why not talk to Him about it?

Chapter 40

Prayer Power

A magnificent southern thunderstorm was entertaining me one evening. As I watched the display of cosmic fireworks from my side porch, suddenly there was a mighty explosion right in our own back yard, an extravaganza of sight and sound. Lightning had struck the transformer and in a moment we lost all light and power—for days. That was interesting because giant towers trooped through the fields just a half mile away, bearing unlimited supplies of light and power. How like many Christians—the power flows all around them, but they aren't connected.

The Source of Power

The power connect is an attitude, as we saw in chapter fifteen: yield and trust. Until we have an obedient and believing mindset or heart orientation, the deal is off because the Holy Spirit doesn't force His way on us. But if we meet that simple condition—the same faith response that connected us to Him in the first place—we are poised to let the power flow. Yet the power flow is more than an attitude; it's an activity. It's through prayer, the human conduit of divine energy, that Holy Spirit power and light flow. When it comes to world evangelism, since the Spirit acts in response to the believing prayer of an obedient people, prayer is the most important part of the missionary enterprise. As E. M. Bounds said, "Much prayer, much power; little prayer; little power, no prayer, no power."

The "How" of Prayer Warfare in the Spirit

Paul gives straightforward instruction on prayer for missions in his letter to the Colossians.

> I want you to know how much I am struggling for you and for those at Laodicea, and for all who have not met me personally. (2:1)

> Continue earnestly in prayer, being vigilant in it with thanksgiving; meanwhile praying also for us, that God would open to us a door for the word, to speak the mystery of Christ, for which I am also in chains, that I may make it manifest, as I ought to speak. (4:2–4, NKJV)

> Epaphras . . . always laboring fervently for you in prayers, that you may stand perfect and complete in all the will of God. (4:12, NKJV)

If we pray for our missionaries at all, it may be a routine mentioning to God of some brief request we've read or been given. But the kind of prayer Paul describes is so different: "struggling," "earnestly," "always laboring fervently." It sounds like a spiritual battle in prayer against unseen enemies that fight to hold captive those we aim to release. And notice that our prayer isn't to be occasional but continuing, regular—daily, at least. Furthermore, our fervent labor in prayer is not only the regular set times for prayer but in-between times. The term *vigilant* is a military term, meaning "on battle alert." We are to be sensitive to the Spirit's intimations of special need for special prayer. In Paul's parallel passage in Ephesians (6:18) he instructs us to pray "in the Spirit."

I was under arrest in central Africa, detained at the border town "airport" because my papers weren't in order. When we had landed at the dusty outpost, the officials admitted the other handful of passengers but said the pilot would have to take me with him. He refused, saying he was going on to Uganda and if he took me there I'd be in really big trouble. I would stay there at the airport, the officials seemed to have decided, until someone flew me out of the country. But what was the chance of that? The future looked bleak, especially if they ever transferred me to the local jail.

As I sat in that small room with my guard, without food or drink, I thought, "today is Thanksgiving Day at home!" I told the guard what we did on that day in the hope that when next he went for his own food he'd remember me. No such luck! What would the outcome be?

Thousands of miles away in a New Jersey nursing home, a ninety-year-old lady I had never met was strangely moved to pray earnestly for me at that very time. She was "on battle alert"; she was "in the Spirit"! The British pilot who had put me down in that tiny outpost was concerned about me, changed his plans, and late in the day returned from Uganda to whisk me away, not on the wings of a Cessna so much as on wings of prayer.

237

Most of us are quite self-centered in our prayers, using prayer to capture some of God's power, if possible, to propel our personal interests. How sad, for all along the Spirit intended to use the channel of prayer for funneling blessing to others, especially to a world yet in darkness. Spirit-filled Christians are world Christians on their knees. As we companion with the Spirit throughout each day, we begin to see the world with His eyes and He catches us up into Himself until our heart beats with His.

One more thing about how we are to pray. When Paul says "with thanksgiving," he doesn't mean merely saying "thank you" when God answers, important as that is, but rather thanking God for the answer even as we ask. In other words, faith-filled prayer. That's the powerful kind. In fact, that's the only kind that prevails in heaven.

The "What" of Prayer Warfare in the Spirit

Paul gives instruction not only on how we're to pray, but also on what we're to pray about.

Pray for the Missionary's Ministry

Paul told the Colossians to pray that doors of opportunity would open up and that the missionary team would have the ability to make the mysterious gospel understandable. That's Spirit-energized ministry, because without the Spirit's intervention, heart doors will remain closed and the gospel will sound like gibberish to those who hear. But your missionary needs not only the gifts to accomplish ministry; he or she must have the fruit of the Spirit or nothing of eternal significance will be done.

Pray for the Missionary's Spiritual Life

You can see this in Paul's instruction to believers in that same passage: "Walk in wisdom toward those who are outside, redeeming the time. Let your speech always be with grace, seasoned with salt, that you may know how you ought to answer each one" (Col. 4:5–6, NKJV).

We could hardly do better than pray those very words for our missionary.

Furthermore, Paul tells the Ephesians in a similar passage (Eph. 6:19–20) to plead with God that he might have courage. Paul, the warrior who faced beatings, stoning, prison, shipwreck (see 2 Cor. 11:23–33), asked prayer for courage? Indeed! He wrote of "fightings without and fears within." The most intrepid missionary needs prayer for faith, for courage, for all the fruit of the Spirit, because, though he may have the most glorious good news, if his life doesn't demonstrate the beauty and strength of Christ, his proclamation will be bad news, not good news.

These, then, are the themes of missionary prayer warfare: the ministry and the life. Another way to put it: pray daily for the gifts of the Spirit and the fruit of the Spirit in the life of your missionary. There's one more thing, however. We need to make it our business to find out the specific needs of the missionary.

On returning from service overseas, I had just completed my report on Japan and stood at the door of the church to greet the people when I felt a tug on my jacket. Looking around I saw a tiny retired school teacher who said, "Robertson, I know you're busy, but please don't leave until I have a chance to talk with you for a minute."

"Why, Miss Ethelyn," I responded, "I'm not busy; let's talk right now." She was one I knew prayed for me continually and fervently, one who was combat-ready and fighting my spiritual wars with me. She had first claim on my attention! We went over to a nearby stone wall, and no sooner had we sat than she began to pepper me with questions about my work. I soon realized she knew more about my work than my fellow missionaries. When she began to ask about the conference I had left in Japan just forty-eight hours earlier, I said, "Miss Ethelyn, how do you know all this stuff?"

"Why, Robertson," she remonstrated, "you're my missionary! I've been praying for you for twelve years. I ought to know *something*, shouldn't I?"

Are there missionaries about whom you could say, "He's my missionary, she's my responsibility for daily prayer warfare"? If you don't have such a prayer partnership already, perhaps it's time to link up with someone out on the frontiers, someone who faces daily hot spiritual combat. Not only do you provide "cover" for your missionary, but you become a full partner in the war—what a high privilege!

If you're not already a co-combatant, how could you get linked up? There are many ways, but primarily through your church. When missionaries visit the church, invite them home for dinner. And don't spend the time reworking the Super Bowl! Pull their story out of them, learn what their prayer needs are. Then pray! Most missionaries send out regular reports with prayer requests. Ask the missionary you choose to put you on their mailing or e-mail list. If you don't have a missionary you could call "my missionary," why not make a telephone call to the church office or write a letter right now? Get started! Because the most important part of the missionary enterprise is prayer.

Chapter 41

Measuring Maturity

$\mathscr{T}$he Holy Spirit has given, is giving, or will give you some wonderful gift, an ability to do an important job for Him (1 Cor. 12). He then wraps that gift in the package of you and gives you as His gift to the church (Eph. 4). After thinking about gifts of the Spirit (chapters 34–37), we turned to the special gift of evangelism, including evangelism-at-a-distance or missionary evangelism. "Apostles" are so important in God's program of reaching the whole world because they are the Spirit's point-men (or women), His only strategy for completing the church and saving humankind. We've seen how all must witness, some must evangelize, some of the evangelists must go to those out of reach of present gospel witness. And we've seen how the "going" will be effective to the extent there is praying. But there's one more thing, and it's another thing that's for everyone.

One of the greatest blockades on the road to victory for King Jesus is something very practical—quite earthy, really—money. And the lack of it for the missionary enterprise is a major roadblock to world evangelism. We seem to have plenty for our own needs and for the needs of our local churches, but when it comes to sending out missionaries, it dries up. In fact, only four cents on each dollar given by evangelicals in the United States is used for world missions. Ninety-six percent of giving is spent at home, on ourselves. Thousands of young adults are fully prepared and ready to go, but the money isn't there. What's the problem?

Immaturity. Spiritual immaturity in God's family is the root problem. We may be startled to discover that Jesus measures *spiritual* maturity by how we relate to material *things*. In fact, he taught far more about our relationships to possessions than He did about prayer! Apparently He considered our check stubs an accurate measure of the level of our spiritual maturity.

Isn't it amazing—plain old down-and-dirty money is God's way of tying together the fruit of the Spirit and the gifts of the Spirit, at least the gift of pioneer evangelism. Notice how He links spiritual maturity with our relationship to possessions in the book of Luke. To calibrate the levels of maturity, let's assign names we can readily identify: infancy, kindergarten, elementary, high, higher, graduate.

Infancy: Non-giving

Jesus actually begins before kindergarten, but we can hardly call infancy a level of *giving*. The infant is basically a self-centered non-giver. Recently I discovered an interesting description of that condition.

Toddler Property Laws

1. If I like it, it's mine.
2. If it's in my hand, it's mine.
3. If I can take it from you, it's mine.
4. If I had it a little while ago, it's mine.
5. If it's mine, it must never appear to be yours in any way.
6. If I'm doing or building something, all the pieces are mine.
7. If it looks just like mine, it's mine.
8. If I saw it first, it's mine.
9. If you are playing with something and you put it down, it automatically becomes mine.
10. If it's broken, it's yours. (No, the pieces are probably still mine.)

An infant is basically a non-giver. Every church has its quota of infants who are there to get, not give. A platoon of the faithful are needed to quell the squabbles, to entertain, to clean up the string of messes.

Jesus told us about this stage of non-giving: "The ground of a certain rich man produced a good crop. He thought to himself, 'What shall I do? I have no place to store my crops.' Then he said, 'This is what I'll do. I will tear down my barns and build bigger ones, and there I will store all my grain and my goods. And I'll say to myself, "You have plenty of good things laid up for many years. Take life easy; eat, drink and be merry"'" (Luke 12:16–19).

How did God respond to this reasonable plan? "Fool! Dead man! Tonight your soul will be required of you." Actually, the self-centered getter is already dead, spiritually. One of the first signs of genuine spiritual life is the desire to give.

Kindergarten: Impulse Giving

Luke introduces a kindergartner to us, one who began to get his kicks, not out of getting and saving and spending, but out of giving. The wealthy little big-time chiseler wanted to see Jesus but couldn't get at him for the thronging people. So Zacchaeus—imported brocade robe tucked up under his sash—climbed a tree to get a view of the famed itinerant preacher. As the procession passed, Jesus stopped and invited Himself to a meal with the despised head honcho of the local Roman tax unit. Was it there on the spot or later over dinner that the conversion took place? That there was a radical conversion we know because of the announcement the host then made: "I give half of my goods to the poor; and if I have taken anything from anyone by false accusation, I restore fourfold" (Luke 19:8, NKJV).

Quite a surge of generosity for an ex-getter! On impulse he risked bankrupting himself. Most genuine Christians in most churches give at the impulse level. That's why it's easier to raise funds for starving orphans in Rwanda than to raise funds for a Bible school library in neighboring Kenya. If you watch religious television, you may feel there is a new crisis every week. But you are probably mistaken. The industry standard for fundraising is twelve to fifteen crises a year. The promotion people know that most Christians most of the time give on impulse. Kindergarten.

Elementary: Legalistic Giving

When a Christian moves from sporadic, negotiable, impulse giving to giving as a way of life, he often becomes a tither. "Will a man rob God? Yet you rob me."

"How do we rob you?"

"In tithes and offerings" (Mal. 3:8). The kindergarten Christian hears that and says, "That's Old Testament legalism." Jesus, too, had problems with the legalists of His day, the Pharisees. In fact, among the terrible woes He pronounces on them is one dealing with their tithing. They were so careful to obey the law of tithing they even measured the harvest of tiny herbal seeds to give God His tenth. At the same time they were not nearly so devoted to the heavy concerns of God: justice and the love of God. "Woe to you Pharisees, because you give God a tenth of your mint, rue and all other kinds of garden herbs, but you neglect justice and the love of God" (Luke 11:42).

Surprisingly, Jesus did not tell them to stop the foolish tithing. "What you should do," he remonstrated, "is concentrate on the big ones, justice and the love of God and *don't stop the tithing*."

The tithe is affirmed by Jesus. Better to give legalistically, apparently, than not to give illegalistically! Tithing is the elementary, basic, primary level of giving, but the majority of faithful church members do not reach that level.

I'd been asked to speak on giving at a large, influential church. There was every sign of dynamic vitality, including a budget of over $3,000,000. In the 1980s, yet! A third of that was for missions, a sure sign of clear biblical priorities. After the message, the church business manager called me aside to share a bit of inside information. "We did a demographic study of our congregation," he said, "and discovered that if every member quit his or her job, went on unemployment, and began to tithe, we could double our budget!"

Tithing graduates the Christian from impulse giving at the kindergarten level to giving as a way of life: the basic, elementary level of giving.

Secondary: Honest Managership

One of the clearest passages on managership has been distorted by centuries of strange interpretations of the story Christ told about the cheating manager (Luke 16). The story is straightforward: an owner discovered that his manager was a cheat and when he announced that he was going to fire him, the shrewd fellow used his boss's assets to win friends for himself by officially canceling large portions of their debts. Jesus was making a single point: even worldlings are smart enough to use available resources to prepare for their future, so why are the "people of the light"—who should know better—so stupid? "I say to you, use your worldly wealth to win friends for yourselves, so that when money is a thing of the past you may be received into an eternal home" (Luke 16:9, NEB).

Then Jesus explained about temporal wealth and eternal wealth—the temporal is very little at best, sort of a test; the eternal is great wealth (v. 10). The temporal is fake, sort of play money; the eternal is the real thing (v. 11). And—the central concept—what you have now is not your own at all. You are just a manager of some of God's property (v. 12). It's impossible to live for both, to work for temporal and eternal payoffs, with equal fervor—you cannot serve both God and money (v. 13). The audience was having a love affair with money, so they scoffed at Jesus' teaching (v. 14). With that he told those cheating managers, those who used God's property for their own benefit, what the final payoff would be: hell (vv. 19–31).

This teaching of Christ rocked my life. As a young adult I continued my childhood pattern of tithing. God got his ten percent first. Always. I didn't feel self-righteous about it any more than I did about paying taxes. But when it became clear to me that I was not an owner at all, just the manager of the property of another, I stood convicted as an embezzler. I was avidly getting, saving, and spending 90% of God's property on myself without a qualm of conscience. I shrank from embracing managership as a way of life, fearing I would be fenced off from the good life. But when I finally gave up and accepted God's view of my possessions, the very opposite of what I feared took place. It was like the cage door swung open and I was free. My intensity about making money was gone, my grief over losses and ecstasy over gains, my apprehension about the future—they all took wings. I was at ease because the corporation of my life belonged to the Infinite One and He guaranteed my life (Luke 12:31). That's what happens when we get honest about who the owner is!

The manager looks at the King's business differently from the tither. The tither looks at his paycheck, calculates the 10 percent and asks, "Where should I invest this money?" The manager, on the other hand, looks at the needs of the business and asks, "How can I rearrange my resources to meet this great need?"

> The angels from their realms on high
> Look down on us with wondering eye
> That where we are but passing guests,
> We build such strong and solid nests;
> And where we hope to live for aye,
> We scarce take thought one stone to lay.

Jesus says, "That's dumb, really dumb. You ought to be using what little I have put under your control temporarily to build your eternal estate, not squander my possessions to build your own petty kingdom here on earth. At least be an honest manager."

Higher: Love Giving

Next we find ourselves in church with Jesus doing something your pastor has never done. If he did, that would no doubt be his last Sunday as your pastor! Jesus watched the offering plate, so to speak, and noted how much each one put in. There He discovered a very beautiful woman. Thin, with hunger-pinched features, no doubt, and shabby in appearance, but how beautiful she was! Out of a heart of love she gave everything she had. "Jesus saw the rich putting their gifts into the temple treasury. He also saw a poor widow put in two very small copper coins. 'I tell you the truth,' he said, 'this poor widow has put in more than all the others. All these people gave their gifts out of their wealth; but she out of her poverty put in all she had to live on'" (Luke 21:1–4).

As God follows the ushers down the church aisles today, how does He measure love? How calibrate the intensity of it, measure the depth of it? Jesus answers: love is measured by the sacrifice it makes.

Bob, a student at Columbia International University, asked for help with a difficult passage he had found in Luke 18. "Let me guess," I responded, "you've got problems with the story of the wealthy young aristocrat, right?"

"Yes," he responded. "Why did Jesus tell him to sell what he had and give it away?"

244

"Well," I said, "the way to life for that young man was blocked by things, his sin of covetousness. For the woman at the well it wasn't money, it was men, so Christ brought that up. Nicodemus, on the other hand, so self-righteous, needed to hear about a second birth. Jesus identified the key issue, the roadblock for each." I was quite pleased with my explanation.

"I see," said my young friend. "If his possessions were the sticking point for him, would you say there are any in America today with a similar problem?"

I wondered where Bob was headed with his line of questioning. "Yes," I chuckled a little nervously. "Just about everyone, I suppose."

"Why then," he asked, "in all my life have I never heard a sermon on the subject?"

"That's a very good question, Bob, because Christ gave exactly the same teaching, not to some wealthy aristocrat, but to anyone who wanted to be His disciple: 'Sell what you have and give alms; provide yourselves money bags which do not grow old, a treasure in the heavens that does not fail, where no thief approaches nor moth destroys'" (Luke 12:33, NKJV).

Does anyone actually do this? Some years ago I wanted to personally thank two of our graduates for their many generous gifts. When we'd have a special need, a gift of a thousand or two thousand dollars would come from this couple. I wondered how they could do this because they were school teachers in a poor district of Appalachia. One day I was in the area and called to see if a visit would be convenient. They were delighted, had something they wanted to tell me. They met me at the highway and escorted me on foot through the muddy ruts that snaked around the hillside. There, nestled in the little mountain cove was the reason they could give so generously: a small log cabin housed all their earthly possessions. Or so I thought.

The husband was so excited. He said, "Robertson, isn't the Lord good?"

"Yes," I responded, "He is. And how has He been good to you?"

"You won't believe how He's been good to me. This week has been fantastic!"

"Tell me about it," I said.

"No," he said, "you have to sit down." So we crossed the rough-hewn planks of the porch into a small living room. Log cabins are often dark because of the small windows, so I'm not sure what kind of rustic furniture he got me seated on, but when I was settled in, he told his story. "You didn't know it, but north of Atlanta, we've had a farm in the family for many years and it's begun to be a headache for us because the whole city of Atlanta has grown out all around our farm."

I said to myself, "Some problem. I wouldn't mind having that kind of problem!" He continued, "This week we were able to sign that property over to Wycliffe Bible Translators! Isn't that fantastic!"

"Yes!" I responded enthusiastically.

He continued. "That's not all. We had another small acreage out in the clay country that was not worth much and we couldn't sell it. Tried for years. Now at last—this week—we were able to sell it to a government agent who will buy it over ten years and give us $1,500 a year. So we've decided to take early retirement, go to the mission field, take care of MK's, and live on what we get from the sale of this property! What do you think about that?"

"I think you're crazy," I responded. "What are you going to do when that money runs out?"

"Oh, we'll be in heaven by then!"

Now, you probably agree that he's a little crazy. But there is one thing we don't even have to ask: whom did he love and how much did he love Him? Love is proved by the sacrifice it makes.

Love-giving graduates a person from the secondary level of honest managership to the higher level of sacrificial love-giving. Mother Theresa was being interviewed on television, and I swelled with pride, along with the young woman who was interviewing her, as Mother Theresa told us how wonderful Americans are. She said, "I don't know if there has ever been a nation that has been so giving. You are such generous people." The interviewer was visibly pleased.

Theresa continued, "Of course, you give out of your muchness." She chuckled and said, "Muchness is a word, isn't it?" She paused, then continued, "You don't really give 'til it hurts."

The young woman's eyes grew large as she looked at Mother Theresa with astonishment, "Must it hurt?"

The angel of Calcutta responded, "Love, to be genuine, must hurt." She understood: love is proved by the sacrifice it makes.

Graduate: Faith Giving

Paul speaks of the gift of faith (Rom. 12:3–8). It seems there are those George Muellers of the world who trust God for miracle provision—finances far above that which could be provided even by sacrificial giving. George Mueller cared for thousands of orphans on God's daily miracle provision. In fact, his faith stretched beyond caring for the orphans as he was able to give millions to foreign missionary work around the world. That's faith giving! I call this the "graduate level" of giving because this gift of faith is not given to all equally.

But there's another sense in which faith must validate any level of giving for God to be pleased. "Without faith it is impossible to please God" (Heb. 11:6). The Pharisees were not the only ones who had problems with Jesus' radical teaching about managership and sacrificial living. The disciples did too. Jesus' teaching cut across the grain of everything they believed about money and things. So He said, "If then God so clothes the grass, which today is in the field and tomorrow is thrown into the oven, how much more will He clothe you, O you of little faith" (Luke 12:28, NKJV).

Indeed, faith must validate every level of giving whether the legalistic minimum, honest managership, or sacrificial love giving. For example, the impoverished widow living on social security must have faith to give ten percent. Furthermore, when she does so, it is certainly sacrificial love. So love also must validate every level of giving. My relationship to my possessions is, according to Jesus Christ, a clear indication of my faith and love, my level of spiritual maturity.

Those levels, then, are not always clear-cut. But they are clear enough for me to evaluate my own life. I know the painful—then liberating—move I made from tithing to managership. And I know very well, as I see the abject poverty of the world that I don't live a sacrificial lifestyle. I have spurts of sacrifice, maybe, but I am far from Jesus' model of giving. How about you? Honesty about our finances may be the hardest honesty of all. As you review your giving for the past year, checking your records if you aren't sure, at what level of giving have you been? Are you pleased with that level? Is God pleased? What kind of lover does that show you to be? What kind of truster?

God's standard for giving is one He Himself models. He created me, so He is owner. I stole His property—took possession of myself. But in love He purchased me at terrible cost, just as if He had no claim on me, making me twice His. If I will only respond with love in obedient giving, He guarantees my livelihood (Luke 12:31), rewards me lavishly in this life as if I were giving what is my own property, and in heaven He rewards me all over again (Luke 18:28–30). That's God's level of giving, love giving.

In response to such love are you ready to move up one step? If you've never been a faithful tither, isn't it time to promise Him that ten percent? Trust Him! He'll take care of you. Perhaps you've been a tither for years, but you did pretty much what you pleased with the other ninety percent. Isn't it time to stop that foolishness and become an honest manager of the property of Another? Whatever level of maturity you've achieved in your walk with God, don't you want to step up? If I'm unwilling to move up from my present level of maturity, it may be because I don't trust God to meet my needs, a lack of faith—or love. If because of your love for Jesus, you're ready to take that leap of faith to the next level, tell Him so. Now.

We've listened to Jesus' teaching about giving at this point in our study because lack of giving is a major obstacle to world evangelism, the main theme of these chapters. But it's a marvelous place to close our Spirit-gifts section because our relationship to things is an objective way of measuring our spiritual maturity. And that's the theme of our whole study of life in the Spirit. Anyone can evaluate your spiritual maturity if you'll let them see your check stubs, Jesus seems to say. So giving ties together the fruit of the Spirit with the greatest of all gifts of the Spirit—evangelism. And because the key to our response about money is love, this study sets the stage for our final chapters, the goal of life: loving oneness with God.

Activity Ten

Glorifying

Chapter 42

A Marriage Made in Heaven

*C*hapel seating was assigned, but I didn't mind. That meant the girl I most wanted to be near was seated right in front of me every day! When she ran those lovely fingers, immaculately manicured, through her thick, chestnut-colored hair, it drove me crazy. Finally I got up enough courage to ask Muriel for a date. I was intoxicated with her infectious laughter, cute face, delightful creativity, deep love for God, and caring ways with people. And she was so much fun. Friendship soon blossomed into love and we talked of marriage. Would it be a marriage made in heaven?

By the time we were engaged, my mind was so consumed with Muriel I wonder if I was worth the gunpowder it would take to blow out my brains. The wedding came, agonizingly slow, and then the ecstatic honeymoon for two innocents in Estes Park, Colorado. Could love ever be more intimate, more satisfying? We had a lot to learn.

Children bond a couple closer, but they also can test the bonds; and though it doesn't always happen that way, love deepened with every shared pain, heightened with every shared joy. Our hearts got so intertwined they seemed like one. Even now at the end of the road, when Muriel's mind barely functions at the borders of consciousness, deep into Alzheimer's, the love grows. I like to think it's been a marriage made in heaven.

There's one marriage, however, I *know* was made in heaven. Did you ever wonder that the chief image of human relationship to God in the Old Testament was of Israel as the wife of God, and a chief image in the New

Testament is of the church as the bride of Christ? There's a marriage made in heaven!

But which is the real, which the reflection? Did the Holy Spirit take the human condition of marriage and draw an analogy with God's relationship to people so we could understand the unseen world better? Or was it the other way around—the plan for a relationship so intimate between God and His beloved required a temporary earthly model for us to understand the ultimate, eternal relationship He intended us to have with Him? If so, it means God made humans on a dual model, man and wife, to show us what His grand plan for union with Him was to be. Either way, that intimate identity with God in love is truly a marriage made in heaven! This incredible revelation of what God intended from the start is the theme of our final activity of the Spirit.

That's what God had in mind from the beginning, but theologians have come up with a variety of answers to the question of what the chief end of a human being rightly is. What would you say is our ultimate goal? Christlikeness? To glorify God? To become holy? To love God? To worship God? To experience loving oneness with God? Let's look at those possibilities and see how they interrelate.

Christlikeness

That's a likely choice since *Life in the Spirit* has been a study of spiraling up into ever greater likeness to Christ. And on reflection, it's clear that Jesus embodies all of the other suggested goals, so you could well choose "to be like Christ" as the comprehensive goal of human creation and redemption. If we were like Christ in all those ways, we would certainly fulfill everything God purposed in our creation and redemption.

But there can be a problem with that answer if we limit the definition of Christlikeness to only part of likeness to Him, and that wouldn't be His ultimate goal for us. We usually limit the idea of "Christlikeness" to having attitudes and behavior like Christ. Something like a synonym for holiness.

Holiness

Holiness is important because without it no one will see God (Heb. 12:14). But it's a limited goal. Most people think of holiness—set-apartness, as the word means literally—as growing away from sinful attitudes and actions. That is surely one purpose God has for us, though hardly the ultimate goal. And there's another problem with making holiness the primary goal. Some hold that striving for holiness can become self-oriented and tend toward legalism. The goal, they insist, should be *God*-oriented, not inward-oriented. No, they contend, the glory of God alone is our ultimate goal.

Glory of God

Focusing on God is certainly biblical and surely all we do should aim at His glory (1 Cor. 10:31), not our own. There's a problem with making the glory of God our ultimate goal, however. Like "Christlikeness" it isn't very specific—it includes everything. So we're left with the task of spelling out in detail how best we can glorify Him. Because glorifying God is quite general, some choose one special way we can do it and make that the goal of life: worship.

Worship

This is certainly exclusively God-oriented and indeed our whole lives should be a worship, demonstrating his worth—"worth-ship," as the word originally meant—putting His worth on display, not our own. But one problem with making either glorifying God or worshiping Him the ultimate goal is the question of why a God of love would be so self-centered as to demand those responses as the whole purpose of making and saving us.

Five-year-old Kent was trying hard to get our guests to notice him and his excellencies. "Oh, Kent, quit showing off," I said. He devoted some deep thought to the subject, apparently, and early the next morning had developed his response: "Daddy, why does God want us to brag on Him?"

We have to be careful to understand what we mean, then, when we speak of God creating us to worship and glorify Him.

~ It's not so much that God desires glory and worship in order for Him to feel fulfilled as it is that God knows we can be fulfilled only as we relate to Him as the glorious God He is. He desires that we conform to the reality of who He is for our own good, because God is love.

~ It's not that God likes to take all the credit so He can feel important, but that He knows we'll destroy ourselves if we take credit for what He does. It's self-destructive to get out of alignment with reality, and that happens when I allow myself to usurp any honor that belongs to God alone. So God wants us to get our lives lined up with reality, recognizing who He is and behaving that way.

~ It's true that our God is a jealous God, but He's not hesitant to see others honored as well. In fact, He constantly honors others. The Bible does speak often, however, of God as a jealous lover—it hurts Him when we love others more than Him, His is the hot jealousy of a husband who puts up with no rival to the affections of His wife. "The affections of His wife"—perhaps we get a clue of what God is after by considering the fundamental command of both the Old Testament and the New.

252

A Marriage Made in Heaven

Loving God

When God came in person to reveal His purpose for humankind, He said, "'Love the Lord your God with all your heart and with all your soul and with all your mind.' This is the first and greatest commandment" (Matt. 22:37–38). "First" and "greatest"—that should make clear what God is after. Jesus quoted this commandment from the foundational revelation of God's will in the Old Testament, what the Jews called the *Shema* (Deut. 6:5) and then explained its importance. Everything else, He said—everything taught in the Bible, "the Law and the Prophets"—hangs on this command, along with the command to love one's neighbor (Matt 22:40). So perhaps we'd be safe to make loving God our chief end. Except for one thing. Love, by definition, is mutual. It's not so much that we love Him, but that He loves us (1 John 4:10). So we must search for a more complete statement of God's ultimate purpose for us.

Loving Oneness with God

As we saw in chapter 38, God is love in His very nature (1 John 4:8, 16), so from all eternity the Father, Son, and Spirit were bound together in bonds of living love. And from the overflow of that love He designed a creature to love Him back. Loving oneness with Himself was His purpose all along. That's why He calls His relationship to us a marriage! When a man "knew" a woman in Bible times, it meant they became one in intimate identity. That's why we say the goal of life is knowing God—an identity so close it could be likened to marriage. Closer than that—it could be likened to the unity the Father and Son have with one another. So now we see that being like Christ really is the ultimate goal! Being like Him not only in character but also in relationship.

> My prayer is not for them alone. I pray also for those who will believe in me through their message, that all of them may be one, Father, just as you are in me and I am in you. May they also be in us so that the world may believe that you have sent me. I have given them the glory that you gave me, that they may be one as we are one: I in them and you in me. May they be brought to complete unity to let the world know that you sent me and have loved them even as you have loved me.
>
> Father, I want those you have given me to be with me where I am, and to see my glory, the glory you have given me because you loved me before the creation of the world.
>
> Righteous Father, though the world does not know you, I know you, and they know you have sent me. I have made you known to them, and will continue to make you known in order that the love you have for me may be in them and that I myself may be in them. (John 17:20–26)

Astounding! So intimate, so exclusive, so permanent is the love relationship He planned for us that the only way to exhaust its meaning is to say it's like the

Father's love for the Son and the Son's love for the Father! That goal is the reason the two of them made the greatest of all sacrifices—"He died for us so that we, alive or dead, might live in union with Him" (1 Thess. 5:10, author's paraphrase).

Perhaps you've always read that prayer of Christ as pleading for unity among believers. Read those incredible words again. You may find in His prayer such an undercurrent, the by-product of the main theme. But His central request, the evidence that will convince the world, is clearly the miracle union of God with us, oneness with the Father, the Son, and the Holy Spirit. That loving identity of life was what God was after from the beginning—His purpose in creating us in His likeness, His purpose in redeeming us from our wayward alienation from Him. It's beyond comprehension. It's like trying to explain to a five-year-old the glories of married love. He doesn't have a clue. So it is with us. But it's not just here and now.

If the unbeliever can't understand what a glorious thing it is to be united with Christ, no more can we understand ahead of time the ecstasies of union with Christ in heaven following the "marriage supper of the Lamb." We just don't have the capacity to understand a whole new dimension of human-divine relationship. We haven't grown up to it yet, we've not undergone the final transformation into God-compatible beings. But one day we will experience God in all His fullness, and that's what He's been after all along. Now that's a marriage made in heaven!

By the lives we live (holiness) and the words we speak (worship) our purpose (loving God) is to shine the spotlight on God's glorious person. That's to glorify God! But all of this is aimed toward restoring the original relationship, loving union with God. If the totality of who Christ is, both His character and His relationship with the Father, is what we have in mind, then the comprehensive, ultimate goal is to be like Him, Christlikeness.

Did you notice how difficult it is to separate these objectives and put them in some order? Your order differs from mine, no doubt, and mine will probably change tomorrow. They are so interactive, so interdependent! Whatever your order, isn't it glorious? Why, it's like a marriage, a marriage made in heaven! To reach that goal is the reason we've been studying the activities of the Spirit: "We know that we live in him and he in us, because he has given us of his Spirit" (1 John 4:13). Don't you feel the urge to pause now and thank God for all I those glorious purposes He has in mind for you?

Chapter 43

All Glory, Worship, and Honor

Loving oneness with God has two sides to it, of course: God's love for you and your love for Him. In this chapter we'll think about your love for Him. Focusing on the loved one is the true evidence of love, but it's not just proof of where your heart is. Focusing your attention on God is also how you express your love for God, and how you can grow in it too. To glorify and worship God, then, is an essential

- ~ evidence of love,
- ~ expression of love,
- ~ means to deepen love.

Glorifying God, worshiping, and honoring Him overlap, but there is a slightly different emphasis. When we honor and glorify God, the focus is on how we show Him off to others; worship, on the other hand, is directed wholly to Him.

Glorifying God

Here are some of the ways we can put the spotlight on God, honor Him, and cause others to see His majesty, beauty, wisdom, power, holiness, love, justice, and truth:

- ~ Living a life that authentically reflects His character
- ~ Praising Him to others in conversation and song
- ~ Winning others to faith so more people will honor Him
- ~ Always giving Him credit for the good that happens and
- ~ Defending Him against false accusation

The list goes on, but those are some important ways to put God's glories on display. It doesn't always have to be a "major production," however. Once in a while my lot is thrown with a person who is forever praising God for the most insignificant things—"The Lord got me a parking place just when I needed it" or "I was late to my appointment and the Lord gave me all green lights." I often have such experiences, but I rarely talk about it. Their hearts, however, are so full of gratitude it's forever just bubbling over. That's what it means to glorify God.

Worshiping God

For many genuine Christians there isn't much true worship in a "worship service," and there isn't much warm devotion in their "devotional time." Yet God longs for those who will worship Him "in spirit and in truth" (John 4:23). What is true, in-the-Spirit worship?

Prostration

In both Old Testament Hebrew and New Testament Greek the word *worship* originally meant to prostrate one's self before someone or something. It could be to a god or an important person. Originally the idea of kissing was included—kissing either the ground or the feet of the object of worship. I experienced that once.

In a dusty desert region of Tanzania we had to travel miles to a lonely outpost to call home. Waiting my turn at the telephone, I was startled when a young man—a total stranger—came up to me, fell to his knees and began kissing my feet. I tried to push him away but the missionary who brought me there cautioned me, "It's just his way of showing respect. Let him do it!"

When Israelites used the term translated "worship," the kissing part disappeared—their God was invisible! And they prayed in many positions—standing, kneeling, lying in bed, sitting. Still, when deeply moved, they prostrated themselves. What do you think of pictures of Muslims at prayer, bowing to the ground en masse? Maybe they're on to something we're missing. The chief word in the Old Testament for a right relationship to God is not "love" or even "faith." It's fear! In our democratic way of viewing life, we've left royalty far behind. We like to think of the "man upstairs," the lover of our souls, the friend. And how blessedly true that He's our friend, our lover. But we may be in danger of losing the sense of imperial majesty, the grandeur, the awe, the unapproachable holiness of our God.

I had prayed in all the "biblical" positions for prayer except one: prostration. Asked to speak on "The Holy Spirit and Worship," I studied the idea of worship in Scripture. As I worked through all the biblical data on the subject, the thought occurred to me, why don't you prostrate yourself before His Majesty? I didn't want to—it didn't fit my culture. Besides, my floors aren't carpeted! After a day or two of resistance, I finally said, "Well, it's no big deal. Give it a try." I was surprised at the outcome—a sense of humble awe swept over me. That's to worship in its original sense. To acknowledge Him for who He is— that's to give Him the glory He deserves.

Worth-ship

Since prostration was a way of showing honor and the highest honor was reserved for their God, Jewish people gradually began to include the inner spirit of that outward form—the fealty, the adoration. So when the first English translators looked for the right word to translate the Bible term of prostration, they came up with "worth-ship" because bowing down is what they did before people of worth. In time, the term gradually came to mean not only the praise and adoration of one's heart, but all the outward evidences in religious symbols, rituals, activities. "Worship," it was called.

One of those worship activities in the Christian church is music, so gradually, in twentieth-century America, "worship" came to mean praise and adoration in song. We no longer speak of a "song leader" but of a "worship leader" and we mean music. Maybe that's OK because Paul instructs us to use psalms and hymns and spiritual songs—all varieties of praise—in public worship. But, he adds, be sure it's from the heart: "singing and making melody in your heart to the Lord" (Eph. 5:19, NKJV). Where does that true worship come from? It's the direct result of being continuously filled with the Spirit, Paul teaches (v. 18). How important music is to true worship!

But music is only one way to proclaim God's worth. Actually the most important and most pervasive worship is to make God's worthy character visible in a daily life that is worthy of Him. Living in the Spirit will demonstrate who God is. People can see God's glorious attributes on display in the Spirit-filled Christian through attitudes, words, and actions that remind people of Jesus. That's to worship! But usually when we think of worship, we think of singing.

Worship in Song

Psalms of praise. There's one sure way to use words in praise that will please God—His words! To pray to Him the very words of Scripture is to guarantee a good reception, and if the words are worship-words, that's to worship in truth. It must be important, for the Spirit gave us a whole book of praise and worship, the Psalms. For example,

> Praise the LORD, O my soul;
> all my inmost being, praise his holy name.
> Praise the LORD, O my soul,
> and forget not all his benefits—

who forgives all your sins
and heals all your diseases,
who redeems your life from the pit
and crowns you with love and compassion,
who satisfies your desires with good things
so that your youth is renewed like the eagle's.
The LORD works righteousness
and justice for all the oppressed.
The LORD is compassionate and gracious,
slow to anger, abounding in love.
     (Psalm 103:1–6, 8)

Hymns of praise. But Psalms is not the only hymn book. A close second is found in an unlikely place—at the end of the New Testament. John was overwhelmed with dreadful visions of future doom, but he constantly bursts into praise. In the book of Revelation he reveals some of the worship that will one day be offered to God on high. As he lets us in on that celestial worship, he's inviting us to join him in adoration as a preview of the glorious worship in which we will one day participate. Let's join him in that worship now:

Holy, holy, holy
is the Lord God Almighty
who was, and is, and is to come.

You are worthy, our Lord and God,
to receive glory and honor and power,
for you created all things,
   and by your will they were created
and have their being.
     (Rev. 4:8, 11)

Worthy is the Lamb, who was slain,
to receive power and wealth and wisdom and strength
   and honor and glory and praise!
To him who sits on the throne and to the Lamb
be praise and honor and glory and power, for ever and ever!
     (Rev. 5:12–13)

Amen!
Praise and glory
and wisdom and thanks and honor
   and power and strength
be to our God for ever and ever.
Amen!
     (Rev. 7:12)

Great and marvelous are your deeds,
   Lord God Almighty.
Just and true are your ways,'
King of the ages.
Who will not fear you, O Lord,
   and bring glory to your name?
For you alone are holy.
All nations will come
   and worship before you,
for your righteous acts have been revealed.
   (Rev. 15:3–4)

KING OF KINGS AND LORD OF LORDS
   (Rev. 19:16)

If you have a recording of the "Hallelujah Chorus" in *The Messiah*, this might be a great time to listen to it again. And sing along!

Perhaps, because of the pressures or griefs in your life or because of foreboding about an ominous future, you do not feel like joining John in such worship. Your heart is just too heavy to sing joyfully. How could John be so exuberant in his praise when throughout the book he so incessantly tolls the solemn gong of doom? The secret is found at the beginning of his book: "On the Lord's Day I was in the Spirit, and I heard behind me a loud voice like a trumpet" (Rev. 1:10). "After this I looked, and there before me was a door standing open in heaven. And the voice I had first heard speaking to me like a trumpet said, 'Come up here, and I will show you what must take place after this.' At once I was in the Spirit" (Rev. 4:1–2).

John the Seer was "in the Spirit" and to be in the Spirit, no matter how threatening the circumstances, is to overflow with praise and worship to the mighty Victor. By the Spirit we can worship always. In fact, if we're filled with the Spirit that's exactly what we'll do! Remember, the heavy heart lifts on the wings of praise.

Songs of praise. Of course, words of Scripture aren't the only way to worship. Your hymnal is filled with songs of praise and adoration. And church isn't the only place to sing God's praise!

To God Be the Glory
To God be the glory, great things he hath done;
So loved he the world that he gave us his Son,
Who yielded his life an atonement for sin,
And opened the life-gate that all may go in.

Chorus:
Praise the Lord, praise the Lord, Let the earth hear his voice!
Praise the Lord, praise the Lord, Let the people rejoice!
O come to the Father, thro' Jesus the Son,
And give him the glory, great things he hath done!

Great things he hath taught us, great things he hath done,
And great our rejoicing through Jesus the Son;
But purer, and higher, and greater will be
Our wonder, our vict'ry when Jesus we see.
(*Chorus*)

Some people don't sing much. Perhaps they don't feel they have any musical talent or perhaps there isn't a song inside to bubble out. I don't know what they'll do in heaven. The beauty is this. If we let the Holy Spirit have His freedom, He can introduce the life of heaven to our drab existence through our singing—off-key is OK—as we let loose with praise to our God in the shower, in the car as we drive along, in the kitchen as we wash the dishes. Or right now.

Worship in your own words. Now that others have inspired you with their expressions of worship, we're ready to worship Him in our own words. Perhaps you'd like to write out in your spiritual life journal a prayer of worship. If you're courageous, try putting it into verse—a hymn of worship! If you did that, you might write three stanzas:

1. First, tell God everything about His person you admire—His marvelous characteristics. That's worship.
2. Next, review the major activities of God since the start of time, His works of creation and redemption, and praise Him for each of those activities you admire or are especially grateful for. That's praise.
3. Finally, thank God for everything He has done for you personally. Be sure to include some of the ordinary earthly blessings as well as the spiritual. That's thanksgiving.

Isn't He wonderful! To love God is to worship and adore Him and to tell others incessantly about His greatness. Even if worship has not been a major activity until now, may today mark a new beginning of a life filled more and more with worship of the God who is worthy of all glory, honor, and praise!

Chapter 44

Best Friends

I'm sure every one of the disciples would have said, "Jesus is my best friend." They walked the village streets and dusty country roads together and they listened intently as He talked—"no one ever spoke like this man." But they didn't just listen—they talked too, and without inhibition. Such an intimate companionship! Do you ever wish you could have been there?

Jesus anticipated our loneliness, what it would be like not to have His companionship; so He promised to send another Comforter who would not just walk with us but who would actually be in us forever, even the blessed Spirit (John 14:15–21). "I've loved you with an everlasting love," He said, "I won't leave you as orphans."

Love, then, is more than my love for God expressed in worship and praise. Much more. It's His love for me! I was on my knees, weeding the front lawn, when a friendly stranger paused to chat, a bricklayer on his day off. I could soon tell he was a believer, so I said, "I think you love the Lord."

"Oh, I does. I truly does," he said. He paused, then continued, "But that ain't important. What's important is—He love *me*!" And off he walked down the sidewalk, his calloused hand in the pierced hand of his true Lover. As in marriage, love is the bridge that must reach out from both sides if ever there is to be a union.

Levels of Intimacy

The octogenarians across the dinner table were puzzled. All their lives they'd been reaching out, winning people to faith. But, they now agreed, the younger

261

generation had them baffled. I told them several things I'd heard or read, then mentioned what my son-in-law, very gifted in reaching youth, had told me. "Terry says they want intimacy."

"Intimacy. Now what do they mean by that?" the three old ladies said in unison. I hadn't thought of definitions, but I had to make a stab at it. "Well, I guess they mean a relationship that's open, vulnerable, trusting, sharing . . ."

What does the word mean to you? Consider the levels of intimacy in a human relationship:

1. Muriel and I met and liked one another. We'd get together occasionally and talk about things of mutual interest.
2. Then love began to suffuse the relationship, so each of us began to move out of our comfort zones. Muriel tried to figure out football and I dragged myself to art museums. But there were certain topics we didn't touch.
3. Eventually we reached the stage of mutual trust and agreed that nothing is off-limits—we'd fully share our hearts. No secrets.
4. Then we were married and intimacy was complete. Or was it? We hadn't been together long enough to have pain. But we did enjoy one another's companionship and moments of exquisite delight.
5. We hit the hard times and ran to embrace one another in shared agony.
6. Finally it came to the place where fun wasn't all that fun if Muriel wasn't with me; heartache was almost unbearable if she didn't share it. It was as if the other was there even when they weren't and when we were apart, the desire to be together became a gnawing hunger. There was freedom and comfort between us that outsiders couldn't disturb.

What level of human relationship parallels most closely your present experience of God? Actually, there's a seventh level, a closer intimacy than Robertson and Muriel could ever experience because they're finite humans. Such a level of intimacy can be experienced, though—with God, as we shall see. Let's explore three levels of union with God.

Intimacy with God

Basic Friendship

Josh was furious about his Christmas gift. It wouldn't work right. Suddenly, he threw it across the room where it crashed through a valued lamp shade. In the following months, Josh tried, with varying degrees of success, to bridle his temper. Ours was an unlikely friendship. He was only three, and our conversations didn't rise to great heights. When we went to the amusement park, Josh refused the tame rides and I got ill on his favorites. When we returned from the circus, he announced to his embarrassed mother that the best act was "the elephant poop."

Josh taught me something about God and me. Now there's an unlikely friendship! I certainly can't converse on His level. Sometimes I may get angry with a gift God gives me, say a bad thing, do a foolish thing, enjoy an ugly thing. Maybe you do too.

Now consider this: still He loves you! Against the backdrop of this lopsided love affair, Jesus calls us friends (John 15:15)—not slaves or even children, both of which we are—but friends! Josh has been my friend now for several years. He's especially hard to resist when a smile breaks across that pixie face as he offers a gift of atonement, some well-loved toy, hugs me tight, and says, "Sorry, Pawpaw." Josh moved to a distant city and entered first grade. A few weeks later I received a letter, the first from my buddy: "I Luv Yoo Yoo Are The Bes Fred I everhad."

It's so good to be best friends with God! But there's a level of intimacy deeper than basic friendship.

Daily Companionship

My youngest son, Kent, has always had a prayer life I envied—from high school days on. But I wasn't prepared to discover what I did when he recently came to stay with me for six weeks. I hadn't finished cleaning the guest room when he arrived, so when he went out for an errand I finished up. As I picked up a scrap of paper from the floor I noticed a cryptic message: "Get up at 3 A.M. every day and stay awake." Sure enough, every morning at three the light in the kitchen would go on and stay on. It was good for me to know what was happening; that way I wouldn't intrude on Kent's time with his beloved.

Jesus is his beloved. In reporting on his work among the slum dwellers of Calcutta to the students and faculty of Columbia International University, he reminisced about his student days. He told of how he decided not to get married, as Paul had taught (1 Cor. 7), so he could serve God more fully. Then he said, "I was walking down the campus road toward the dining hall when I was met by a parade of dating couples, out for an evening stroll. They seemed so happy. Then the thought struck me, 'They can't even imagine what a great time God and I are having.'"

Later I was talking with him about his prayer life and how, in my judgment, he was jeopardizing his health with all this fasting and prayer. He seems so God-intoxicated. "Dad," he said, "I think I have more fun with God than you do!" I'm afraid he does.

Constant Awareness of His Presence

At age twenty I discovered the motto of Frederic Franson, the pioneer who founded five Scandinavian mission agencies at the close of the nineteenth century. Franson's life theme was CCCC: Constant Conscious Communion with

Christ. The moment I heard it, my heart leaped. "That's what I want, Lord!" I cried out. And God heard my prayer. For about two months that summer I was not only always conscious of the Lord's presence; I seemed to be constantly, consciously conversing with God. But then it slipped away. I pled for the return of that experience, but it never came back. I'm not sure why He gave me that foretaste of heaven nor why He withdrew it. Was it something like Paul's brief visit to "the third heaven," not intended to be permanent, not designed for daily human experience? Yet the mystics down the ages testify of a life pattern of constant conscious communion with Christ. Perhaps God would give you that high level of intimacy if you sought it; don't let my experience deflect you.

In the meantime, until that day when we all have such a life-suffusing experience in His presence, I can promise something very special: a constant relationship of intimacy, an uninterrupted awareness of the Spirit's presence. As we mentioned earlier, it's much like a child, preoccupied with her toys and games, nevertheless fully aware of her mother's presence. She knows when her mother is in the room, enters freely in and out of conversation, and rests in that abiding relationship.

What is your level of intimacy with God today? Basic friendship? A special time of intimate companionship every day? Constant awareness of His presence? Don't settle for "a superficial relationship with a friendly stranger," as someone has described it. Don't be afraid of intimacy. He won't reject you because you don't measure up. No one measures up. He loves you and longs for your companionship. Run and embrace Him—He's waiting, eagerly.

Chapter 45

Celebrate!

*W*e've considered several levels of intimacy, but the highest and best lies ahead. That will be the grand climax, all the Spirit's work in us consummated as we find ourselves in a condition that reaches far beyond our most untamed imagination: "filled to all the fullness of God!" What a celebration! That too will be the Spirit's work.

The Spirit's Last Great Activity

> If the Spirit of him who raised Jesus from the dead is living in you, he who raised Christ from the dead will also give life to your mortal bodies through his Spirit, who lives in you. (Rom. 8:11)

Here's a beautiful story of that occasion:

> Then I heard what sounded like a great multitude, like the roar of rushing waters and like loud peals of thunder, shouting:
> "Hallelujah!
> For our Lord God
>   Almighty reigns.
> Let us rejoice and be glad
>   and give him glory!
> For the wedding of the
>   Lamb has come,
>   and his bride has made
>   herself ready.

Fine linen, bright and clean,
    was given her to wear."

(Fine linen stands for the righteous acts of the saints.)

Then the angel said to me, "Write: 'Blessed are those who are invited to the wedding supper of the Lamb!'" And he added, "These are the true words of God." (Rev. 19:6–9)

The Spirit and the bride say, "Come!" (Rev. 22:17)

What a Day That Will Be!

In a sense we're already married to God, united with Him forever. But in another sense, the consummation of that marriage is yet to be. You might call our present relationship an engagement and the Holy Spirit our engagement ring. "God . . . set his seal of ownership on us, and put his Spirit in our hearts as a deposit, guaranteeing what is to come" (2 Cor. 1:21–22; see also 5:5 and Eph. 1:14). Exciting as the engagement has been, how our present experience of God will fade into the dim recesses of memory when the marriage is consummated! The climax of all the Spirit's work is to usher us into the banquet hall to introduce us to our beloved where we shall meet Him "face to face" (1 Cor. 13:12). And the Spirit's work will be complete when "we shall be like him, for we shall see him as he is" (1 John 3:2).

Many of God's promises about eternity will be fulfilled when we die and are instantly with Him. Others will be fulfilled when the bride, the church, is completed and Jesus returns to take her to the grand celebration. Since the Bible doesn't explain all the delightful mystery of it, I'm not sure exactly what will happen when; they all sort of merge in my thinking. But whenever He completes it—what a glorious anticipation! As I think about eternity, here are some of the things I look forward to:

~ Jesus—Seeing Him, feeling His warm embrace, being united with Him in a union so intimate I don't have the capacity now even to imagine.

~ The Father—Seeing Him smile and hearing His commendation, "Well done." I want to tell Him how grateful I am for His love for me, so great He let go His own Son for me. In fact, for the first time I'll be able to worship Him as I've always longed to but never seemed able.

~ The Spirit—I want to tell Him how deeply I appreciate all He's done for me. In detail!

~ Being reunited with my son, Bob, my parents, and other loved ones who got there before me, and, especially, my precious Muriel fully restored.

Celebrate!

- ∽ All sorrow, pain, sickness, weakness, sin, failure gone forever.
- ∽ Jesus' smile when I give Him my wedding present—my life investment for Him.
- ∽ Being transformed into the likeness of Jesus, the spiral complete.

Do you resonate with any of those hopes? What do you most look forward to? What a celebration that will be!

But maybe you don't look forward to the approach of the grim reaper, or even the second coming of Christ. Not everyone does.

Not Everyone Wants to Die

One of my best friends, John, was dying an agonizing death of bone cancer. When I visited him in his home he said, "Robertson, you're so spiritual you probably want to go to heaven. But I don't. I've got too many things to do for God right here on earth." He declined rapidly and soon I heard he had made his final trip to the hospital. I flew into town, rushed to the hospital and found his room. I no sooner entered the door when John said, "Robertson, I've got something to tell you about death. It takes too long." I reached his bedside and groped for words of comfort, but he continued: "You've probably got it all worked out theologically, but I can't figure out the purpose of all this pain and suffering."

"No, John," I responded, "I haven't got it figured out. But I do notice one thing it's done for you. A few weeks ago you didn't want to go to be with Jesus. Now you can hardly wait."

John grimaced. "You're right, pal." A few hours later he had his desire.

As you think about death or, better, about that grand celebration at the end of time, how do you feel about it? Here are some possibilities:

- ∽ I'm with John. I'm happy to contemplate that last great day and glad I'll be there, but I'm in no hurry; I've got too much important and fun to do right here. I want to stay around as long as I can. I just hope God doesn't send me a messenger of pain like John's to change my mind!
- ∽ I'm with Paul. I'm so excited I can hardly wait to be with Jesus. It's like my wedding day.
- ∽ I'm more than a little apprehensive about that day; I'm afraid my wedding gift to Jesus won't amount to much.
- ∽ I dread the day. What an embarrassment I'll be to Jesus and to myself.
- ∽ I wish it would go away; I'm not even sure I'll be there.

If you think the Spirit would be pleased if you felt differently from what you now feel about that day of consummation, what's gone wrong? We began our walk with the Spirit in eternity where He designed us to be God-compatible, and we've kept "in step with the Spirit" (Gal. 5:25) through His work of transforming us, a spiral up from one degree of Christ's glorious likeness to another. We're headed toward the grand finale when the Spirit will complete His work. But somewhere we must have gotten out of step because we don't rejoice with the Bridegroom in anticipating that glorious wedding day. If that's your situation, don't you want to get back in step with the Spirit?

Getting Back in Step

To get back in step, perhaps it would help to turn back to the table of contents and see if you can identify the work of the Spirit you've missed out on. If you find a possible missing step, or perhaps a bit of a stumble in your spiritual pilgrimage, why not read that section again and see if the Spirit is drawing you to do something about it now in preparation for your wedding day? If He is, do it now!

Does it bother you when I say things like that? At the end of some of our chapters I've given a gentle nudge to action because I'm convinced that simply studying about life in the Spirit without experiencing it will do more harm than good. It would just build callouses of unassimilated spiritual truth instead of producing life transformation. So when I've suggested a response, even an immediate response, I hope you won't feel I've gotten too personal. If you've already moved beyond what I advocate, perhaps you won't object as I reach out to help others. If, on the other hand, you've found those occasional suggestions helpful, perhaps you'd find even more helpful the original *Life in the Spirit* interactive study on which this book is based! One busy mother of small children wrote after completing that study:

> Because of the way you describe how life can be lived, it's what I want, what I've always wanted, and really, what I've known practically all my life. But to be led by the hand, as it were, through the steps of a Christian life and be held accountable to decide whether I'm willing to do what it takes to make each step. And even enticed into it! Of course, I'd do practically anything to have the life you describe as the "normal Christian life"! And to be reassured over and over again from your experience and from God's word that this is possible, it kept me faithful to the point where now I see for myself that it's true.

I really do want to "see for myself that it's true," don't you? So now, before we part company, let's turn once more to reflect on what the spiral up is like, what it means to live out all of life "in the Spirit."

Conclusion

Life in the Spirit: Spiraling Up

*W*e've come to the conclusion of our study of life in the Spirit. Perhaps for you it's not the end but a new beginning. It has been for me. As I walked through Scripture with you I experienced many fresh encounters with the Spirit and with His truth. I've been spiraling up, too! To bring that about, the Spirit is constantly at work in our lives. Here are the ten activities of the Spirit we've considered:

- ~ Creating
- ~ Revealing
- ~ Redeeming
- ~ Indwelling
- ~ Transforming
- ~ Filling
- ~ Overcoming
- ~ Gifting
- ~ Sending
- ~ Glorifying

Life in the Spirit: Summary

We started at the top of the spiral since the Spirit *created* us in God's very image. When we chose to abandon that love relationship and headed for hell, the Spirit gave us a great *revelation* of truth—of our true condition and of God's salvation, so hope was born. Next the Spirit stopped our downward spiral by doing two or three things simultaneously. As we responded to His truth with repentance and faith He *redeemed*, forgave, and regenerated us, changing our very nature, and came to *live in us*. In fact, in some mysterious way, He *filled* us with Himself. This began the great spiral up, *transforming us*, the process theologians call experiential sanctification. For most of us it wasn't to be an unbroken upward spiral, however.

Through drift or rebellion we broke fellowship, we made the Spirit sad. We were no longer filled—He was no longer in full control and God wasn't pervasive, the dominant characteristic of our lives. But whenever we would reenter that tight relationship through yielding to His will and trusting Him, the process would begin again. We would again become overcomers in our spiritual war. In these ways the Spirit produced through us all kinds of Jesus fruit, ever-increasing likeness to Jesus' own character.

But that isn't all. The Spirit also custom-designed a pattern of unique abilities, supernatural *gifts* for us to serve Him. Isn't it marvelous? He provides everything to be what we were designed to be (fruit) and do what we were designed to do (gifts). Why, that's all of life!

One of those gifts is the ability to win others to faith. Whether or not I have the gift of evangelism, though, the Spirit is *sending* each of us as witnesses to God's saving grace. Thus, through every Christian as a witness and some gifted in evangelism the Spirit builds His church. Not just at home, though. Part of His sending activity is to commission some from among us to go where Christ is not known because God loves the whole world.

Finally, the Spirit will one day wrap it all up, bringing to completion all His plan for restoring us to our original condition, image-bearers and intimate companions of the triune God. What a consummation! We call it His *glorifying* activity because that's when He brings us to our glorious destiny. But more, that's when our God will be supremely glorified by the return and total transformation of the rebels. Then together we'll celebrate the wedding!

O Holy Spirit, what a wonder you are!

> O for a closer walk with God,
> A calm and heav'nly frame,
> A light to shine upon the road
> That leads me to the Lamb.
>
> Return, O holy Dove, return,
> Sweet messenger of rest;
> I hate the sins that made You mourn,
> And drove you from my breast.
>
> The dearest idol I have known,
> What e'er that idol be,

Help me to tear it from Thy throne,
And worship only Thee.

So shall my walk be close with God,
Calm and serene my frame,
So purer light shall mark the road
That leads me to the Lamb.

—William Cowper, 1772

Don't Be Afraid!

When our children were small I would occasionally take speaking engagements away from our home base in Japan. The children developed a celebration response when I would return. Once, when I came in the gate, four-year-old Kent was playing in the back yard. He'd flooded it to make a gigantic mud pie and was thickly coated with sticky black goo from head to toe. He sighted my entrance and sounded the alarm: "Daddy!" he shouted and ran to embrace me. Here I was, all dressed up in my one preacher-suit. What should I do? Oh, hug him good, of course.

His older brothers and sisters—all five of them—swarmed out to greet me. Then each dashed to prepare my welcome—one got a chair, another plugged in an electric fan. As if that weren't enough, another got a fistful of hand fans and began to vigorously churn the hot, humid air. Someone else took my mud-spattered jacket. Kent stood in the background and silently watched. Suddenly he disappeared. In the kitchen he pushed a chair over to the wall cabinet where he knew the powdered drink mix was stashed. He'd never done it before, but his daddy was hot and thirsty. He poured an ample supply into a tall glass and, though he didn't know about stirring, he did know about water. Chair to the sink. The glass was too tall, so he anchored it with two chubby, muddy fingers grasping the rim on the inside.

When Kent brought it to me, what do you suppose I did? No, I couldn't pitch it out into the garden, for the little guy was watching me like a hawk.

"Did you make this all by yourself?" I asked. Standing first on one foot, then the other, twisting his grimy T-shirt up till his whole dirty midriff stuck out, he nodded two silent, quick jerks. Under his close surveillance I took a sip of the gritty, brown drink. Kent waited a moment and then, with eager anticipation, he asked, "Did you like it?" You think I lied, don't you? But I didn't. I told the very truth.

"Kent, I loved it!" Oh, I didn't love the gritty brown water, but it was his love-gift to me. I loved it!

When the Lord returns and we gather to celebrate, the gift offered by the best among us will have in it a muddy finger or two. But if it's the gift of our true love, He'll be well pleased. "I love it!" He'll say, and our joy will be complete. Our next stop on the spiral up is the marriage made in heaven. Rejoice! Don't be afraid.

When I reached this place in our study, my heart so filled with gratitude I found this prayer overflowing into my journal. I invite you to join me in prayer.

Holy Spirit of God, what a wonder You are! From beginning to end You made it all happen. And You not only do for me; You love me and want to be with me. That I can't understand, but I love You, too, and want to be Your intimate companion always. Hold me close and when I start to drift away, draw me back. I want to become all that a mortal can be, so here I am, Yours to do with as You will.

Father and dear Son, how can I ever express my gratitude for Your great gift at Calvary and Your great gift at Pentecost? I cannot, so I offer You all of me with the hope that it will bring You some small joy.

On the authority of Jesus' name I come. Amen.